THE

Daily Bible®

EXPERIENCE

F. LAGARD SMITH

HARVEST HOUSE PUBLISHERS
EUGENE, OREGON

The Daily Bible® Experience

Copyright © 2008 by F. LaGard Smith
Published by Harvest House Publishers
Eugene, Oregon 97408
www.harvesthousepublishers.com

ISBN 978-0-7369-0036 (pbk)
ISBN 978-0-7369-8004-3 (eBook)

Library of Congress Cataloging-in-Publication Data

Names: Smith, F. LaGard (Frank LaGard), - author.
Title: The Daily Bible experience / F. LaGard Smith.
Other titles: Daily Bible devotional
Description: Eugene, Oregon : Harvest House Publishers, 2020. | Reprint.
   Originally published: The Daily Bible devotional. 2008. | Summary:
   "Inspired by the very strong sales of the Daily Bible (2.1 million
   copies sold) this devotional is for those who want to go deeper and add
   to their daily Bible readings. While designed to be used as a companion
   alongside the very popular Daily Bible, it can also be used by itself"--
   Provided by publisher.
Identifiers: LCCN 2020018592 (print) | LCCN 2020018593 (ebook) | ISBN
   9780736980036 (trade paperback) | ISBN 9780736980043 (ebook)
Subjects: LCSH: Devotional calendars.
Classification: LCC BV4811 .S386 2020 (print) | LCC BV4811 (ebook) | DDC
   242/.2--dc23
LC record available at https://lccn.loc.gov/2020018592
LC ebook record available at https://lccn.loc.gov/2020018593

Printed in the United States of America

20 21 22 23 24 25 26 27 28 / LSCK-CD / 10 9 8 7 6 5 4 5 3 2 1

To Randy and Mary Emily
for their constancy of friendship,
encouragement, and shared dreams.

WITH APPRECIATION

To Bob Hawkins Jr. and the editorial staff at Harvest House Publishers, who nudged, cajoled, and insisted that I take on this daunting task.

To Hope Lyda, who indulged my linguistic quirks and honed my words with finely crafted creativity; and to Peggy Wright, who carefully scrutinized the copy.

To Ruth, who happily encouraged my countless hours spent working on the project and painstakingly proofed each devotional with an eye for readability and meaning.

To the staff and students at the Cochran Library at Sweet Briar College and the Lipscomb Library at Randolph College, who graciously welcomed a bearded stranger busily writing away in their midst.

To Gilbert and Patricia and all the staff at What A Blessing Bakery in Amherst, who sustained body and soul for the journey.

And to my heavenly Father, whose elegant hand of providence made this work possible with surprising but impeccable timing.

Welcome to the Journey

Welcome to *The Daily Bible Experience,* a companion volume to the bestselling *The Daily Bible.* Readers familiar with *The Daily Bible* will know that it is a chronological arrangement of the New International Version, narrated for clarity and insight and divided into 365 readings. By design, the 365 devotionals in this book are written to correspond with each day's reading in *The Daily Bible.* Rich insight will be gained if the two books are read in tandem each day—the Scripture text first, followed by the accompanying devotional. However, if you are not following along in *The Daily Bible,* the devotions in this book each begin with a brief passage taken from the day's reading, allowing them to stand alone. May this unique chronological panorama of God's interaction with mankind—from creation to John's visionary new creation to come—inform, inspire, and draw you higher. Along the way, my hope is that together we can explore timeless, often-troubling questions about the nature of God, the mystery of his providential working, and the profound complexity of our own response to such a sublime Creator.

Needing consolation, comfort, understanding, hope? This book is for you. Wanting to be boldly challenged in your faith life? This book is for you. Desiring fresh insight into Scriptures with which you may already be familiar? Hopefully this book is for you as well. In a spiritually vacuous, fast-paced world, even a few moments of quiet reflection spent each day in the presence of our Maker can uplift and transform.

Welcome to the journey.

F. LaGard Smith

The Wondrous Spark of Creation

So God created mankind in his own image, in the image of God he created them; male and female he created them.

GENESIS 1:27

If you and I are to truly believe that we're made in the image of God, shouldn't there be evidence that we are indeed *godlike*? Dare we even be so presumptuous knowing that our first forebears were made from the dust of a tiny planet in the remotest corner of a vast universe by a creator God whose intelligence and power defies imagination? How is it remotely possible that we could be like such a God? God is spirit and we are but dust. Then again we're not just any old dust. We are dust that breathes…and dust that dies. And—if the end of the story be told—we are souls made for eternity. So when we begin to search for parallels between us and our Creator, we typically speak of ourselves as intelligent, morally conscious beings, communicators, and spiritual beings beyond mortal flesh. Yet, is it possible that we have overlooked the obvious—that we too are *creators*?

No, it doesn't mean that you and I are purposed to create a cosmic universe from nothing. It simply means that, like him, we too can dream big dreams and have the creativity to make them happen! In crafting this intricate universe, God was a genius engineer, architect, scientist, musician, mathematician, and artist. And all to his glory. To be made in the image of the Creator is to be a creature who creates! Whether it be breathtaking beauty in music or art, sheer genius in math, or molding a child into a precious person of faith, God has gifted us all with a tiny touch of his own creative spark.

■ **A question worth pondering is: How will I use that creative spark in me today, and will it be to the glory of God?**

The Problem of Sin

If you do what is right, will you not be accepted? But if you do not do what is right, sin is crouching at your door; it desires to have you, but you must rule over it.

GENESIS 4:7

When God declared that all he had made was "good," he set in motion a necessary consequence with regard to the moral law, which was as much a part of his creation as the laws of nature. *Good* is only "good" if there is an opposite reality of *evil* from which *good* can be distinguished. Taking a huge risk, God has placed us in a moral universe of good and evil, knowing full well that we might choose the evil he never intended for us instead of the good he created for our benefit. Adam and Eve had the same choice as you and I and chose badly, as did Cain. And with each of those bad choices came built-in consequences that none of us can avoid—shame, guilt, fear, and regret.

Why, then, would we ever choose to sin? Perhaps because sin usually masquerades as good. It looks, tastes, and feels "good" because in the proper context the same act might actually *be* good. Or perhaps we choose to sin because we have convinced ourselves in a variety of subtle ways that we cannot help but sin. How many times have we told ourselves, for example, "But I'm only human" or "Nobody's perfect"? Cain may have rationalized his sin in much the same way. The problem is that his brother Abel was equally human, and yet he was able to make the right choices that Cain was not willing to make. The frustrating problem of sin is not that we *can't* make right choices, but that we *don't*. If, like Cain, we are called to "master" sin, it must surely mean that we *can*.

■ **So the question of choice is: The next time I'm faced with some enticing temptation (perhaps a familiar one), will I choose what merely *feels* good or what truly *is* good?**

_____

_____

_____

_____

_____

A God with Feelings

The LORD regretted that he had made human beings on the earth, and his heart was deeply troubled.

GENESIS 6:6

Have you ever considered that the creator God of the universe is profoundly affected by how you and I live our lives on this earth? Or that he takes genuine delight when we live the way he envisioned we would live, but is heartbroken when we disappoint him? Unlike the idols of wood and stone worshiped by pagans, the amazing thing about our God is that he seeks a personal relationship with us and is truly touched by how we respond to his overtures of love. If there is some way in which we are like God, there must be some way in which he is like us. Who among us doesn't know the hurt of being spurned by the object of our affection? If broken relationships are painful for us mortals, how much more so for the One who is immortal? Or do we think that God, being God, sheds no tears?

A God who sheds no tears would also be a God who takes no delight. If all we had to go on was the horrific destruction of the flood, we might believe that God is a cold-hearted, angry, vindictive God who doesn't care. But when Noah found favor in God's eyes because of his exceptional righteousness, he enabled us to see that our God is both just and loving. Even though God's heart breaks at the sight of our sin, he takes great joy when we rise above a corrupt world and walk in righteousness before him. Though this sinful world remains vulnerable to the wrath of a holy God, the good news is that God has a tender heart for those whose own hearts are equally broken when they disappoint him.

■ **The painful question is: When I repeatedly disappoint God, do I understand that I have genuinely and truly broken his heart?**

The Language of Pride

Come, let us build ourselves a city, with a tower that reaches to the heavens, so that we may make a name for ourselves.

GENESIS 11:4

Have you ever taken pride in learning a second language? Do you realize that there never would have been second or third languages had it not been for the sin of pride? Isn't this the reason we have the story of Babel? We know, of course, that the word *pride* can have two very different connotations—one good and one bad. For example, it is good to take pride in your accomplishments, especially when they are achieved only with great effort, and to have enough personal pride to do a job right or keep your possessions neat and tidy. And what doting grandparent doesn't have button-popping pride in their newborn grandchild (with endless pictures to prove it)? We can even speak with justified pride about being followers of Christ. There is no need for false humility when we're proclaiming our Lord and Savior!

It is that other kind of pride that gets us into all sorts of trouble—that insidious pride which boasts and brags, schemes and manipulates, exaggerates and falsifies. That cosmetic pride that vainly attempts to cover up deep-seated insecurities we are unwilling to confront. Above all, there is that self-assured, defiant, "terrible twos" kind of pride that pretty much says to God, "I can do it my way, thank you very much!" The language of pride is mostly "babel." It may fool others, and even ourselves, but it doesn't fool God. He knows that human pride is at the very heart of all sin—elevating our will above his. How could we possibly ever take pride in that kind of pride?

■ **So the humbling question is: What kind of pride do others see in me—an appropriate sense of pride, which they will notice with respect, or a self-focused pride shouting to the world that it's all about me?**

Following God's Call

The LORD had said to Abram, "Go from your country, your people and your father's household to the land I will show you."

GENESIS 12:1

Have you ever thought long and hard about what it means to follow God's call? Right up front there are challenging questions to ponder: Does God call all people to go wherever he chooses (including those millions who face starvation, disease, and violence daily)? And how can we ever be certain it is God's bidding that prompts us rather than our own selfish desires? By what means does God actually call us? Are there voices, signs, or perhaps just unexpected doors that open or close? And what are we to think when we eagerly follow what we believe to be God's call, only to experience such great disappointment that we wonder whether there was really any call in the first place?

But all those questions are moot if, like Abram, you and I have no doubt whatsoever about either the call or the destination. The question that matters is whether we are willing to leave every secure, comfortable aspect of our lives behind and launch out in faith to do what is completely counterintuitive. Given God's track record, it's unlikely that he is calling us to a better-paying job with a grander house in a more upscale neighborhood. More likely he is calling us to abandon all of that to serve in ways that would utterly mystify family and friends. "Are you out of your mind?" is the response a lot of people would have to our answering a true call of God. For a secular world obsessed with ease and security, the line between faith and insanity is thin indeed.

■ **The uncomfortable questions are: Do I trust God enough to drive into some unfamiliar neighborhood to share his love and mine? Do I trust him enough to leave my comfort zone and to serve wherever he calls me?**

Commitment to Keeping Covenants

I will establish my covenant as an everlasting covenant between me and you and your descendants after you for the generations to come, to be your God and the God of your descendants after you.

GENESIS 17:7

Promises, promises. At every turn God seems to place high value on making and keeping promises. Remember his covenant to never again destroy the earth by water, and how he set the rainbow in the heavens as a sign of this commitment? More than once God covenanted with Abraham about a great nation that was to come through his lineage and about a land that even today we speak of as "the Promised Land." And with each new covenant come more and more signs, such as name changes, mysterious flames between animal carcasses, and circumcision for Hebrew males. How very odd! Yet stranger still is the very idea of God making covenants. Why should the Creator of the universe design to make promises of any kind to his creatures, including even lowly animals? It's not exactly as if leopards and toads have the capacity to reciprocate covenant agreements!

In society we often make legally binding contracts that contain specific covenants, the breach of which obligates the parties to compensation or specific performance. In such contracts, typically, there is equality between the contracting parties and, also, something of value which prompts the parties to obligate themselves. But when God makes a covenant, the parties are hardly equal, and there is nothing we might give that could obligate God to keep his promises. So when God makes a covenant, he is bound solely by a moral obligation consistent with his holy character. This only highlights the importance of keeping our own covenants, especially when human courts might actually sanction their breach, as with divorce.

■ **So the probing question is: What solemn covenants have I made that I will honor at all cost, even if there might be an easy way out?**

_____

_____

_____

_____

_____

The Power of God

Then the LORD said to Abraham, "Why did Sarah laugh and say, 'Will I really have a child, now that I am old?' Is anything too hard for the LORD?"

GENESIS 18:13-14

Wouldn't you think that a God who created the entire universe from nothing has the power to make anything happen that he sets his mind to? So why do you think Sarah laughed at the possibility of having a child at her advanced age? Even when she knew full well that God—not just some strange visitor—had made such a promise, Sarah thought it was up to her to make it happen through Hagar. Like Sarah, most of us tend to assume we must make things happen through our own effort. Even when God promises to take care of us, we don't always take him seriously. Will he really destroy a city full of wicked people? Will he really provide children against all odds? Where is our belief?

There is reason to believe that God has a sense of humor, but he is never joking when he makes promises. Nor does he lack the power to accomplish whatever is necessary to bring about either his will or our best interests. Has God promised us something? He will do it! Has God warned us about something? We'd be well-advised to take that warning seriously! We would be equally foolish to think that God has promised us things he has never actually promised, whether it be having children or perhaps restoring an alienated child's love. But if what we hope for never happens, it won't be because God lacks the power to make it happen. Whenever God thinks something is best for us, *impossibility* is not a word in his vocabulary.

■ **The only question to be asked is: Is there something I've desperately tried to make happen on my own without thinking that if God wants it to happen, he has the power to make it happen?**

Rationalizing Sin

Abraham replied, "I said to myself, 'There is surely no fear of God in this place, and they will kill me because of my wife.' Besides, she really is my sister, the daughter of my father though not of my mother; and she became my wife."

GENESIS 20:11-12

D o you find it intriguing that Abraham—the ultimate icon of trusting faith—has a specific moral weakness that keeps resurfacing? And he gives in to this weakness despite the fact that he has already gotten into trouble because of it. Perhaps the most fascinating aspect of Abraham's moral lapse is how he so easily rationalizes his sin, even as he continues putting his wife, Sarah, at great risk. Yet given what Abraham perceived to be a real possibility, that he could be killed for telling the truth, we also might have been tempted to lie! But because God had previously intervened to save Abraham when he was in a similar situation, maybe, just maybe, Abraham should have figured that God could protect him again.

Not many of us are forced to make moral decisions in the face of potential death. It is with the second part of Abraham's rationalization that we most relate—that Sarah was *in fact* his half-sister. Had he not told the truth? Yes, but not the *whole* truth. The truth that he told, in the way that he told it, had the same effect as an outright lie. Consider this: Before Abraham lied to others, he first had to deceive himself into believing that telling a half-truth was just as honest as telling the whole truth. What's more, it was undoubtedly easier to deceive himself the second time around. What a vexing problem sin is! Rather than learn from our mistakes, it's often easier to rationalize our sin the more often we do it!

■ **So the troubling question is: What persistent sin do I engage in and have rationalized so repeatedly that it now hardly seems to be sin at all?**

_____

_____

_____

_____

A God Who Provides

So Abraham called that place The LORD Will Provide. And to this day it is said, "On the mountain of the LORD it will be provided."

GENESIS 22:14

What strikes you most about the story of Abraham being called to offer his son Isaac as a sacrifice? That a loving God would put Abraham through such a daunting test of faith? That Abraham actually trusted God enough to do the unthinkable? That Isaac himself trusted his father enough to let him tie him on an altar, fearfully anticipating that he was about to die? Any way you look at it, it's an extraordinary story. When you race ahead in history to the story of the Son of God being crucified on a cruel Roman cross, you begin to make connections Abraham himself could never have guessed. There's the Father giving up his only Son. There's the obedient Son praying, "Not my will, but yours be done." And, most amazing of all, there's the Lamb being sacrificed for the sins of the world. But even that sublime analogy does not alter the hard reality of what happened on that bleak mountain that day.

The text itself focuses on the importance of God as provider. The message is clear that whatever the need, large or small, God provides. Yet you might wonder if that message has a hollow ring to those for whom God seemingly has *not* provided: the hungry, the oppressed, the abused, the ignored, the homeless, the fearful, and the dying. Has God provided for them in any meaningful way? Are we simply to spiritualize away their immediate physical or emotional needs, contenting ourselves that God will take care of them in some transcendent spiritual realm? Or have we forgotten that often we ourselves are the "rams" caught in the thicket—whom God has provided to meet the needs of those suffering in our midst?

■ **The challenging question is: Who is depending on me to provide for the distressing needs that God has put me in a position to supply?**

Praying for Success

Then he prayed, "LORD, God of my master Abraham, make me successful today, and show kindness to my master Abraham."

GENESIS 24:12

Deciding what to pray for is not always as easy as we might wish. Some prayers are so obvious that there's no time or need to decide anything. When a loved one is suddenly in the throes of death, for example, we immediately beg God for prolonged life. But most moments lack that kind of immediacy and clarity, thus demanding conscious thought about which requests to choose to take to God. The list of possible petitions is endless. Everything from world peace to "our daily bread" is open for discussion with God. He knows our needs even before we utter a single word, yet he invites us to lay our every concern before him. Is there anything too trivial to pray about? Certainly nothing is too trivial, but you can hardly imagine that God would be pleased to hear purely selfish requests or prayers invoking his help in doing unrighteous deeds.

So what does God think when we pray for success, as Abraham's servant did? Is he pleased with such a prayer? Given the success of the servant's mission, it certainly appears that God looked with favor upon his request. In fact God answered that prayer specifically and in every detail. The issue, of course, is how we define success. If the success for which we pray is determined by the world's definition of success, we could be in for a great disappointment—even if we coincidentally happen to attain it. Of one thing we can be sure: God will never give us what is not good for us. Only when we pray for success in accomplishing the good that God has called us to can we be assured of his blessing. Even then, when we are clearly on a mission for God, perhaps we pray too little for success.

■ **The question for discernment is: For what specific success should I pray, assured that God will bless me?**

Selling Ourselves Short

So Esau despised his birthright.

GENESIS 25:34

What was Esau thinking! Maybe we could understand it if Esau was literally starving to death, but to give up your inheritance just because you are hungrier than usual makes no sense whatsoever. Did Esau have no appreciation for the virtues of deferred gratification? It wasn't just one man's inheritance that was blithely thrown away. Not in a million years could Esau ever have guessed all that would hinge on his single rash decision, but the consequences would be felt for countless generations to come, even to this day. Much to their great chagrin, countless others have seen in their own lifetime the destructive, wide-ranging results of a single rash decision they themselves have made. Hardly ever is the following generation untouched by the foolish actions of the preceding generation. Indeed repercussions "to the third and fourth generations" would not be unusual.

Why, then, do we mimic Esau so often, rashly throwing away great opportunities and expectations for paltry substitutes that rob us of what might have been? What looks or feels so good about those unworthy "bowls of stew" we recklessly risk trading a whole lifetime for? Are we really so desperate for immediate gratification that we never think of the long-term consequences? If perhaps impulsiveness is more to be expected of impetuous youth, how do those of us who are older explain our momentary stupidity? Maybe it's that we too easily forget the big picture, which young people have yet to fully see. When every moment in life is seen in its proper, larger context, there is less of a chance that we will act rashly at any given moment. Beyond that we may need to take a higher view of ourselves. Just remembering how valuable we are in God's eyes would go a long way toward keeping us from selling ourselves short.

■ **So the cautioning question is: If I know I'm vulnerable to doing something beneath me should the occasion arise, have I thought hard enough about the horrendous consequences that possibly could result?**

Enslaved by Family Grudges

Esau held a grudge against Jacob because of the blessing his father had given him.

GENESIS 27:41

Are you haunted by childhood memories that have shaped your life in ways you seem unable to escape? Do you know siblings who can never quite shake the thought that they were not loved in the same way as the other children? Maybe they are right. Sometimes parents do have favorites and cannot mask their preference for one child over another. Anyone who is not on the receiving end of such disparity can never fully appreciate how devastating preferential treatment can be to tender, formative minds. Just imagine the feelings of insecurity and the exaggerated need for love and acceptance that could emerge, perhaps being manifest in dangerous ways at a later time in life. Imagine how a parent's early emotional trauma might in turn influence the reactionary patterns displayed toward his or her own children.

Sadly, those who live a lifetime perceiving themselves to be victims of parental favoritism are virtually enslaved to a long-standing grudge against one or both parents or even the more favored child, as was the case with Esau. Yet a sober caution arises out of Esau's case. The fact that Jacob was favored by Rebekah does not discount the fact that Esau was favored by Isaac, and that Isaac had acted in good faith when he was deceived by Jacob. Is it possible, then, that immature minds might sometimes misinterpret parental decisions as reflecting a favoritism that never exists? As children of a God who plays no favorites, have we never wrongly interpreted our heavenly Father's actions as favoring others more than ourselves? It would be heartbreaking to live one's life in the shadow of a grudge based on hard reality. But it would be tragic if such a long-standing grudge was baseless all along.

■ **The question begging to be asked is: Am I willing, by God's grace, to rise above whatever early childhood experiences I may have had, even if they gave me a false start?**

Working Too Hard at Love

Again she conceived, and when she gave birth to a son she said, "Now at last my husband will become attached to me, because I have borne him three sons."

GENESIS 29:34

The story of Jacob and his competing wives is a tragic, farcical soap opera, complete with predictable jealousy, spite, and petty infighting. How could a race to bear children between two wives, who happen to be sisters, be anything other than a recipe for disaster? Throw in two conspiring maidservants, and the stage is set for a no-holds-barred family fracas. Of course it's the classic "tangled web" we might expect from the deception that spawned it. Had Laban not tricked Jacob into marrying the older sister he didn't love, none of this would have happened. Poor Leah! What's a girl to do to win the affection of her man? Bearing as many children as possible seemed to be the answer. Surely that would gain his favor.

Love is a funny thing. The harder you try to make it happen, the more it slips away. One sure truth about love is that it can never be bought, earned, or manipulated. True love may be a response to another's overtures of affection, but it can never be artificially contrived. Sadly, it's a lesson many insecure spouses have learned the hard way. Sadder still, it's a lesson many religious folks have yet to learn about God's own love. Those who are insecure in their faith often think they can win God's approval by amazing displays of exhausting, mind-numbing human effort. Interminable ritual, harsh self-flagellation, and endless good works are all seen as direct lines to the heart of God. But if God loved us first (which he did), what in the world did we ever do to deserve it? Because God's own love is a gift, maybe we're working way too hard at love.

■ **The question of securing affection is: Am I operating under the deceptive premise that the more I work at pleasing God, the more he will love me?**

A God Who Watches

It was also called Mizpah, because he said, "May the LORD keep watch between you and me when we are away from each other. If you mistreat my daughters or if you take any wives besides my daughters, even though no one is with us, remember that God is a witness between you and me."

GENESIS 31:49-50

You cannot be certain with what motive Laban spoke about God's being a constant witness between himself and Jacob, whether of distrust or of divine affirmation of their mutual commitment. But the name given to the heap of stones they erected as witness to their agreement—*Mizpah*—was altogether appropriate. *Mizpah*, meaning "a watchtower," was intended to be a lasting witness to the vow they had taken to act honorably toward each other. But what good would that heap of stones be as a watchful reminder of their vow if each of them moved away from the heap? Out of sight, out of mind?

Today we don't stack stones to remind us of solemn vows. The sign of our commitment might be a wedding ring, or perhaps our baptism into Christ. While a wedding ring might always be on our finger, we aren't often near the pool of water in which we were baptized to be reminded of the commitment it represents. Even a wedding ring can easily be ignored when you are away on a business trip or some place where you won't be recognized. Or maybe *Mizpah* applies to the young person away at college, no longer under the watchful eyes of parents. On all those occasions, thinking of the word *Mizpah* would be wise, for no matter how far away we might be from the object of solemn commitments we have made, God is always there and watching. "As God is my witness" leaves no room for escape from his roving eyes.

■ **So the question for all wanderers is: Just how troubled am I at the thought that, with God always watching, there is no such thing as secret sin?**

Choosing Your Battles

But they replied, "Should he have treated our sister like a prostitute?"

GENESIS 34:31

There is little doubt that Simeon and Levi thought they had done the right thing by killing the men of Shechem to avenge Dinah's brutal defilement. Didn't they administer justice where justice was due? So why was their father so upset with them? Had he not taught them to stand on principle, to do the right thing, to valiantly fight for truth and justice? But perhaps they had forgotten that other lesson—the one about choosing your battles. As everyone knows, it is possible to win a great battle yet lose the war. Jacob knew that Simeon and Levi's momentary (and ridiculously easy) victory would invite far more serious trouble in the long run. He might also have suspected that his sons acted more out of hot-blooded anger or swashbuckling bravado than any pure sense of doing justice. Even righteous battles can be tainted by mixed motives.

The problem for all of us is that there are almost limitless battles to be fought in the larger war against evil. To throw up our hands in despair is certainly not the answer, but neither is it wise simply to charge up every hill worthy of being assaulted. Even if we are prepared to assume the risks of being a hero, have we stopped to consider the collateral damage that could be inflicted upon others? To act on principle virtually always requires careful consideration of more than just the obvious central issue. The grave responsibilities of waging any battle are rarely as recognizable as the glaring wrongs begging to be put right. The tricky bit is knowing what that right thing is…and the right way to go about it.

■ **So here is the truly tough question: When I see some wrong needing to be made right today, will I wisely consider all the potential strategies and ramifications before whipping out my sword?**

When Marriage Is Dangerous

Esau took his wives from the women of Canaan.

GENESIS 36:2

Marriage is always a risk. For two people to truly become one, each has to give up a fair amount of freedom and independence—a process necessarily requiring a great deal of self-emptying compromise. Fortunately the abundant benefits gained in the exchange ensure that marriage is an ongoing institution. But it doesn't alter the fact that compromise is a part of marriage—even in the choice of one's mate, compromise is to be expected. One need only look at one's self to realize that the unsuspecting fiancé is making the best of a bad bargain! And let's not overlook the compromise required when two extended families are involuntarily roped into sharing holidays and grandchildren. For hapless in-laws, compromise takes on a whole new meaning!

The story of Esau and his Canaanite wives is a poignant reminder that some risks in marriage are greater than others. We're not just talking about a "night person" marrying a "morning person," or a big-city guy hitched to a country gal. Countless marriages have survived differences in nationality, race, culture, language, tax brackets, and even religion. The greater concern is not whether the marriage itself survives, but how fundamental differences in faith can profoundly affect a person's relationship with God. The sad story of Esau's marriage to pagan wives is a story of a personal faith being put at risk. Of most deeply held moral values being compromised. Of a bloodline of faith in God being adulterated, perhaps for generations. Time and again, God's people have married outside of faith, only to find that they are irrevocably wedded to whatever lesser gods are revered by their mate. Little wonder that God repeatedly warned against such dangerous marriages and had to keep picking up the broken pieces.

■ **The crucial question is: What can I do to ensure that the next generation doesn't make the mistake of thinking that faith differences within a marriage pose no serious risk?**

The Hypocrisy of Double Standards

Judah said, "Bring her out and have her burned to death!"

GENESIS 38:24

Hardly any of us is free from the pitfall of operating under double standards. What's "good for the goose" isn't always so "good for the gander," especially if we happen to be the "gander." In fact the difference between a "goose" and a "gander" can loom large. When it comes to sexual misconduct, for example, cultures often hold one standard for the male and another for the female. Men and boys are cut some slack when it comes to sexual promiscuity, whereas, even in a sexually liberated society, women are expected to be more chaste. Apparently that was the case as far back as Judah's day, when it was socially acceptable for him to sleep with a prostitute, but outrageous for his daughter-in-law Tamar to have been that very prostitute!

Of course it's not just sexual sin that succumbs to double standards. Consider how Joseph's brothers judged his youthful arrogance to be a deplorable sin, but thought nothing of killing him and then lying to their father to cover up the plot! Even when they decided to sell him into slavery instead of murdering him, an exaggerated sense of self-importance would pale when compared to their sinister conspiracy. Not many of us are without fault when it comes to the hypocrisy of double standards. We may rightly decry the sins of others, yet fail to acknowledge our own, more reprehensible sins. (Have you ever noticed that certain sins seem to be acceptable among Christians compared with the never-acceptable sins of "people in the world"?) It's good that we express moral outrage at the sin in others, else sin ultimately would lose its well-deserved stigma. But harsh judgment of others should always prompt us to look more closely into the nearest mirror.

■ **The introspective question is: What "respectable" sin in myself am I overlooking as I pass stringent judgment on the "foul" sins of others?**

Dreams That Come True

The reason the dream was given to Pharaoh in two forms is that the matter has been firmly decided by God, and God will do it soon.

GENESIS 41:32

Do dreams ever really come true? Down through time both God's people and pagan worshippers have attributed supernatural meaning to their dreams. Even today some live their lives by their dreams— and a whole industry of soothsayers, psychics, and gurus is available to interpret those dreams and give spiritual counseling based on those nightly visions. We'd all have to admit that dreams are both fascinating and mysterious. Why do we dream at all? Are our dreams anything more than the brain's post office working overtime at night, sorting our thoughts in bizarre patterns? Did God actually intend for us to take our dreams seriously? From reading the Bible it would be easy to think that God speaks to us through our dreams, as he did time and again with those he called to special duty. But is that just ancient history?

Without discounting the possibility that God could speak to us through dreams just as he did repeatedly over centuries of unfolding providence, perhaps it would be more beneficial to reflect on how we use "dream talk" today. For example, there's that "dream house" we would love to have, or the "dream vacation" we hope to take someday. For the teenage girl thinking of marriage, it's that "man of her dreams" who is all-important. For the guys, it's that "dream team" that sets off male testosterone. Given all this superficial "dream talk," it seems we are long past the point of expecting our dreams to be messages from God. But here is a point to ponder: If dreams often reflect something that has been weighing heavily on our minds, might God have more to say to us in our dreams if we thought more about God when we are awake?

■ **The crucial question is: Are my dreams mostly about temporal things in a material world rather than nobler things in a spiritual realm?**

_____

_____

_____

_____

The Fine Art of Forgiveness

And he kissed all his brothers and wept over them. Afterward his brothers talked with him.

GENESIS 45:15

You're all too aware that the harm done to you is worthy of fair retribution. Yet you also know that there is no wrong which cannot, and should not, be forgiven. Caught on the horns of that moral dilemma, what's a person to do? Whether Joseph got it completely right when he negotiated a reconciliation with his brothers is unclear. One cannot help but wonder why he seemed to be playing mind games with them. That he kept running off to weep in the midst of those "games" suggests he wasn't merely toying with them out of some baser sense of revenge. So why make them jump through all those hoops? Maybe they needed to be brought to full recognition of how serious their sin had been. Or perhaps it wasn't about them, but about us—showing us how God's grace fills our sacks with silver even though we have greatly offended him.

When we think about those who have done us wrong, it is hard to forgive and forget. Sure, we can always *say* that we forgive them, knowing that is what we *ought* to say. We may even pray for them (likely in a condescending manner). But can we ever imagine kissing them and weeping over them? If perhaps we could bring ourselves to do that with alienated family members, could we do that with others? The secret to tough forgiveness seems to be, first of all, acknowledging our own sins (Joseph himself had not been without fault), and beyond that, allowing some space for the offender to truly repent without being humiliated. (If the tables were turned, wouldn't we want that for ourselves?) Forgiveness with honor on all sides is not an exact science, but a fine art that only a heart of hopeful faith can acquire.

■ **The challenging question is: If I'm struggling to forgive someone in my life, am I even praying about how that might be done?**

Second-Guessing Motives

The land became Pharaoh's, and Joseph reduced the people to servitude, from one end of Egypt to the other.

GENESIS 47:20-21

Something doesn't ring quite right about Joseph's selling grain to his desperate countrymen, taking their land in payment, and making them Pharaoh's indentured servants. Because they had contributed to the surplus grain, why should they have to sell themselves in order to eat the fruits of their labor? At first glance it would appear that Joseph is taking advantage of helpless, starving people. So are we wrong to think that this man, who had the moral fortitude to flee from seduction by his master's wife and to treat his brothers better than they deserved, is a man of faith to be emulated? Is this just another example of "chinks in the armor" that even the Bible's spiritual giants seem to have? Or could it be, instead, that we risk misjudging Joseph's motives by too hastily jumping to conclusions?

If you have ever had your own motives called into question, you can appreciate that folks don't always understand decisions which might seem out of character for you. Had they known all the relevant facts, your choices might not seem strange after all. So perhaps Joseph had good but not obvious reasons. Suppose, for example, it was Joseph's intent to preserve the dignity of his countrymen, who otherwise would have been embarrassed to receive charitable handouts. (It does seem the people were happy enough with the arrangement.) Or maybe Joseph thought this was a way to keep from playing favorites between the "haves" and "have-nots." The point is that we just don't know, and because we don't know, we would do well not to rush to judgment. That should be the case especially with those who have a track record of acting on principle. Good reputations do not just happen overnight and are well worth protecting.

■ **So the obvious prudent question is: Would I do well to consider that others might be making "stupid" decisions based on information I don't have?**

God's Mysterious Providence

You intended to harm me, but God intended it for good to accomplish what is now being done, the saving of many lives.

GENESIS 50:20

How is it that God can work his divine will through the actions of fallible human beings whose last thought would be that they are God's agents for good? Over the centuries, gallons of ink have been spilt by theologians grappling with the puzzling conundrum. The problem is not whether the sovereign God of the universe has sufficient power to accomplish his will on earth (that's a given), but whether you and I can simultaneously pursue our own adverse purposes within the parameters of God's own will. To put it another way, is it possible for God to control the outcome of the game without necessarily moving each and every chess piece on the board at each turn? Or more to the point, even if our actions somehow contribute to God's own master plan, are you and I nevertheless responsible for how we act?

That last question is the easy one. Few, indeed, would argue that we are not personally responsible for our evil deeds. But if so, how does God take our abject moral failures and turn them into his own triumphs? Not just *my* moral failures or *yours,* but collectively the sullied lives of the whole of humankind—all to his ultimate purpose and glory? *Somewhere* along the way, individual men and women would have to be specially chosen instruments of God to inexorably move "his story" along to its rapturous consummation. It was to be true even of Joseph's brothers, who would play a key role in fathering a nation, which would be God's chosen instrument to bring a sinful world to its Savior. And if those flawed fellows, why not us?

■ **The breathtaking question is: Is it possible that God might intend, even after I am gone, to save lives through something an unworthy soul like me has done during my lifetime?**

Reverence with Awe

"Do not come any closer," God said. "Take off your sandals, for the place where you are standing is holy ground."

EXODUS 3:5

With all due respect, God's encounter with Moses on Mount Horeb is unearthly to the extreme. A bush that burns without being consumed. A staff that turns into a snake. What's going on here? To believe the story is to believe that God is playing tricks with the laws of nature…and seems to hint that he has plenty more tricks up his sleeve. But don't you wonder even more about what God's voice sounded like to Moses? Did Moses simply take for granted that he was having a normal conversation with the Creator of the universe? We have read the story so often that familiarity breeds contempt. Or could that be the very message of the day—that our familiarity with God has actually robbed us of the respect due to God?

Maybe it is partly God's own fault. After all, he did deign to come into "our world," touch human hands, and speak to mere mortals eye to eye. He even called us *friends*! Yet there are still those haunting words to Moses: "Do not come any closer." Stand back. Keep your distance. Dare we approach the great I AM with anything less than utter reverence and absolute awe? What respect do we show when "Oh my God" becomes merely a thought-less exclamation in everyday conversation? Where is the reverence when "traditional" worship so numbs the worshipper that the focus turns to stained glass and steeples, or when "contemporary" worship ends up exalting self or superstar entertainers rather than the Holy One of heaven? How often do we come in and out of God's presence in prayer with hardly a pause before moving on with the conversation? Do we go through entire days without considering that we live our lives on holy ground?

■ **The potentially shameful question is: Has my God become so familiar that I've forgotten what I ought to remember most about him?**

Bargaining with God

But when Pharaoh saw that there was relief, he hardened his heart and would not listen to Moses and Aaron, just as the LORD had said.

EXODUS 8:15

When you have had your fill of frogs, what do you do? A lot of people would be tempted to pray that God would get rid of them! No, not those ugly, jumping kind of frogs perturbing Pharaoh, but those emotional "frogs" that plague us beyond the breaking point—illness, catastrophic disease, divorce, job loss, a rebellious child, the death of a loved one. Try as we might to kiss those frogs and turn them into benevolent princes, magic is pure fantasy. And so we pray. Not just pray, but foolishly make all sorts of bargains with God, as if God cannot see right through us! "Please, God. I'll never take another drink." Or, "God, if you'll only solve this problem for me, I'll never again let you down." Oh, it's not that we are insincere at the moment, just notoriously fickle and unreliable. Nor do we fully appreciate that God is not in the genie business to grant our every desperate wish—not even his own Son's heart-wrenching plea in an unbearable hour of suffering. (On which occasion, notably, there was no bargaining.)

As it happens, sometimes the "frogs" in our lives disappear as quickly as they come. Maybe they just go away on their own. Then again, since God has been known to make the impossible happen, might we then have second thoughts about that rash bargain we've struck? Many have! When the relief so desperately prayed for actually comes, commitments lightly made in the panic of the moment often vanish just as quickly. We can even rationalize that the problem went away on its own, thank you very much! Interestingly, how we react exposes the difference in character between hearts of wax melted by the sun and hearts of clay hardened by the same sun.

■ **The searching question is: If God should honor my bargain and come to my rescue, which kind of heart would it expose?**

Living with Purpose

But I have raised you up for this very purpose, that I might show you my power and that my name might be proclaimed in all the earth.

EXODUS 9:16

Out of the billions of people who have ever lived, was it inevitable that *you* should be born? We like to think, of course, that each soul is important. But why *you* or why *me*? And was it by sheer accident of nature that we were brought into this world by our particular parents, sort of like a gum-ball machine—you just get the next one, whichever happens to drop into position? Could we have been born of another race or into another social strata? Might we have lived in a different part of the world, or spoken a different language? For many couples it's an intentional decision to bring a child into the world, but odds are that most children are just little surprise bundles that come along. A surprise to everyone but God.

The mystery of life belongs to God. What we do know is that God has purposely anointed any number of men and women as his special emissaries. It is possible that in some cases he simply worked with whatever lives were available from a natural process of human procreation—putting certain people in positions where they could best serve his divine will. That could well have been the case with Pharaoh, whom God raised up to play this crucial role in the deliverance of God's people. For all the rest of us, the meaning of our existence is less specific but equally clear. We do not live without purpose. Whatever our circumstance of birth, Scripture gives us abundant reason to believe that we too have been raised up so that God might show us his power, and through us, in some way unique to ourselves, to proclaim his name in all the earth.

■ **The question of purpose is: What might God show me of his power even today, and what unique opportunities will I have to proclaim his mighty name?**

The Next Generation

And when your children ask you, "What does this ceremony mean to you?" then tell them, "It is the Passover sacrifice to the LORD, who passed over the houses of the Israelites in Egypt and spared our homes when he struck down the Egyptians."

EXODUS 12:26-27

Why do children ask so many questions? Because they have so much to learn! Eager little sponges soaking up everything around them, children have a curiosity and excitement which many of us, sadly, have lost along the way. Their fascination with wiggly creatures, mud puddles, and the beauty of butterflies is but a prelude to their more probing questions about life's most profound mysteries. Any child old enough to know the story of Adam and Eve will certainly want to know whether they had belly buttons. And how did all those animals on the ark go to the bathroom? Out of the mouths of babes come even more serious questions about God himself: Where did God come from? If he was God, why did he need to rest? Does God ever get lonely?

What we adults blithely take for granted (or have already given up on learning), children have a driving need to know. And have you ever noticed that the *what* questions get overshadowed by all those *whys*? "Mommy, why don't puppies go to heaven?" "Daddy, why did Jesus have to die?" And whether or not they ask it aloud during a time when the communion is being shared, inquiring young minds are still asking that ancient question: "What does this ceremony mean to you?" (Despite the *what*, of course, it's really a *why*.) As with the ancient Hebrews, God has gifted us with a ceremony tailor-made for the transferring of one generation's faith to the next. Like the Passover, the Lord's Supper provides a wonderful opportunity to pass along the gospel story to young hearts eagerly receptive to faith.

■ **The sobering question is: What *does* this ceremony mean to me, and has it appeared important enough each week that young minds are being led to faith?**

Trusting in God's Deliverance

Moses answered the people, "Do not be afraid. Stand firm and you will see the deliverance the LORD will bring you today…The LORD will fight for you; you need only to be still."

EXODUS 14:13-14

Ever known what it is like to be "between the devil and the deep blue sea," as the saying goes? For the Israelites, of course, it was the *Red* Sea and not the devil, but Pharaoh. Still, theirs was a desperate situation with nowhere to turn. Most of us are all too familiar with such dire predicaments from time to time. Either way we turn, we're dead. Whichever choice we make, we're wrong. Whatever we decide to do, there are potentially adverse consequences. So when there's no "lesser of two evils," but two equally unacceptable evils, what is a person to do? The good news, if any, is that usually in such predicaments we don't really have any choice anyway. There is nothing to decide, and nowhere to turn—except to God.

One cannot possibly know what hopeless predicament you might be facing right now, or perhaps will encounter in the near future. But one wonders whether such predicaments might be God's way of getting our attention, of reminding us that we cannot live our lives without his intervention, of comforting us with the thought that whenever the *next* predicament arises we need not be anxious about the outcome. If you think back for a moment, you can probably remember any number of high-anxiety moments when all seemed lost. Maybe it was a health problem, or a disastrous relationship, or some grave moral error that God has already brought you through. Are we then to believe that, having rescued us once, he is unable to rescue us again? Even though we can never predict how God will suddenly "part the waters," no sea can overwhelm, nor the devil destroy, when God is on our side.

■ **It is a question of trust: Am I thinking it's solely up to me to fight the hopeless battles only God can fight?**

Putting God to the Test

And he called the place Massah and Meribah because the Israelites quarreled and because they tested the LORD saying, "Is the LORD among us or not?"

EXODUS 17:7

How would you like it if you could just step outside your door each morning and pick up your Frosted Flakes for breakfast? Or strike a rock when you are thirsty and out comes your favorite beverage? Pretty cool, huh? Then again, what would we think if we joined a tour crossing the desert only to discover there was neither water nor food of any kind? How long would it be before we started complaining to our tour guide about the lack of amenities? It is not difficult to empathize with the Israelites. Given similar circumstances, we would be pretty upset ourselves. Turn that hypothetical desert tour into a traumatizing real-life tragedy, and we too might be wondering: "Is the LORD among us or not?" Why has God abandoned us under such dire circumstances?

For the Israelites, each step of their journey out of bondage became a test of God's power and provision. No matter how many times he came to their rescue, the insecure Israelites seemingly needed more and more assurances of God's presence. If he delivered the goods, then God retained the people's loyalty. If he didn't deliver, how could they possibly put their trust in such a powerless God? Do you and I ever put God to similar tests? Even if we might never actually articulate it, is there something in the back of our minds that says, for example, "If you'll just heal my loved one, then I can believe that you are real"? What would we think if our prayers seemed *never* to be answered? Would we no longer believe? Or, come to think of it, do we have it all backward? Is it perhaps *God* who is testing *us* in these trying circumstances?

■ **Here is the real question I need to ask: Is my faith in God so fragile that nothing short of daily miracles can sustain it?**

Incremental Holiness

Little by little I will drive them out before you, until you have increased enough to take possession of the land.

EXODUS 23:30

Do you get the idea that God is serious about his people being holy before him? First, the command comes down, "Don't touch the mountain." And should anyone violate that order, he is to be stoned or shot with arrows—not run through with a sword, which would require at least indirectly touching the defiled offender. So it's no touching and no touching anyone who does touch—a stringent set of rules, indeed! Then, there are those famous Ten Commandments that God orders the Israelites to strictly observe. To us those rules of holy living might seem obvious, but consider how revolutionary they must have been at the time. Don't forget that Israel's pagan neighbors would have felt comfortable having multiple gods and idols.

So how is Israel to become a holy nation in the midst of wicked, idolatrous nations? The Israelites cannot remain in isolation forever—there is a promised land to conquer. But God knows that confronting too many enemies too soon will end in failure. No, not militarily, for God could conquer the land in the snap of a finger! It is spiritual defeat that God is concerned about. Spiritual maturity takes time. In a world of rampant immorality, holiness has many battles to fight. So the divine strategy is "little by little." One enemy at a time, one day at a time. This ought to give comfort to anyone struggling with sin along numerous fronts. God knows that holiness is a process, not an overnight victory. Fighting too many battles simultaneously can result in discouraging self-defeat. Yet we mustn't forget God's promise—that if we steadfastly commit ourselves to obeying his commands, he will ultimately drive out all of our enemies!

■ **The question for us strugglers is: Am I tempted to use God's "little by little" strategy as an excuse, or am I truly striving toward greater holiness one courageous day at a time?**

A Patterned Sanctuary

Then have them make a sanctuary for me, and I will dwell among them. Make this tabernacle and all its furnishings exactly like the pattern I will show you.

EXODUS 25:8-9

Everybody needs a home—even God. Not that the universe isn't his home; nor, more so, heaven itself. Yet in a special way, God desires a home in the midst of his people where he can invite us in to have fellowship. Considering his deity, it is an astounding thought! Though some folks don't seem to care what kind of house they live in, God obviously has definite ideas about his house—right down to the last detail. It is equally obvious that God has good taste. Nothing but the very best for God! Not just gold, but pure gold. Not just any fabric, but fine linen. For a God who calls us not to be materialistic, it is curious that he should place such a high priority on finery in his own house. Then again, perhaps his reasons for high-ticket items and ours are worlds apart.

When God draws up blueprints for his house, he expects his plans to be implemented without the slightest deviation. How many times did he tell Moses to build his sanctuary *exactly* as instructed? No independent contracting, please. No "do-it-yourself" notions. No human innovations. When God gives us a pattern, we are to stick to it, jot and tittle. Only his own meticulous pattern assures the intended relationship between form and function, whether it be in Israel's ancient tabernacle or, more crucially, in the sanctuary God has called each of us to be. If we are to be the sanctuary in which the Spirit of God makes his home, how can we expect to substitute our own designs for his, yet achieve the function and purpose he intends?

■ **The question is one of some urgency: If God expects nothing but the finest wherever he dwells, how comfortable can I expect him to be while living in my sanctuary?**

Equality of Atonement

The rich are not to give more than a half shekel and the poor are not to give less when you make the offering to the LORD to atone for your lives.

EXODUS 30:15

Are we so familiar with blood sacrifices for atonement that we skip over this obscure reference to paying a half shekel for atonement? And what's this about the payment being made as a "ransom" during the taking of a census? Is God holding his people for ransom; otherwise, they don't count? The whole thing smacks of being some kind of unseemly sin tax, but how any amount of money could buy reconciliation with God is a mystery. God can't be bought off or bought out! Nor would he respond to a bribe. So something else must surely be going on here. Perhaps there is a clue in the half shekel each person is to give, *whether rich or poor*. When other sacrifices and offerings are required, there is always a "discount" for the poor. If they cannot afford one kind of animal, they are permitted to offer a less costly one. In God's economy, offerings and gifts are always to be given on a sliding scale of one's personal prosperity. Yet here God is quite clear that everyone is to pay precisely the same half shekel.

That this unusual, one-time payment is associated with the census may in fact indicate a striking equality among the Israelites. In Israel everybody counts! Rich or poor, male or female, priest or servant—everyone of sufficient age to bear spiritual responsibility has an equal relationship with Israel's God. The rich can't buy God's special favor, nor will the poor be robbed of any blessing. Even today the threshold question of who is numbered among God's people does not have multiple answers depending on one's economic or social status. Whether then or now, praise God, salvation is for all, on equal terms.

■ **The question for me is: If God regards each and every soul as equal before him, am I making class distinctions that really shouldn't matter?**

A God Who Relents

Then the LORD relented and did not bring on his people the disaster he had threatened.

EXODUS 32:14

If you hadn't read it, you wouldn't believe it—the God of heaven and earth changing his mind! And all because one human being implored on behalf of other human beings! If there were other gods, God's "fickleness" is not a rumor you'd want to start among them. What kind of a god changes his mind? Well, actually, the only God there is. The same God who once said he was grieved to have made man. The same God who all but wiped mankind off the face of the earth in the flood. The same God of justice who has every right to punish man's disobedience. The same sovereign God who can do whatever he wants, all to his glory! And amazingly, this same sovereign God listened to Moses' passionate plea and actually acquiesced to it.

More amazing still are Moses' bold arguments to God. Moses first reminds him that a pagan world would be delighted to see that Israel's God was no different from all their own gods. Then there was the reminder of God's repeated promises to Abraham, Isaac, and Jacob. Would he dare break his promises? Yet what irony—Moses asking God to change his mind by recalling God's promises *not* to change his mind! When it comes to his promises to bless, we can be sure that God will never renege. (Of course it would not be a change of mind for him to withhold blessings where he has set conditions we ourselves fail to meet.) But when it comes to God's promises to punish or destroy, the picture gets slightly more complicated. For all the times when God punishes precisely as he has promised, there are those other times when a merciful God surprises us and relents from imposing what is justly deserved.

■ **The persistent vital question is: Have I learned anything from a merciful God about when to keep my promises and when to change my mind?**

Excessive Generosity

So all the skilled workers who were doing all the work on the sanctuary left what they were doing and said to Moses, "The people are bringing more than enough for doing the work the LORD commanded to be done."

EXODUS 36:4-5

News flash: Church Collects So Much Money, Everyone Told to Stop Giving! Not a likely story line these days, but that is exactly what happened when Moses called for offerings in support of the tabernacle's construction. It was a job to count the shekels pouring in! And it wasn't limited to gold and silver, but yarn and linen and precious gems. Whatever was needed was provided—and then some. The secret to this astonishing fund-raising success? "Everyone who was willing and whose heart moved them" brought offerings. Which only begs the question: Why were some hearts so incredibly willing? Remember we are talking about giving up even personal jewelry—perhaps with family memories attached. What would prompt us to give up family heirlooms for the Lord?

Have you ever considered the difference between regular offerings and special contributions for targeted causes? You can certainly be generous each Sunday when the offering plate comes around, but when some particularly urgent need tugs at your heart, have you found yourself suddenly digging deeper and pulling out extraordinary amounts of money in ways you might never have expected of yourself? Most likely those occasions follow in the wake of human tragedy where, intuitively, we identify with the possibility that it might have been *us* rather than strangers far away. Yet if appeals for building funds normally do not grab us the same way, maybe it is because they rarely embody a fresh, exciting idea that we can get swept up in. It's grand visions that move us, not structures. Just imagine. Wouldn't it be interesting to see how much might be contributed to really worthy causes if building budgets weren't all about structures, but *building* and *rebuilding* lives?

■ **The tugging question today is: If I'm not giving with extraordinary generosity, have I no grand visions that prompt such giving?**

_____

_____

_____

_____

_____

Anointed for Holiness

Take the anointing oil and anoint the tabernacle and everything in it; consecrate it and all its furnishings, and it will be holy.

EXODUS 40:9

Just how oil of any kind applied to ordinary utensils, furnishings, and clothing is supposed to make those items "holy" is a mystery. Surely no magic potion has such power. Yet it is clear that God wants everything in the tabernacle anointed with oil for that very purpose. And is that not what it's all about: purpose? Surely the lampstands, tables, and basins themselves did not become intrinsically holy. They were being dedicated to a uniquely holy purpose. In so many ways, God has a habit of turning the ordinary into the extraordinary—all for the sake of holiness. That should not be surprising. How can a holy God associate himself with anything that isn't itself holy? Would we expect God to dwell in any place that isn't holy? And just look what happened when the tabernacle was fully anointed—"the glory of the LORD filled the tabernacle"!

Do you want God in all his glory to dwell in your own home like that? Maybe it's time we anointed our houses, clothes, cars, and investment accounts to make them holy for the Lord—to "set them apart" for a holy purpose, to dedicate all that we have to God's use and service. We needn't literally use oil, of course. Again, it is not the oil itself that is magic. It is dedication to God's purposes that makes things holy. Yet lest we forget, Aaron and his sons were also a crucial part of the anointing process. As God's priests they too had to be made holy. Which only makes this business of anointing all the more important. Because each of us has been called to be a priest of God, as well as a tabernacle in which his Holy Spirit can dwell, no anointing is more important than making ourselves holy for his divine purposes.

■ **The compelling question is: Am I, and all I have, truly anointed for the Lord's holy purpose?**

Discerning the Law

Aaron replied to Moses, "Today they sacrificed their sin offering and their burnt offering before the LORD, but such things as this have happened to me. Would the LORD have been pleased if I had eaten the sin offering today?" When Moses heard this, he was satisfied.

LEVITICUS 10:19-20

The law is the law is the law. Nadab and Abihu failed to fully appreciate this hard truth when they decided to add some sweet-smelling incense to the holy fire of the tabernacle. Can you blame them? With all that pungent burning flesh around, fragrant incense to mask the odor was probably a good idea. As far as that goes, it is also possible that Nadab and Abihu acted with more noble motives, thinking God would be especially pleased if they gave him something of a bonus. How were they to know that even the best of intentions is no substitute for faithful obedience? Besides, their father, Aaron, had been persuaded by the Israelites into making a golden calf when he knew full well that idols were strictly forbidden. And was he struck dead? Nadab and Abihu certainly were!

Which makes it all the more intriguing that Aaron and his remaining sons were not struck dead for not eating the goat of the sin offering as they had been commanded. Isn't the law the law? When Moses confronted the two sons, Aaron intervened to take personal responsibility for the blatant irregularity. Considering the tragic loss of his other two sons that day, Aaron implored as to how he could possibly have participated joyfully in the eating of the sin offering. Though forbidden to mourn, was Aaron actually expected to celebrate? Does the law make no room for exceptional circumstances? Is the law devoid of all sympathy? Given Moses' satisfaction with Aaron's explanation, we are presented with a powerful lesson about the enforcement of God's laws: Compassionate exceptions to obedience are not to be compared with calculated deviations from obedience.

■ **The ever-difficult question is: Am I sufficiently discerning to distinguish between aberration and innovation?**

Dealing with Discrepancy

The LORD said to Moses, "This applies to the Levites: Men twenty-five years old or more shall come to take part in the work at the tent of meeting, but at the age of fifty, they must retire from their regular service and work no longer."

NUMBERS 8:23-25

If you know your Bible well, you know that in other passages the Levites are called to serve at the age of thirty, not twenty-five. Does this mean, as skeptics argue, that the Bible has so many inconsistencies it can't be trusted? Few skeptics have read their Bibles closely enough to know the distinction between mere differences and genuine inconsistencies. Nor are they willing to give the same benefit of the doubt they happily apply to articles in the morning newspaper. So is there any legitimate way to reconcile the five-year gap in question? Though speculative, it wouldn't be unreasonable to suppose that a five-year period of apprenticeship preceded the actual service of the Levites. Is that such a leap?

There will always be skeptics, but a mistake often made, even by true believers, is lifting verses out of context and missing the meaning or reading a verse with wooden literalness without considering qualifying nuances. If, for example, all you read is the passage cited above (or interpreted it too literally), you might conclude that at the age of fifty the Levites were forever forbidden to do work of any kind. However, the whole picture changes with the very next verse: "They may assist their brothers in performing their duties at the tent of meeting, but they themselves must not do the work." Just as there might be residual duties after the age of fifty, there could well be emerging duties prior to thirty. The point for us is to read the Scriptures to get the full picture—looking first for the obvious, then looking again for the not-so-obvious.

■ **The ironic question for us believers is: When I engage the biblical text, am I sufficiently "skeptical" to make sure I get the right picture?**

A God-Centered Community

The LORD said to Moses and Aaron: "The Israelites are to camp around the tent of meeting some distance from it, each of them under their standard and holding the banners of their family."

NUMBERS 2:1-2

Suppose you were asked to design a planned community, complete with houses, shops, schools, churches, and hospitals. Would you want there to be a grid with streets crisscrossing like tic-tac-toe or, perhaps, streets ringing the inner city in concentric circles like a target? And what would you put in the center of the community? A park? City hall? The business district? When God planned a community for the Israelites, he put the "church" smack-dab in the middle, with "houses" streaming out in every direction—north, south, east, and west. Of course the tabernacle wasn't exactly a "church" as we might think of a steepled church today. In fact, the earliest church wasn't a "church" at all if what we have in mind is bricks and mortar. Unlike the temples of Solomon and later Herod, the first Christians did not have any buildings for the sole purpose of worship for over two centuries. They just went from house to house. Nothing fancy. No pulpit. No pews. No steeples. Just a gathered group of believers sitting around tables enjoying fellowship with each other and with God.

So where do you put the church in the community when there is no church building? How about in the families that comprise the community? That way the church is not just in the middle of the community, but on every block. And where is God's dwelling place when it is set within families themselves? Smack-dab in the middle, of course. In godly families, worship is always at the center of everything a family does, whether work or play, mealtime or prayer time. When God is at the heart of a family, and family after family centers itself on God, an entire community can be wondrously transformed—as if God planned it that way.

◼ **The intriguing question is: If I were a community of one, where would God's special place be?**

The Principle of Substitution

The LORD said to Moses, "Count all the firstborn Israelite males who are a month old or more and make a list of their names. Take the Levites for me in place of all the firstborn of the Israelites, and the livestock of the Levites in place of all the firstborn of the livestock of the Israelites."

NUMBERS 3:40-41

Given a choice, which would you rather have: the real thing or some substitute? Most of the time, of course, we would prefer the genuine over the substitute. Why settle for a vinyl imitation when you can have genuine leather? Then again sometimes substitutes are to be preferred, as with sugar substitutes or milk substitutes, when there is some health advantage to not using the real thing. So what are we being told when God substitutes the Levites for the firstborn of all Israel? Since the Levites were specially chosen to offer Israel's sacrifices, is it possible that God is signaling the importance of substitution's role in those very sacrifices?

When it comes to paying the penalty for sin, God seemingly has a particular affinity for substitutes. Perhaps it is just a practical necessity. For if everyone has sinned and the penalty for sin is death, then imposing the death penalty directly on every sinner would quickly mean an end to human life on earth. So what is God to do but provide some substitute for that penalty—as in animal sacrifices? Does that not explain why human hands are laid upon the animal being sacrificed—to make a visual connection between the death of the slain animal and the worshipper's sins? An innocent bull or lamb is taking the place of a guilty sinner! Only when we come to understand the vital role substitution plays in ransoming our lives from the death penalty we deserve can we begin to fully grasp the profound implications of the sinless Lamb of God being slain for your sins and mine.

■ **The follow-up question is: Is there some struggling soul in distress for whom I might be a sacrificial substitute?**

Running Out of Cope

He asked the LORD, "Why have you brought this trouble on your servant? What have I done to displease you that you put the burden of all these people on me?"

NUMBERS 11:11

Have you ever felt like you've taken absolutely all you can stand? That you cannot cope any longer? If so, you're not alone. To be honest, maybe we haven't a clue about the far more serious challenges others may face, or maybe we have less capacity for dealing with despair than others. Whatever the circumstances, if we can't cope, we can't cope! Suddenly life is overwhelming. And just as suddenly we might well find ourselves having a pity party with God. It's then that we, like Moses, are tempted to lay the blame for our troubles squarely at God's feet. "What have I done to displease you?" is only slightly different from "It's all your fault!" But are we right to assume a connection between our current travail and our relationship with God? Was Moses cursed with the leadership of Israel because God found him displeasing, or had God greatly honored him as a man with broad shoulders?

When Moses asks "Did I conceive all these people? Did I give them birth?" it's hard not to think of countless parents who have given birth to special children requiring extraordinary wisdom and patience. How ever do they cope? Certainly they could be excused for having a quiet word or two with God about why he might have thrust upon them such a daily trial. Perhaps your own challenge seems equally unbearable. If so, there is reason to take heart. Just as God provided a means to help Moses cope, so too will he provide for you. For those of us who haven't been equally honored, could it be that we are the very ones God is setting in place to help another cope?

■ **A hopeful question is: With others around me coping despite great challenges, do I have any reason to truly despair?**

Crowned with Humility

Now Moses was a very humble man, more humble than anyone else on the face of the earth.

NUMBERS 12:3

Isn't it ironic that some of the most humble people we've ever known, or known about, are also those who have every reason *not* to be humble? More than anyone on the face of the earth in Moses' day (or in any other era), Moses had reason for extraordinary pride. God himself reminded Miriam and Aaron that, unlike ordinary prophets to whom he spoke through visions and dreams, God spoke directly to Moses, face-to-face! How many of us wouldn't be puffed up with pride to be considered that important? All we have to do is listen to Miriam and Aaron boasting about being prophets. Spiritual leaders of all types are especially vulnerable to pride. Aren't they far more gifted and "in the know" than most folks? Doesn't God's Word come flowing through them to the teeming masses? Don't strugglers of all sorts turn to them for guidance? It's hard to be humble when you're special.

It would be fascinating to know what made Moses so humble. Was it the faltering speech he was concerned about at the burning bush? Or perhaps the haunting memory that he had once killed a man and tried to cover it up? Maybe it was his youthful experience in Pharaoh's household, witnessing enough pomp and pride for a lifetime. Whatever else might have contributed to it, we probably have already made a false assumption. Rather than having more reason than anyone to be prideful about God's speaking to him directly, might not Moses have been humbled precisely because, day in and day out, he was in God's very presence? Think about it. If you were close enough to be face-to-face with God, how comparatively insignificant would you feel? In the immediate presence of the sovereign God of the universe, how could anyone *not* be humble!

■ **The question with the obvious answer is: If I wanted to be more humble, how best would I go about it?**

Nothing but the Finest for God

You must present as the LORD's portion the best and holiest part of everything given to you.

NUMBERS 18:29

God is a practical, common-sense God. If we look closely enough, we can see that what God commands by way of moral law, or doctrine, or worship ritual usually has some purpose other than his simply being arbitrary or capricious. We are not being asked to jump through hoops merely for God's amusement. Down to the last detail, what God asks us to do is ultimately for our own good. The typical rules even earthly parents lay down don't just come out of thin air. Usually they are directed at some higher good. Would we expect anything less from our heavenly Father? So it should not be surprising that the Israelites are instructed to tithe in support of the priests and Levites, who are too busy doing God's work in the sanctuary to support themselves otherwise. It's a practical problem solved—nice and easy, done and dusted.

But then we discover that God requires the Levites themselves to give a tenth of the tithe! It can't be needed for support of the work in the tabernacle. In this case does God perhaps have in mind something beyond the practical? The clue seems to be in the requirement that the Levites are to present "the best and holiest part" to the Lord. This was also true of the tithe and required of each sacrifice brought before the Lord. The best and the holiest. Always the best and the holiest. Is it just a matter of vanity that God would demand nothing but the finest for himself? Or is he still being his usual practical self—all for our ultimate good? In one fell stroke, to give of our best to God teaches obedience, sacrifice, nobility, prioritizing, selflessness, and a host of other important lessons. What could be more practical?

■ **The question beyond mere practicality is: Of all that I give to God today, will it truly be the best and holiest?**

Records That Reflect

At the LORD's command Moses recorded the stages in their journey.

NUMBERS 33:2

Journaling is back in fashion, though it has been practiced for centuries, all the way back to the time of Moses. Keeping track of our travels, activities, and appointments is a good way to record our life, day by day. If all we are talking about are facts and figures, the journal might be nothing more than "The Book of the Wars of the Lord," curiously alluded to in the text and containing what seems to us today as gibberish. Of course it would have meant much more to Moses and his contemporaries, perhaps bringing back memories of exciting encounters or sudden skirmishes along ravines now washed away. The simple journal God commanded Moses to keep of Israel's various encampments tells us little other than Israel's bold exodus from Egypt and the death of Aaron. Even in the two passing comments about water (or lack of it), notably missing are the embarrassing moments associated with Israel's thirst.

The more intimate the journal, the more we think of it as a diary—perhaps even a secret diary. The book of Numbers itself is a far more revealing account of Israel's triumphs and disasters. In this journal, the Israelites (including Moses and Aaron) are fully exposed. No sin or moral flaw is kept secret. For those of us privileged to read that diary, there is plenty of food for thought. By some irony we may even keep a personal journal of what thoughts come to mind when we read *their* diary. Or perhaps how our own lives have changed since the last time we read those same words. Looking back through journals past, might we be surprised at where we have spiritually camped along the way? At what stage were we then; what stage now? Most intriguing of all, at what stage will we be this time next year?

■ **The potentially disquieting question is: If I were to record all my thoughts and deeds done today, would I want others reading the entry?**

_____

_____

_____

_____

Foolishly Testing God's Word

He answered, "Must I not speak what the LORD puts in my mouth?"

NUMBERS 23:12

Playing both ends against the middle takes real bravado. Poor ol' Balaam would certainly love to have all that silver and gold, so he is careful not to gratuitously offend King Balak. But Balaam also knows he is dealing with a powerful God, not just a fluke or small-time divination. So Balaam does the judicious thing and tells Balak he is in no position to curse or bless Israel unless God puts it on his tongue. To King Balak's chagrin, of course, it's always blessings on Israel—not curses—even after three attempts. Seems like everyone in the story lives by the adage, "Third time's a charm." First, there's King Balak thinking that he can either wear God down or get lucky the third time around. Then, there's Balaam hoping that the third time would bring Balak his curses—and resulting fortune for himself. Finally, there's Balaam thinking that beating his skittish donkey three times will sort her out and get him on his way!

Ah, the talking donkey (famously known as "Balaam's ass"). If that inspired donkey were still around today, wouldn't it be a riot to hear her say, maybe even to chortle, "Must I not speak what the LORD puts in my mouth?" When that is true of a donkey, how could it not be true of Balaam? And when it is true of a cagey old prophet for hire, how could it not also be true of you and me? Has God spoken to us through his revealed Word? Then, despite those times God has mercifully relented from punishing some deserving culprit, we can rest assured he is not going to change his mind about what he actually requires of us. Not the first time we test him, or the second time, or yet some "charmed" third time.

■ **The question for wishful thinkers is: If perhaps I am hoping against hope to find a Scripture to circumvent some obvious biblical teaching, what kind of stupid donkey am I?**

In Praise of Moral Outrage

When Phinehas son of Eleazar, the son of Aaron, the priest, saw this, he left the assembly, took a spear in his hand and followed the Israelite into the tent. He drove the spear into both of them, right through the Israelite man and into the woman's stomach.

NUMBERS 25:7-8

In today's politically correct, nonjudgmental climate, Phinehas most likely would be thrown in jail for life or even executed. What was this self-appointed guardian of cultural values thinking? You can't just go around imposing your own morals at the end of a spear! Maybe…but God seemed especially pleased with what Phinehas did. Were you to ask Phinehas if he himself were perfect, he'd tell you right out that he wasn't. Were you to ask him if everyone who sinned ought to be put to death, he'd probably look at you as if you were crazy. So did he, a fellow sinner, have any right to take justice into his own hands and put these two particular sinners to death? The times were different, of course. God himself struck thousands of people dead for their sins—24,000 in this plague alone. Still, was Phinehas right to go ballistic?

Sin of any kind is always grievous. Yet some sins rightly evoke heightened moral outrage. Merely consider the brutal rape of a young child or the senseless murder of a helpless pensioner. For Phinehas, undoubtedly it was the brazen insolence with which the couple's sin was committed in the midst of a wider moral rebellion. But have you noticed lately that moral outrage is in short supply? Not even today's impudent, in-your-face moral obscenities draw much response from society's caretakers or even from us religious folks. Oh, we may moan about how society is going to the dogs, but where is the clenched fist, defying the defiant? Have we become so desensitized that even the most outrageous immorality is rarely met with determined confrontation?

■ **The more personal question is: If sin is always open and outright defiance against God, why am I not more outraged at my own sin?**

Disinherited Children

For the LORD had told those Israelites they would surely die in the wilderness, and not one of them was left except Caleb son of Jephunneh and Joshua son of Nun.

NUMBERS 26:65

Had not God covenanted with the children of Israel that he would bring them into a land of promise and bless them with a bountiful inheritance? Is God now being unfaithful to his many promises? What this second census powerfully underscores is that none of the fighting men of Israel who were over the age of twenty just forty years earlier had survived the wilderness wanderings except for Caleb and Joshua, the courageous spies. Nor was it natural attrition that had decimated the ranks. It was God's own judgment against his rebellious offspring, intentionally cutting them off from their inheritance. Unlike human situations where disfavored children are unceremoniously cut out of the will, the Israelites were literally cut off from the face of the earth!

An inheritance is always by grace and favor. The person who has a legally valid will need not bequeath his or her estate to anyone in particular, though typically it is the spouse and then the children who inherit. In many ancient cultures, with lingering effect even today, it is the firstborn son who inherits all. Most importantly, the testator can always decide to disinherit someone previously named in the will. Without question a sovereign God could do that! But had he not *promised*? As God's children, we make a grave mistake if we assume God's promises are wholly unconditional. Whereas God's initial covenants with mankind were clearly one-sided, all of his later covenants have been based upon mutual promises and obligations. While God will never breach his side of the covenant, is it not possible that we could write our own selves out of our inheritance? In case we are in any doubt about that, we might just ask a whole generation of God's children.

■ **The reassuring question is: If I hold to the faith that is the key to my eternal inheritance, need I have any doubt, whatsoever, that I will receive it?**

_____

_____

_____

_____

_____

The Importance of Eradication

But if you do not drive out the inhabitants of the land, those you allow to remain will become barbs in your eyes and thorns in your sides. They will give you trouble in the land where you will live.

NUMBERS 33:55

Sometimes a warning is really a prediction. All it takes is changing an "if" to a "when." Looking back some 3500 years, it's clear that it was only a matter of time before the "if" of God's warning turned into the "when" of predictable consequences. Israel's constant flirtation with her idolatrous neighbors would bring terrors for centuries. It did not take a clairvoyant to see what inevitably would happen. Israel's track record was already pretty dismal. The Israelites were a fickle bunch—one day praising God, the next day being seduced by cheap imitation gods. One day trusting God for victory, the next day cowering with fear. The Israelites lacked full and complete commitment to the Lord. And given that fragile faith, they always underestimated the power of their enemies. Indeed, they seemed to be altogether fascinated by them, strangely drawn to them, and almost envious of them!

As long as you are fascinated, drawn, and envious, it is hard to wipe out your enemies completely. Oh, maybe there are daily skirmishes and sometimes even furious all-out assaults. But there is never quite that knockout punch because, after all, you're still fascinated, drawn, and envious. Call it a love-hate relationship. Call it compromise. Call it anything you want. The problem is that anything less than complete eradication of the enemy means that there is no escape from the endless cycle of war, appeasement, fraternization, accommodation, acceptance, betrayal, conflict, and, once more, war. Spiritual enemies are enemies for a reason! With spiritual enemies, there can be no peaceful coexistence. It's them or us. Complete and total victory, or ongoing, never-ending conflict.

■ **The disturbing question is: Am I kidding myself to believe that I can rid my life of most major sin and still live comfortably alongside the few "insignificant sins" I allow to remain?**

In Proper Retrospect

Only be careful, and watch yourselves closely so that you do not forget the things your eyes have seen or let them fade from your heart as long as you live.

DEUTERONOMY 4:9

Notoriously, Lot's wife looked back and turned into a pillar of salt. Why did she look back? A good guess is that she was looking back wistfully, unable to completely tear herself away from her past and move on. Her past is unknown to us, of course, but given the wickedness of the cities of Sodom and Gomorrah, perhaps it had something to do with the evil web that had provoked God's fiery wrath. Were the unrighteous friends and neighbors she hurriedly left behind more important to her than they should have been, given their perverted values? Whatever her reasons, she paid a high price for looking back—as is often the case when we look back in ways we shouldn't. Have you ever noticed that some people seem unable to tear themselves away from the past and move on with their lives? Maybe they simply can't get over a devastating divorce. Or perhaps it is the death of a loved one, especially a child cut down in the blossom of youth.

By contrast with these unhealthy ways of looking back, Moses actually cautions against forgetting the past. Don't forget how God has moved in your life in the past! Don't forget how richly he has blessed you in your righteousness or how punishment has always followed on the heels of sin! Don't forget how many times God's promises have already come true! In times of fear and uncertainty or when your heart aches with unbearable pain, don't let slip from your heart the security, comfort, and wisdom that can come from thinking back on what God has already done for you. A healthy heart knows what to remember and what to let slip away.

■ **The sobering question is: Am I trapped in time, unable to escape the past, or is my rearview mirror an invaluable aid to the journey ahead?**

Godly Parenting

These commandments that I give you today are to be on your hearts. Impress them on your children. Talk about them when you sit at home and when you walk along the road, when you lie down and when you get up.

DEUTERONOMY 6:6-7

For many believing parents in particular, homeschooling has become an option to be preferred over public education. The problem is not simply that public education has officially turned its back on God, daring not to mention anything overtly spiritual for risk of a lawsuit. It is also clear that, although the Bible does not directly enter the debate over education, parents have been given primary responsibility for the training of their children. They alone must decide whether public, private, or in-home tutelage is in their child's best interest—not just educationally, but spiritually. For what does it profit a child to gain a superior education in the eyes of the world, yet lose his or her own soul? Not that educating the soul precludes a superior education. Indeed, scholarly faith-informed learning provides the foundation for a far superior education to anything a purely secular world has to offer. Yet whatever road a child's formal education takes, it is moral and spiritual training that counts most.

So whether we are parents or perhaps extended family, what do we talk about with children all day long? How often do we bring up moral values or spiritual concerns? Listen closely to most conversations adults have with children, and we are likely to hear a constant stream of talk about sports, social activities, songs, movies, clothes, food, or—if they are old enough—perhaps girlfriends or boyfriends and plans for college. For younger children maybe there is a Bible story at bedtime, and hopefully nightly prayers. But as children grow into teenagers, most of the God-talk seems to fade away. Are we surprised, then, that so few grown-ups talk about God?

■ **The vital question is: What might I say to some young person today to stir a greater interest in being a faithful child of God?**

Treating Cause and Effect with Caution

Understand, then, that it is not because of your righteousness that the LORD your God is giving you this good land to possess, for you are a stiff-necked people.

DEUTERONOMY 9:6

Whoever said you shouldn't look a gift horse in the mouth was quite right. (Why risk disappointment by examining the horse's mouth and discovering it's really an old nag? Because it is a gift, at least it's a *free* old nag!) A flip-side corollary is the adage, "You shouldn't judge a book by its cover," which is to say that appearances can be deceiving. In fact there is often no connection between the quality of the cover and the quality of the writing inside. In a variety of ways, we seem always to be making connections that don't necessarily hold true. Consider, for example, Moses' warning about what will happen when the Israelites take possession of the Promised Land. The more they prosper, the better they eat, and the finer their houses, he warns, the more danger there is that they will forget God. Failing to make the *right* connection (between their success and God's power), they will arrogantly make the *wrong* connection (between success and their own efforts). Appearances can indeed be deceiving.

The same goes for any foolish notion that these stiff-necked Israelites might be receiving the Promised Land because of some meritorious righteousness on their part. Far from it! Although Moses speaks passionately about a cause-and-effect connection between obedience and blessings, the reverse is not always true. To be sure, obedience will always be blessed, but sometimes God blesses us for his own reasons wholly apart from our obedience (or even disobedience). Because appearances can be so deceiving, we would do well not to examine too carefully any "gift horse" God might give us. We might end up disappointed to learn that it has nothing whatsoever to do with our own effort or righteousness.

■ **An intriguing tangential question is: If my primary motivation for obeying God is to receive his blessings, will I still receive them?**

Marked for Holiness

Do not cut your bodies for the dead or put tattoo marks on yourselves. I am the LORD.

LEVITICUS 19:28

Lately tattoos are all the rage. Young and old, pop star and housewife, Hell's Angels biker and Wall Street broker—they've all got them. Some have them discreetly hidden from view, but most want their tattoos noticed. Of course tattoos are not all that novel. An older generation will recall young sailors coming home from war proudly displaying on their shoulders Cupid's heart bearing the name of their favorite girl. Tattoos lost some of their appeal when many returning servicemen discovered that the "Peggy Sue" they so adored had married someone else!

Because tattoos have an ancient association with pagan practice, it's hardly surprising that tattoos were taboo in God's eyes. One cannot help but wonder if God is pleased with deliberate desecration of our earthly "temples." But because the prohibition against tattoos is part of the warnings against idolatry, something far more serious is at stake spiritually. To the extent that pagan tattoos were a sign of "ownership" by a false god, it meant that one was marked for life as a pagan for all the world to notice. For the Israelites such implications would have been unthinkable. While a believer today would likewise want to avoid pagan allusions, the irony is that God has set his own mark on us in a different kind of way—also for life and for all the world to see. As Christ's disciples we bear his indelible imprint, displaying love, devotion, and loyalty as surely as any tattoo dedicated to "Peggy Sue." In this case, praise God, it's not an embarrassing ink-design on our body, but a lasting impression on our soul.

■ **The question naturally arising is: Is our mark of being a Christian proudly displayed or discreetly hidden?**

Misusing God's Name

You shall not misuse the name of the LORD your God, for the LORD will not hold anyone guiltless who misuses his name.

DEUTERONOMY 5:11

To listen to some foul-mouthed folks talk, you'd think you were listening to a sermon. It's always "God" this and "Jesus Christ" that—as if by casually invoking the names of deity, they can somehow reduce God to their own level. Ironically, they only reinforce the exclusive authority of God and Jesus Christ. (What nonbelievers ever include Buddha or Mohammed among their curses?) Strangely, it is reassuring that when disaster strikes, the first thing you are likely to hear is "Oh, my God!" For many it is as close as they will ever come to uttering a prayer—and at least they intuitively know to whom it ought to be directed. Trouble is, most of these same folks are just as likely to say "Oh, my God!" when they're served a huge piece of cake!

When people thoughtlessly use the expression "by God," it is far from the formal courtroom oath whereby witnesses swear, "so help me God." When that particular oath is violated, we call it perjury. By extension, taking God's name in vain is always perjury because it always involves a misrepresentation. Surprisingly, the most unexpected misuse of God's name comes from those who use the name "Christian" as an adjective to describe any number of organizations that don't live up to that name. To describe something as, say, a "Christian ministry" or a "Christian university" without thinking and acting Christianly is a misuse of the Lord's name made all the more monstrous by its false pretension. Yet the single greatest abuse of the Lord's name is when a person appropriates the name "Christian" to himself or herself while doing nothing but bringing dishonor to that holy name.

■ **The piercing question is: What kind of God-talk will people hear from me today, and—more important—what kind of God-walk will they see?**

Chasing Away Scapegoats

The goat will carry on itself all their sins to a remote place; and the man shall release it in the wilderness.

LEVITICUS 16:22

If the team has a losing season, fire the coach! Never mind that he or she couldn't possibly have made "silk purses" out of the "sow's ears" they were given to work with. And if a giant corporation fails, you know someone is going to get fired, deserving or not. The more blameless a person is, the more vulnerable that person becomes to those who are unwilling to take responsibility for their own actions. By definition a scapegoat is *supposed* to be innocent. The whole point of the exercise for Israel was to lay the nation's corporate sins on an obviously innocent goat and run it out of the camp, symbolically bearing the burden of the people's guilt. It could be said that the scapegoat was the lucky one. By sheer fortune of the draw, the *other* goat got roasted!

We mustn't forget that the "other goat" was just as much an innocent scapegoat, even as it was vicariously sacrificed for the sins of Israel. If sometimes the ceremonial rituals of ancient Israel seem more than a bit bizarre, they are God's remarkable ways of teaching us about sin and forgiveness. About vicarious atonement. About the need for sin to be "run out of the camp" so that sinners might be deemed guiltless. Prophetically, it is also a graphic picture of the innocent Lamb of God who one day would be taken outside the city walls of Jerusalem as a scapegoat vicariously bearing away your sins and mine. Tragically, he would also be the sacrificial Lamb, taking our place when it is we alone who deserve to die.

■ **The troubling question is: Does my gratitude match the extent of Christ's love when he willingly became a scapegoat for the sins I will commit this very day?**

_____

_____

_____

_____

Keeping Faith Alive

The fire must be kept burning on the altar continuously; it must not go out.

LEVITICUS 6:13

On again, off again. Fits and starts. Look at some people's faith life, and it is the story of the hare, not the tortoise. And why is it so difficult to stick to a diet or maintain a regimen of exercise? What happens to our resolve? Why do our commitments seem so hard to keep? At the first of the year, we do our daily Bible readings with disciplined consistency, then there's that unexpected interruption that makes us miss a day, followed by another day when still other events overtake us. Before we know it, we've gotten out of the routine, and the Bible lies unopened for weeks. No wonder God instructs the priests and Levites to keep a fire burning continuously on the altar. Anyone who has ever built a fire knows it is a lot easier to add fuel periodically and stir the embers than to let the fire go out and have to start all over again.

Of course it's not about the fire itself. What God wants is daily, continuous, uninterrupted devotion—certainly for his own glory, but also because he knows how much we ourselves are shaped and nourished by daily acts of worship. To be constantly into the Word is to be continuously reminded of right priorities and values. To make little sacrifices each day is to prepare us for times when we may be called upon to offer extraordinary sacrifices. To regularly exercise our spiritual gifts is to strengthen ourselves to serve even more. To pray day by day is to be secure night after night. Above all, to make God the Lord of each day is the only way to make sure he is Lord of a lifetime.

■ **The question for some of us is: If I've let myself get out of the daily habit of being in touch with God, might this be the very day my faith gets back on track?**

Unintentional Sin

If any member of the community sins unintentionally and does what is forbidden in any of the LORD's commands, when they realize their guilt and the sin they have committed becomes known, they must bring as their offering for the sin they committed a female goat without defect.

LEVITICUS 4:27-28

We hear it all the time (often coming out of our own mouths): "But I didn't mean to!" "But I didn't know…" Isn't ignorance of the law an excuse? Not really, but four-year-olds seem to think so! And what if we're operating on the basis of mistaken facts? Is it fair to be punished for innocent mistakes? All we have to do is recall that speeding ticket we received when we really and truly didn't see the reduced speed limit sign. Despite being a notoriously merciful judge, it is clear from Israel's laws that God is serious about sin. A sin is a sin is a sin, even if it is committed unintentionally. And guilt for that sin must be expunged, regardless of whether the offender is an ordinary individual, a civic leader, or even the entire community.

It would have been hard for any Israelite to claim ignorance of the law. As part of the very essence of the nation, God's ordinances were declared publicly and repeatedly, in both sweeping breadth and minute detail. So how could you commit a sin unawares? Suppose, for example, you touched a dead body thinking it was still alive. Only later, when you discover it was actually dead, do you realize you've violated the law—not willfully, but negligently. Seems pretty harsh, doesn't it? Maybe it was God's idea to place such a high premium on obedience so as to nix any flimsy excuses. Or, more likely, to instill a pervasive awareness that every thought and action has potential spiritual consequences.

■ **The unsettling question is: If I unknowingly commit a sin against someone today, what will they be thinking of me until I finally discover what I've done and make amends?**

Communal Responsibility

Then all the elders of the town nearest the body shall wash their hands over the heifer whose neck was broken in the valley, and they shall declare: "Our hands did not shed this blood, nor did our eyes see it done. Accept this atonement for your people Israel, whom you have redeemed, LORD, and do not hold your people guilty of the blood of an innocent person."

DEUTERONOMY 21:6-8

Reading the passage above, we can but gasp at the chilling cry of those who centuries later would shout for Jesus' crucifixion, saying, "Let his blood be on us and our children!" Did they not realize the gravity of the responsibility they were assuming? One thing they apparently did not consider was the ordinance requiring an offering by the nearest town when a murder victim was found and there was no known perpetrator. It was up to the community to see that the blood was atoned for—otherwise the blood was on their own hands. (In fact, how can we ourselves say of Jesus' crucifixion, "*We* didn't do it, nor did we see it being done," as if to deny that our sins too demanded his death!)

None of us live to ourselves. God has set us in communities with spiritual responsibilities toward all who live within the community. In one sense the sins of others are also our sins. Consider the unknown murderer, for example. Whose son or brother was he? Who taught him in school? Who might have set a bad example for him when he was only a child? Just how many people in the community does it take to turn an innocent newborn into a cold-hearted murderer? Maybe none, as with Cain. But when we read disturbing headlines in the morning paper, at least spare a thought that it might never have happened if the whole community had been more spiritually responsible.

■ **The challenging question is: As I go about my community today, what vulnerable lives will I be touching for good or for ill?**

_____

_____

_____

_____

_____

Jubilee Freedom!

Consecrate the fiftieth year and proclaim liberty throughout the land to all its inhabitants. It shall be a jubilee for you; each of you is to return to your family property and to your own clan.

LEVITICUS 25:10

When a couple has been married for fifty years, it is time to gather the whole family together, throw a party, and celebrate their golden wedding anniversary. Jubilees are occasions for jubilation! For the Israelites the year of Jubilee was certainly an occasion for joy because debts were forgiven, property was returned to original owners, and servants were set free. Whether it be a birthday, an anniversary, or perhaps the jubilee of a long-established congregation, the passing of five decades should be an occasion for joyful celebration.

Quite brilliantly, God often paints a picture for Israel, which is a perfect preview of things to come for followers of Christ, right down to the last detail. Think, for example, of the parallel between Jubilee and the Jewish feast of Pentecost. Just as Jubilee is the fiftieth *year,* Pentecost is the fiftieth *day* (after Passover). On the first Pentecost following Christ's resurrection, an extraordinary jubilee occurs. "What must we do?" asked the shocked crowd of Pentecost celebrants when told they had crucified the Messiah. The remarkable answer was, "Repent and be baptized…for the forgiveness of your sins, and you will receive the gift of the Holy Spirit." Like Jubilee's turning back of property, *repentance* is a turning back of one's life. Like Jubilee's redemption, *forgiveness* is the discharging of debt for sin. And, just as with Jubilee's freedom for those enslaved, the *gift of the Spirit* accompanies freedom from spiritual bondage. With this "good news" of the gospel comes even more good news—no one has to wait fifty years to share the joy!

■ **The question for each of us is: Have I prepared the way for my own spiritual jubilee by doing what the celebrants on Pentecost did?**

Water, Water, Everywhere

The person to be cleansed must wash their clothes, shave off all their hair and bathe with water; then they will be ceremonially clean.

LEVITICUS 14:8

Perhaps you have seen pictures of the millions of Hindu worshippers submerging themselves over and over in the polluted waters of the Ganges. Maybe you've been to the Dome of the Rock in Jerusalem and watched Muslim worshippers wash themselves before entering the nearby mosque for prayers. And maybe you've seen the ancient *mikvehs* throughout Jerusalem where the Jews of ancient times performed their own ceremonial washings. After a while you begin to understand the adage, "Cleanliness is next to godliness." So is it any surprise that Christian baptism plays such an important role? Even Christ began his ministry by going down into the waters of the Jordan to be baptized by John—not to be cleansed, as the penitent sinners that day, but to fulfill all righteousness.

Of course it's never about the water itself or about washing the body clean. Just ask Naaman, who thought the Jordan too dirty for his Syrian dignity. Or merely consider the grungy Ganges, into which pour all things foul. For God, water is simply the medium of choice for his creative artistry. When he wanted to create the world, his Spirit hovered over water. When he wanted to re-create a sinful world, he did so through the rising waters of the great flood. When he wanted to create a chosen nation, he brought Israel through the divided waters of the Red Sea. And now when he wants to create new creatures out of sinful men and women, once again he paints with water. Other religions have the right idea, just not the right artist.

■ **The question for reflection is: If God has painted me pure in the waters of baptism, have I allowed myself to become polluted?**

The Making and Keeping of Vows

Whatever your lips utter you must be sure to do, because you made your vow freely to the LORD your God with your own mouth.

DEUTERONOMY 23:23

At a wedding the central feature is the exchange of vows between the bride and groom. Whether an arranged marriage or one driven by love and romance, the vow says to God and the whole world that the marriage will last "until death do us part." Sadly, the importance of vows has become a lost art. Not just *keeping* them, but also *making* them. Apart from marriage vows, or perhaps those of certain religious orders, we don't think a lot about the making of vows. Oh, we might hear someone say in frustration, "I vowed never again to…" But did they really take a vow? Not likely.

In ancient Israel it was not uncommon for people to make vows to God. The Nazirite vow, for example, was a vow of separation and abstention, expressed particularly in not shaving one's hair and abstaining from wine. Unlike Samson, Samuel, and John the Baptist—all of whom were Nazirites for life because their parents dedicated them thus—others took the Nazirite vow for the special purpose of focused holiness, somewhat like a fast. Distinct from both forms, followers of Christ make an implicit vow for life when they personally commit themselves to his lordship. And with each observance of the Lord's Supper, that vow is effectively renewed. But have we possibly missed something by not making more Nazirite-like vows in pursuit of godly dedication? Maybe it would be a good idea to forego shallow New Year's resolutions in favor of serious vows to God—and then keep them!

■ **The challenging question is: Might there be a meaningful vow of dedication I can make before God today that will bring me ever closer to his holiness?**

A Most Intriguing God!

When you enter the land the LORD your God is giving you and have taken possession of it and settled in it, and you say, "Let us set a king over us like all the nations around us," be sure to appoint over you a king the LORD your God chooses.

DEUTERONOMY 17:14-15

Is not this passage incredibly odd? Throughout the history of Israel, God repeatedly warns the Israelites against desiring a king. *He* is their king! Besides, for every good king there are many more bad ones. They oppress their subjects, tax them to death, and fight senseless wars. So why would the Israelites ever want a king? More to the point, why would God ever let them have one? Stranger still, what was God thinking to include regulations for Israel's kings before they even asked for one? And if Israel's having a king was truly against God's will, why did he insist that they choose only kings he himself appointed!

Of course just knowing in advance that Israel would demand a king speaks volumes about God's omniscience. And because he had that foreknowledge at the time he was proclaiming the laws by which Israel would function for centuries, it makes sense that God would include rules regulating kings. Yet that still doesn't explain why God would tolerate kings unless, perhaps, there was something keenly important to be learned. Without earthly kings how would we understand God's own kingship over a spiritual kingdom? Without bad kings how could we appreciate good kings—especially the righteous King of kings? And how else could we learn to honor our secular leaders, whether kings, presidents, or governors? If God thinks government itself is important, there will always be specific individuals who govern—even the worst of whom might well be serving purposes we'd never guess—at the prompting of a most intriguing God!

■ **The fascinating question is: Does God ever allow me to act *against* his will in order to bring me *within* his will?**

Mixed Signals from the Law

Anyone who beats their male or female slave with a rod must be punished if the slave dies as a direct result, but they are not to be punished if the slave recovers after a day or two, since the slave is their property.

EXODUS 21:20-21

For its time, the Law given through Moses was uniquely enlightened, demonstrating a sense of justice unknown in any other culture. Even the classic punishment of "eye for eye, tooth for tooth"—often thought to be vindictive—was in fact a limitation on the extent to which revenge could be brought. If modern minds think capital punishment for lesser offenses than murder to be unduly harsh, then having designated cities of refuge to prevent blood avengers from taking the life of one who had killed another accidentally must seem revolutionary.

Yet what can one say about this *enlightened* Law when it provides punishment when a slave dies from his master's beating, but not when the slave is able to get up after a day or two, *since the slave is his property*! The modern mind rightly recoils from humans ever being regarded as property to be bought and sold, whether beaten or not. How could God ever permit the institution of slavery? Is this just another case where God is painting pictures—perhaps showing how we slaves to sin have been set free to be servants of righteousness? If so, it's a painting for which millions of oppressed souls have paid an incredibly high price! It is only a desperate guess, but maybe God is taking people where he finds them and gradually leading them to higher moral ground. For a morally immature human race, maybe it had to be baby steps first. No answer should leave us completely comfortable, other than that a righteous God is to be extraordinarily trusted.

■ **The question for doubters is: If I am ever tempted to give up on God when I don't understand how he acts, what would be my alternative?**

Dignifying the Poor

When you make a loan of any kind to your neighbor, do not go into his house to get what is offered to you as a pledge. Stay outside and let the neighbor to whom you are making the loan bring the pledge out to you.

DEUTERONOMY 24:10-11

One of the most laudable aspects of the laws of Moses is the detailed attention given to respecting the dignity of all Israelites, no matter what their station in life. Requiring contributions for the poor is not surprising. What is extraordinary are all the rules protecting the poor from humiliation. Consider, for example, that marvelous provision to stay outside a debtor's door when claiming a pledge. The man may need a loan, but there is no reason to rob him of his pride! And what about not taking anything necessary for a man's livelihood as a pledge? Or not keeping a man's cloak in pledge overnight, lest he freeze to death? Or paying the poor worker his wages promptly at the end of every day?

Even with today's unprecedented prosperity, the poor are still among us. How we should meet the needs of the poor is an age-old debate. Do we give them handouts? Teach them to fish instead of giving them fish? Attempt to meet their needs through government programs or channel our benevolence, instead, through church or personal contributions? Then there are always those pesky street beggars to deal with. To give or not to give? Lost in all the debate is not so much *whether* to give or *how much* to give, but how to give in such a way as to honor the dignity of those to whom we give. What the poor need most is not a handout, but a hand up. Not just benevolence, but opportunity. Not simply charity, but dignity. To give the one without the other is to impoverish the poor all the more.

■ **The question for serious reflection is: How can I generously put money into the pockets of the poor without simultaneously robbing them of their greatest asset?**

Sexual Taboos

Do not defile yourselves in any of these ways, because this is how the nations that I am going to drive out before you became defiled.

LEVITICUS 18:24

Sexual practices and values seem to fluctuate constantly. Like hemlines that rise and fall, sexual expression is both defined by the times and, in turn, defines the time. In a sexually liberated generation, it seems that almost anything goes. Practices once thought outrageous and shocking by grandparents are but casual recreation for their grandchildren. What once carried widespread public stigma is transformed overnight into the subject of comedic humor and public acceptance. Naturally, those who disapprove are said to be, not just narrow-minded, but bigoted. But how can sexual standards be so flexible? Is morality of any kind ever that malleable? And when sexual practices have become so liberal that anything goes, where do we go from there? In ancient Israel God had a definite answer: It's time to get serious about radical sexual purity.

Even a sexually liberated society finds it difficult to believe that pagan sexual practices once included cult prostitution, incest, and—dare it be said—bestiality! No wonder God said those practices had defiled the very land. Yet if those detestable practices were not obviously and naturally taboo, what does it say of our own times now that the formerly detestable practices of both heterosexual and homosexual promiscuity have gained such widespread respectability? Nothing is quite the barometer of a culture's moral values like sex. Because of the profound spiritual implications of sexual intimacy, if one can throw off the shackles of sexual restraint with impunity, then there are no moral boundaries that cannot be safely traversed. That culture wars are fought mostly on battlegrounds of sexual issues is not happenstance.

■ **The quite personal question is: Just how far have I myself succumbed to accepting the morally unthinkable as respectable?**

Spiritual Isolation

In cases of defiling skin diseases be very careful to do exactly as the Levitical priests instruct you. You must follow carefully what I have commanded them. Remember what the LORD your God did to Miriam along the way after you came out of Egypt.

DEUTERONOMY 24:8-9

When suffering from a cold, we sometimes say (half seriously, half joking) "Unclean! Unclean!" to anyone approaching. The phrase has ancient roots all the way back to the rules of hygiene given to the Israelites. The laws of Moses were as practical as they were ceremonial. Whenever there was an infectious disease, the course of action was isolation and avoidance. Sometimes strict quarantines are the only way to stop a contagious disease from spreading. So there's nothing surprising about sending infected people outside the camp. The surprise comes when Israel is warned to follow the rules precisely, *remembering what God did to Miriam*! If you recall when Moses' sister, Miriam, was critical of Moses' marriage, God regarded it as an open challenge to Moses' spiritual leadership. Miriam's punishment? Leprosy and isolation outside the camp for seven days.

The tie between Miriam's sin and Miriam's leprosy is significant. Although there is no automatic connection between disease and sin, in this case the connection was direct, and it raises the parallel between how one deals with an infectious disease and an infectious sin. Had Miriam been left unpunished for impeaching Moses' authority, it could have emboldened others who were challenging his leadership. When spiritual infection is in the air, the cure is the same as for the physically infected—cut them off! But here's the caution—not forever. Not unduly. It's not the *person* we are trying to get rid of, only the *disease*.

■ **The question to contemplate is: Have I dealt too leniently with those whose spiritual disease might infect me and my family or, instead, dealt perhaps too harshly?**

Dining Separately

You must distinguish between the unclean and the clean, between living creatures that may be eaten and those that may not be eaten.

LEVITICUS 11:47

Jews are renowned for their kosher diet. It derives, of course, from the ancient dietary laws given to the Israelites, drawing a sharp distinction between "clean" and "unclean" creatures. Perhaps there were health reasons for not eating certain foods, or perhaps the aim was to avoid imitating pagan dietary practices. Whatever other purpose the rules might have served, they were a constant reminder to Israel of their need to be *separate* from both pagans and from sin. Did you catch that little rule, "Do not cook a young goat in its mother's milk"? And don't forget those other rules, such as men and women not wearing each other's clothes, not mixing two kinds of seed, and not wearing blends of wool and linen. The persistent message? Come out and be separate!

But, today, how are we to demonstrate separateness as we chow down on pork barbeque while wearing polyester, transgender trousers? What sets us apart from a godless world *might* be our dress, or perhaps food or drink from which we abstain. Modesty and sobriety and self-control are increasingly rare virtues. Yet dressing oddly doesn't necessarily make us separate—only odd. And eating strangely doesn't make us separate—only strange. If we truly want to be seen as separate, it will come in our conversations and values. In our material possessions and financial priorities. In what we listen to and what we watch. Interesting, isn't it? Even today there's a recognizable difference between "clean jokes" and "dirty jokes," between "good clean fun" and "just plain filth."

■ **The practical question of separation is: On a daily basis, do I ever consciously distinguish between what is "clean" and "unclean"?**

Acts of Compassion

If you come across a bird's nest beside the road, either in a tree or on the ground, and the mother is sitting on the young or on the eggs, do not take the mother with the young. You may take the young, but be sure to let the mother go, so that it may go well with you and you may have a long life.

DEUTERONOMY 22:6-7

God not only knows every sparrow that falls, but quite incredibly, also cares what happens to each one! So how would you characterize today's passage? Quaint? Charming? Endearing? It's yet another instance where some seemingly quirky commandment is packed with insight! If we are to have compassion on an ordinary bird, how much more for our fellow man? God has a unique way of developing habits of the heart, such as the virtue of compassion. Just think of it—leaving corners in the grain field for the poor to reap! Treating foreigners with the kindness you'd hope to receive if in a similar situation! Regarding the elderly with due respect and compassion! Can you even begin to imagine a world without daily acts of compassion? Indeed, what would you and I be like if we were devoid of compassion?

We are told that when Jesus saw the multitudes "like sheep without a shepherd," he had compassion on them. And so he fed them—all five thousand. No, not just with food for the stomach, but with food for the soul. Aware that we are wretched, blind, and poor, God shares the gleanings from his glorious bounty. Having himself come into this world as if a stranger, God is touched that we are struggling aliens in a world not our own. The beauty of compassion is that it calls us to our highest instincts for good—putting ourselves in the place of others, instantly recognizing a vulnerability we've experienced, and doing whatever we can to lessen the burden, just as God has lessened ours.

■ **The compelling question is: Whose life might be uplifted today because of some compassion I might show?**

Tassels of Remembrance

The LORD said to Moses, "Speak to the Israelites and say to them: 'Throughout the generations to come you are to make tassels on the corners of your garments, with a blue cord on each tassel…Then you will remember to obey all my commands and will be consecrated to your God.'"

NUMBERS 15:37-38,40

Ever find yourself being forgetful? Even before the senior years arrive, forgetfulness is why we make grocery lists, scribble notes when listening to a speaker, and mark our calendars to remember important days and appointments. In an era when there were no such memory aids, Moses knew all too well that the Israelites would quickly forget the laws he had given them. It wasn't so much that they would literally forget them, but forget to *obey* them. Hence the tassels they were to attach to their clothes. They were daily reminders not to forget their obligation to obey the Lord's commands. Similar to our grocery lists, the tassels were a constant reminder to distinguish between clean and unclean food. Similar to our scribbled notes, the tassels helped them recall what God had said to them through Moses. And similar to our marked calendars, the tassels would impress the importance of each Sabbath, feast, and high holy day.

We don't wear tassels anymore, but "memory verses" might be a modern equivalent. Memory verses are especially important for children because children have such a voracious capacity to store memories in the early years and because they are a great way to transmit faith from one generation to the next. *Obeying* what they put to memory remains the age-old challenge, but even Jesus proved the power of memory in overcoming sin. Whenever confronted by temptation, a protective Scripture instantly popped into mind—a Scripture undoubtedly first memorized as a small boy. For Jesus, the tassels weren't just for decoration.

■ **The critical question is: What "tassels of remembrance" have I memorized lately?**

_____

_____

_____

_____

A False Sense of Security

When such a person hears the words of this oath and they invoke a blessing on themselves, thinking, "I will be safe, even though I persist in going my own way," they will bring disaster on the watered land as well as the dry.

DEUTERONOMY 29:19

Have you noticed that there aren't many "hellfire and damnation" sermons anymore? Either we have foolishly given up on the notion that there really is a hell to take seriously, or we are more soothed by the thought that we'll all share the bliss of heaven regardless of what we believe or do. That said, most folks don't need sermons on hell to intuitively conclude that even the possibility of a state of eternal adversity is sufficient reason to avoid it if given an option. An *easy* option. A nod to God. Just in case. Perhaps that explains the millions of nominal Christians. As long as there is some plausible reason for assuming a saved relationship, surely one isn't expected to be a religious fanatic! Whatever the initiating ritual might be, it satisfies family and friends, and even one's self. Didn't I go through the motions? Didn't I say all the right words?

Shifting the focus slightly, have you ever wondered why certain moral laws are retained on the statute books even though they are rarely enforced? Apparently we feel better about ourselves knowing we've at least officially condemned the conduct! The more personal corollary is as fascinating as it is frightening—as long as we confess our sins, we're tempted to believe it's actually okay to persist in those very sins! If we just throw God a bone, we think surely he will be satisfied! By some irony, solemn vows to God may provide such a false sense of security that our covenants actually end up excusing disobedience!

■ **The compelling question is: Has my commitment to God given me some false sense of comfort that it's safe to act inconsistently with that very commitment?**

The Blame Game

Many disasters and calamities will come on them, and in that day they will ask, "Have not these disasters come on us because our God is not with us?" And I will certainly hide my face in that day because of all their wickedness in turning to other gods.

DEUTERONOMY 31:17-18

Have you seen the bumper sticker which reads: "Feeling distant from God? Who moved?" If there is anything we can count on, it is God's everlasting constancy. Yet because it is we who move away from God, not the other way around, what happens when we forsake God is altogether amazing—we act as if it is God who is moving away, not us! It's as if some rogue planet got out of orbit and then blamed the sun for changing its position. When our focus is on ourselves, ironically *the blame* is never on ourselves! Just ask Adam. "Wasn't me, God. It was this woman you gave me." (Wouldn't you like to know whether the emphasis was on *woman* or *you*? Wow!) And, of course, Eve was all too happy to point the finger of blame at the serpent.

Whether it is a two-year-old caught red-handed, a hardened criminal turning against his coconspirators, or simply every one of us who sins—there's always someone else to blame. The only alternative is to accept personal responsibility for our sin, and that just won't do. Yet how could we ever stoop so low as to blame God himself for our own transgressions and their disastrous consequences? "I didn't ask to be born!" "Bad things are happening to me, so it must be God's fault!" In a sense we may actually be right about that. When God tells us he will hide his face from our wickedness, how can we possibly be blessed in such a state? But if that is the case, who really is to blame?

■ **The penetrating question is: If I am unhappy with God for how things are in my life, is it remotely possible that I'm forcing God's hand?**

Hopeful Disappointment

Therefore, you will see the land only from a distance; you will not enter the land I am giving to the people of Israel.

DEUTERONOMY 32:52

How often have you heard it lamented, "He never got to see his dream come true"? Perhaps it was said of a designer of some grand edifice who died before its completion or of a philanthropist who didn't live to see the object of his generosity brought to fruition. There are also those who have implanted ideas in the next generation, never surviving long enough to see what a blessing those ideas proved to be. And how many parents' lives have been cut short before they could share in the joy of being proud grandparents? We can only imagine the disappointment Moses must have felt when told that he would not personally lead Israel into the land of promise about which he must have dreamed so often.

We should not assume, of course, that every life cut short before a dream is fulfilled implies that a "premature death" (if there is such a thing) is because of sin, as in Moses' case. If our dream is within God's will, it may simply be that God has chosen to use others to accomplish the next phase. No dream or efforts made that are consistent with God's own good pleasure will be unfulfilled or wasted. Are we to think that Jesus' work on the cross was wasted simply because he would not see (through human eyes) his kingdom fully flourish? The good news is that Jesus' triumphant resurrection was our own "distant view" of greater things than earthly dreams. Not even Moses will be denied that eternal Promised Land! So if we are saddened at the thought that we might die before accomplishing all we would like, how can that disappointment possibly compare with the hope of what is yet to come?

■ **The question of current importance is: What foundation will I lay today that others will build on long after I'm gone?**

_____

_____

_____

_____

_____

Crossing Our Own Jordan

Be strong and courageous. Do not be afraid; do not be discouraged, for the LORD your God will be with you wherever you go.

JOSHUA 1:9

Easy enough for God to say! "Don't worry, Joshua. There is no reason to be afraid." Even seasoned veterans know the smell of fear when they launch into battle. And who can blame them? Few battles have ever been fought without casualties. *Somebody* has to die! Then again, not all battles are the military type. There are battles against cancer, for example, every bit as hard fought and frightening as armed conflict. And battles within families, within the workplace, and even within the church. Not all are terrifying, but all of them are discouraging. So God promises to be with us in the midst of whatever battle we happen to be facing this very day. Then again, haven't countless losing armies claimed that God was on their side? Indeed, but Joshua and the Israelites have indisputable proof that God really and truly *is* on their side. How else can you explain their incredible crossing of the Jordan?

Unlike military battles where at least *somebody* has to die, in the great battle of this life, *everybody* has to die. Everybody has to "cross the Jordan" (signifying our crossing from this life into the land beyond)—a phrase that is synonymous with dying. Is there anything more terrifying than death? And yet, in anticipation of Israel's crossing of the Jordan, God provided a miracle to safeguard his chosen people, just as he had done at the Red Sea. For those who have witnessed a lifetime of God working in their lives, death need no longer terrify the soul. Even in death God is with us wherever we go.

■ **The encouraging question is: If God has promised to be on the front lines with me even in the most crucial life-and-death battle I will ever face, why should I be terrified at lesser battles that come my way?**

When Breaking Rules Becomes a Priority

On the seventh day, march around the city seven times, with the priests blowing the trumpets.

JOSHUA 6:4

When you see the words "seventh day" in connection with the Israelites, what instantly comes to mind? The Sabbath, right? But then what strikes you about God commanding the Israelites to march around Jericho seven times on the seventh day? It's possible that the "seventh day" in question was not itself the Sabbath; however, over the course of any seven-day period, one of those days would have been a Sabbath, on which the Israelites were to do no work. Maybe we're missing something, but marching around a city and blowing trumpets sure sounds like work! Apparently a time of war was an exception to normal Sabbath observance, not unlike the priests performing their ritual duties on Sabbaths and high holy days.

As unrelated as it may seem, think back on why Rahab and her family were saved in the assault on Jericho. She was rewarded for having told a lie! Had she not deceived the king of Jericho, the spies would have been caught, and the whole operation put in jeopardy. So is telling a "little white lie" okay? Certainly not where the reasons are merely selfish. But given the right priorities, there are instances where violating the rules apparently has God's blessing. Consider King David and his men eating the consecrated bread and Jesus himself healing on the Sabbath. That God recognizes some circumstances as exceptions to the rule must mean there is a hierarchy of values each of us needs to consider. When the reason for a rule is trumped by a more important rule, black and white has an interesting way of becoming gray.

■ **The difficult question is: Do I think in black and white when I should be thinking gray, or do I perceive gray when there's really nothing but black and white?**

Depreciating an Incredible God!

The sun stopped in the middle of the sky and delayed going down about a full day. There has never been a day like it before or since, a day when the LORD listened to a human being. Surely the LORD was fighting for Israel!

JOSHUA 10:13-14

How often do we attempt to put God neatly into a box—a box more suited to our paltry understanding rather than a box large enough to accommodate his infinite nature, were that even possible? When reading the Scriptures, it's easy to glide right past truly phenomenal acts of God. Assuming you're not in some arctic region, try to imagine the sun not setting as usual tonight. How could that possibly be! Yet the text tells us with a straight face that when Joshua asked God to extend the day, that is precisely what God did! The literal, historical fact is that, at the request of an ordinary human being just like us, the Creator God of the universe put the entire solar system on hold!

What do you think? If for some reason *you* desperately needed twenty-four hours when the sun didn't set, would God honor your request? One of the dangers of reading about God working in such extraordinary ways is that, if we don't personally witness similar mind-boggling acts, it's easy to conclude that God is distant or dead. Or that God wound up the clock of the universe, tinkered with it for a while, then just walked away. Do we still have reason to trust that, if necessary, God would literally move heaven and earth on our behalf? Considering that the Israelites personally witnessed all those extraordinary miracles and still lacked trust, maybe God now works mostly behind the scenes. Even so, ask enough people and you'll quickly find that God is still doing the incredible!

■ **The question to ponder is: Have I been desensitized into thinking that, just because I've never seen the sun stand still, God either *can't* or *doesn't* work in my life?**

Old, but Not Out!

When Joshua had grown old, the LORD said to him, "You are now very old, and there are still very large areas of land to be taken over."

JOSHUA 13:1

You mean God didn't say to Joshua, "You're too old to do the job I have in mind"? Whatever happened to retirement and "the golden years"? Apparently Joshua himself was in no mood to sit quietly in a rocking chair. Here he was at eighty-five, boasting about being just as strong and fit for battle as when he was a virile young man! Because Joshua was still twenty-five years away from his death, we might get the idea that eighty-five was somewhat younger for that time than now. But Joshua was no spring chicken. The text insists that he was old and well advanced in years. Yet that didn't seem to bother God. Indeed, it appears that God finds Joshua's advancing age to be an asset. There is nothing quite like the experience of the years to prepare a person for leadership.

What a contrast with today's marginalization of the elderly. In a youth-oriented culture, advanced age and experience are more likely considered liabilities than assets. As lamentable as that cultural attitude is, it is sadder still when those who are older actually write themselves off as useless. It is understandable, of course, that you would get frustrated when your get-up-and-go has "got-up-and-went"! Not being able to do what you have easily done for a lifetime must certainly be discouraging. If Joshua were still around, you might wonder what he would say to anyone languishing in the doldrums of advanced age. You can almost hear him shouting, "You may be old, but you're not out!" So if you know anyone who thinks they're no longer important to God, do them a favor and give them a piece of Joshua's mind!

■ **The question for each of us is: Whether old or young, am I making each day count for the kingdom?**

Promises Delayed, Not Promises Denied

So the LORD gave Israel all the land he had sworn to give their ancestors, and they took possession of it and settled there...Not one of all the LORD's good promises to Israel failed; every one was fulfilled.

JOSHUA 21:43,45

We have to go back almost seven centuries from the time of Joshua to fully appreciate the significance of today's passage. It was then that God first promised Abraham that his descendants would inherit a land that he would give them. With each succeeding generation, the land promise was renewed. Generations came and generations went without that promise being fulfilled. But the time for fulfillment has finally arrived, and God has made good on his promises. Of course much of Israel's new land has yet to be fully subdued, and for centuries to come, Israel will suffer for failing to completely subjugate the land as God has commanded them. But that's another story. What's important, as this record reflects unequivocally, is that God has done all that he ever promised to do by giving Israel the land.

Why is that historical fact so crucial? Because we need to be able to implicitly trust God's promises for us. Is God a promise keeper? We can count on it! If someone should protest, "But that's a given," we mustn't forget the many generations who lived and died in expectation of a promise that was never fulfilled in their lifetime. How must they have felt? Did they ever doubt God's credibility? For that matter, have *you* claimed a promise of God that has yet to be fulfilled? What's so wonderful about the land promise to Israel is that its belated but certain fulfillment reminds us that God is always faithful, even if not on our timetable. A promise unfulfilled today is no less secure than the promise fulfilled yesterday. Trust is never the issue, only God's timing.

■ **So the timely question is: If perchance God's promises were unfulfilled throughout my entire lifetime, would I trust him any less?**

Making Good Choices

But if serving the LORD seems undesirable to you, then choose for yourselves this day whom you will serve, whether the gods your ancestors served beyond the Euphrates, or the gods of the Amorites, in whose land you are living. But as for me and my household, we will serve the LORD.

JOSHUA 24:15

Ours is a time and culture when the one thing we demand is unlimited choice. Whether it be the lunch menu, our evening's entertainment, or the options available on the latest technological gadgets, we've come to expect endless choices. It's all the more interesting, then, that Joshua would speak not only to the Israelites but also to us when he sets before them the most important choice they will ever make: Who is to be their God—the true God of heaven or lesser, false gods? Ironically, our most troublesome choice today might be between God and choice itself! Among our fundamental freedoms, seemingly, is the right to life, liberty, and... *choice*! Ever notice all the pro-choice bumper stickers? Even people who are not pro-choice on the issue with which that term has become synonymous are so pro-choice in practice that their own demand for unlimited choice in the marketplace unwittingly bolsters the demand for unlimited choice in morals. Once choice becomes God in any arena, inevitably it becomes God in every arena.

So we are back to a choice between the God of heaven (who makes challenging demands on us) and the lesser god of choice (which is the object of our own demands). Correctly understood, our reverence for choice has so much to do with satisfying our own desires that the lesser god we end up worshiping is self! By modern translation Joshua's challenge is to choose this day whom you will serve: God or self. For Joshua that was no real choice at all. As between ourselves and the transcendent God who made us, what kind of choice is that!

■ **The tough question is: Am I so committed to having and doing whatever I want that God takes second place?**

The True Test of Trust

The LORD was with the men of Judah. They took possession of the hill country, but they were unable to drive the people from the plains, because they had chariots fitted with iron.

JUDGES 1:19

Have you ever considered that chapter breaks, verses, and even paragraphs can distort the intended meaning of a passage? Take, for example, today's featured verse. Does anything strike you as odd about it? (Read it again carefully.) If God was with the men of Judah, would even iron chariots present the slightest difficulty? (In some translations, the problem is only exacerbated by the implication that it was *God himself* who was unable to bring about a victory!) Only a short time has passed since Joshua had said, "Though the Canaanites have chariots fitted with iron and though they are strong, you can drive them out" (obviously inferring by the power of God). So maybe the first sentence of our verse belongs with the previous verse, which records that the men of Judah totally destroyed the Canaanites living in Zephath, and also took Gaza, Ashkelon, and Ekron…all because "the LORD was with the men of Judah."

The more powerful lesson, however, would come from keeping the verse break exactly as it is. Standing alone, the verse may actually be telling us that the men of Judah were able to take possession of the *hill country* because there (where they knew they had a fighting chance) they trusted in God, but they lost the battle for *the plains* because the very sight of the Canaanites' iron chariots had made them lose sight of God. It's easy to trust God when you're fighting an enemy on somewhat even terms. The true measure of trust is when the odds are overwhelming, and we still believe. God may be with us in times of shallow belief, but how can he not turn away in the face of sheer disbelief?

■ **The obvious question is: Do I glibly speak of trusting in God when all is well, but cower in fear when the situation looks hopeless?**

Just a Single Generation

After that whole generation had been gathered to their ancestors, another generation grew up who knew neither the LORD nor what he had done for Israel.

JUDGES 2:10

Listened to any children playing lately? They are likely repeating the same games, songs, and expressions you and I grew up with as children. But imagine an entire generation growing up without singing the alphabet song or playing hide-and-seek. Worse yet, imagine a generation of young people who don't believe in God, betray their parents to a big-brother government, and have no scruples about lying and cheating. Given the not-too-distant history of certain political social orders, reality is not far from the imagination. The scariest part? In each instance the radical transformation happened within a single generation.

We all know what it is like to have a breakup in the transmission of a phone call. First there is that intermittent screeching sound, then the line goes dead. Yet losing a phone connection is minuscule compared with losing a connection in values between succeeding generations. Cultural values are transmitted through custom, tradition, and ritual. When a civilization (or church) quits telling its story to the next generation, it isn't long before cultural screeching begins. Decry as we might the evils of the younger generation, the story of cultural and moral values is theirs to *hear*, not to *tell*. Where there is a runaway generation, an older generation has opened the gate. The only explanation for a generation growing up without knowing what God had done for Israel is that—at an identifiable point in time—an entire generation of Israel's parents had failed to tell their children about God. Whether it be a whole society, the church, or an individual family, there is always only one generation difference between faith and disbelief.

■ **The crucial question for any parent is: Do my children know about the three little pigs, but precious little about the three persons of the Godhead?**

Reluctant Role Reversals

"Certainly I will go with you," said Deborah. "But because of the course you are taking, the honor will not be yours, for the LORD will deliver Sisera into the hands of a woman."

JUDGES 4:9

She was a woman in a man's world. A highly competent woman from the look of it. Unlike the other "judges" of Israel who were primarily military leaders, Deborah was a *real* judge to whom the people came to have disputed cases adjudicated. To appreciate how strikingly unique Deborah's role was, we need only consider that, for centuries, the entire political and religious structure of Israel had been decidedly male. So what accounts for her extraordinary position in Israel? We are given a good clue in her song of celebration when she observes "Villagers in Israel would not fight; they held back until I, Deborah, arose, until I arose, a mother in Israel." And again, "When they chose new gods, war came to the city gates, but not a shield or spear was seen among forty thousand in Israel." That would be forty thousand cowardly *men*! Forty thousand men too numbed by the allure of idolatry to fight off their enemies or even take responsibility for running the affairs of local villages. Deborah wouldn't be the only woman to step in when men have stepped out.

The story of Deborah (and that courageous woman Jael) demonstrates the obvious about women—that they are certainly capable of doing whatever task needs to be accomplished. Yet the necessity of their having to take the initiative only highlights the relationship between a major breakdown in male leadership and the breakdown in society. The issue is not what a woman has the *ability* to do (what *can't* she do!), but what a man is *called* to do. This was no liberating moment for Israel, when the roles of men and women were permanently reversed, but rather an occasion for sharp rebuke of Israel's irresponsible men. It's a matter of honoring one's calling.

■ **The question for both men and women is: Am I fulfilling to the best of my ability whatever role God may have given me?**

Fleecing from Faith or Doubt?

Then Gideon said to God, "Do not be angry with me. Let me make just one more request. Allow me one more test with the fleece, but this time make the fleece dry and let the ground covered with dew."

JUDGES 6:39

Perhaps you have heard someone talking about "putting out a fleece." What various people mean by that expression runs the gamut from genuinely seeking God's will in a matter of decision, all the way to throwing some important decision to the winds of fate or sheer chance. Gideon's famous fleece may not have been so much an act of faith as an act of doubt. Had Gideon merely been seeking confirmation from a God in whom he fully trusted, he only needed to put the fleece out once. When he insisted on putting the fleece out a second time, we wonder if there was more doubt than trust. Yet we mustn't be too hard on Gideon. How, indeed, do you and I know with any confidence what God's will is? Are we just supposed to take the first thing that comes along as our indicator of where God is leading us? What if it is only a coincidence? What if we too quickly seize on something that simply appeals to what we ourselves secretly want?

Gideon had good reason not to thoughtlessly seize the first possible indicator of God's presence in his life. Using what seemed to be common sense, Gideon initially concluded that God must have abandoned Israel. What else would explain all the trouble they were in? Then realizing that his first assumption was obviously wrong, Gideon took on a healthy skepticism about how God acts. Crucially, it seems that God was not angry with Gideon for putting the fleece out twice. Instead of going off half-cocked, making doubly sure of what God wants may not be such a bad idea.

■ **The question for all of us is: Even if I may not instantly or easily know which direction God is leading, do I at least stop, look, and listen?**

Godly Leadership

But Gideon told them, "I will not rule over you, nor will my son rule over you. The LORD will rule over you."

JUDGES 8:23

When I'm king of the world…" How many times have you heard or said that? Seems like everybody wants to be king, or president, or whoever it is that's in charge. Oh, not that most folks would ever want to take on all the responsibilities attendant to the office. But every now and then, most of us would love to be in a position where we could put right whatever we think is being done wrong. Of course there are those who absolutely love the prestige and power that go along with being in charge. Can't get enough of it. No office too big, no position too high. Would do almost anything to move up the ladder. Since politicians seem to have more than their fair share of ambition, just how envious might they be of Gideon, who was handed power on a platter? All he had to do was reach out and take it. Yet to everyone's surprise, Gideon refused the honor, saying instead that God would rule over them. What must they have thought!

Ironic isn't it? The Israelites wanted Gideon to be their king because he had saved them from the Midianites. Yet it wasn't Gideon who had saved them, but God—and they refused to honor God as Lord and King! What Gideon understood that they didn't was the difference between human and divine leadership. Although there is a proper place for human leadership, it can never rightly supplant divine rule. Sadly, it's a lesson lost on kings, presidents, CEOs, union bosses, college deans, scout leaders, church pastors, and even parents. "Servant leadership" might have become an overworked catchphrase, but it is a good reminder to leaders of every type as to who is really in charge.

■ **The question for all would-be kings is: Unless I'm willing to let God be king of my own world, how can I possibly be king of any other world?**

When Vows Become Shibboleths

When he saw her, he tore his clothes and cried, "Oh no, my daughter! You have brought me down and I am devastated. I have made a vow to the LORD that I cannot break."

JUDGES 11:35

What was Jephthah thinking when he vowed to sacrifice the first thing that came out of his house! Wouldn't the odds be pretty good that the first to greet Jephthah might be a family member rather than a goat? You have to hand it to him, though. As excruciating as it was to discover the object of his vow was his only child, Jephthah didn't shrink back from honoring that vow—rash or not. Then again, a *human life* was at stake…or was it? Did Jephthah really offer his daughter as a burnt offering? Although the text says that "he did to her as he had vowed," there is also the lament of her friends that she would never marry and the enigmatic reference to her being a virgin. What difference would any of that make if in fact she was sacrificed—unless it was her future happiness as a bride that was "sacrificed"?

What we know for certain is that Jephthah's commitment to God outweighed even family loyalty and personal happiness. Lesser men would have renounced the vow the moment they spied their precious daughter. Surely God would understand! Indeed, didn't his making a vow in the first place demonstrate that Jephthah was a man of faith? Perhaps, but Jephthah himself recognized the crucial difference between passive *faith* and active *faithfulness.* Given the telltale pronunciation test Jephthah's men later used against the Ephraimites, it is interesting how it worked out. By being true to his word no matter the cost, Jephthah passed God's own "Shibboleth" test where others woefully failed. For when God asks us to say "faithful," there is no safety in simply saying "faith."

■ **The searching question is: How high a price am I willing to pay to translate my faith into unflinching faithfulness?**

Choosing at the Crossroads

But Ruth replied, "Don't urge me to leave you or to turn back from you. Where you go I will go, and where you stay I will stay. Your people will be my people and your God my God."

RUTH 1:16

Many who've heard this well-known passage either read or sung at a wedding would be surprised to learn that it is taken from a conversation between a woman and her mother-in-law. It does sound more like a lover speaking, doesn't it? Of course the endearing sentiment so lovingly expressed during the wedding ceremony has often led to a future one could not possibly have imagined. And when the extended family becomes more "interesting" than first expected, one might have second thoughts about "your people" becoming "my people"! Nevertheless, countless couples have boldly tied their fate to their beloved, left family and friends behind, and headed off for parts unknown, all for the sake of love. In Ruth's case, fortunately, it was a story with a fairy-tale ending in which they lived happily ever after.

The intriguing question is: Whatever happened to Ruth's sister-in-law, Orpah? Although Naomi encouraged both of her daughters-in-law to remain, the text gives us an important clue as to why only Orpah stayed behind. "Look," said Naomi, "your sister-in-law is going back to her people and her gods. Go back with her." The choice was not really about whether to leave relatives and friends. Naomi knew it was fundamentally a choice between gods. So did Ruth. Despite being given the clear option to choose otherwise, Ruth chose the God of Israel. The true God. This left Orpah choosing false gods—and a culture that did not honor godly values. Was hers, then, a fairy-tale ending, or as one can imagine, a life ending in bitterness, grief, and regret? Defined as we are by our choices at critical junctures in our lives, the only real issue is whether we decide to go with God.

■ **So the question is: When I reach each crucial crossroad in my life, is God foremost among my considerations?**

On Angels' Wings

Then the woman went to her husband and told him, "A man of God came to me. He looked like an angel of God, very awesome. I didn't ask him where he came from, and he didn't tell me his name."

JUDGES 13:6

Have you ever seen an angel? If not, do you think you could recognize one? Surely those wings would be a dead give-away, wouldn't they? Or maybe the harp, or that radiant white robe! Despite all those artistic depictions of winged angels, the fact is that most of the angels in Scripture are fairly nondescript. No wings. No harps. What, then, was so "awesome" about the man to whom Samson's mother spoke that prompted her to think he might be an angel? And why didn't Samson's father, Manoah, realize that the mysterious visitor was "the angel of the LORD" until the angel ascended in the flame? Seems this was no ordinary angel, but one of those amazing, pre-Christ personifications of God! Reading between the lines, this story is a technicolor preview of the incarnate "Angel of the Lord" who one day would ascend back into heaven after himself becoming the ultimate "burnt offering."

Since angels serve as God's messengers to mankind, Christ's role in bringing the good news of God's grace to a sinful world is nothing short of angelic. Which must surely raise a question about today's faddish fascination with angels that has precious little to do with the gospel of Christ. No crystal angel displayed as a talisman from a rearview mirror, or set on a coffee table, or imagined as a personal guide to the spirit world can begin to approach the reality of bona fide angels sent from God. When mystical "guardian angels" and other fairy-like "angels" become spiritual substitutes for the Angel of angels, the saving power of the gospel message becomes as weakened as Samson without his hair.

■ **The question for a superstitious New Age is: Am I more fascinated with magical, mystical pseudo-messengers wearing frothy-white wings than with the omniscient, soul-saving Message himself?**

False Comfort from Religious Trappings

And Micah said, "Now I know that the LORD will be good to me, since this Levite has become my priest."

JUDGES 17:13

Let's see if we have this right. Micah builds himself a shrine, puts some forbidden idols in it, and makes his son a wholly unauthorized personal priest. Then when a wandering Levite comes along, Micah hires him as the new in-house priest and says to himself, "God will certainly bless me now." Is this fellow completely delusional? Here he is openly engaged in idolatry and convinced that the same God who has prohibited idolatry will be pleased that he has hired a Levite as his priest! What can we say except that Micah is not alone. He is not the only person who has sought spiritual comfort in thinking some fellow human being could absolve him of his sins—or been relieved that respected religious councils have declared righteous what is patently unrighteous.

As lawyers are well aware, an expert witness can be found to testify on behalf of almost any issue. Sometimes it's because there are conflicting schools of thought that can be legitimately tapped. Other times it's because there are unscrupulous individuals who will testify on whichever side their bread is buttered. Sadly, among the religious elite there are also some who, whether knowingly or unknowingly, sell their souls to the highest bidders and bless what God has not blessed. They flourish because there are enough of us who, like Micah, content ourselves that when we have a "man of God's" stamp of approval, we must have God's blessing as well. What better way to fool ourselves than to wrap our spiritual rebellion in religious trappings? But maybe spiritual rebellion isn't the problem. When "men of God" themselves can so easily lead the unwitting faithful down unauthorized paths, are *we* not the ones who have sold our souls to *them*?

■ **The potentially disturbing question is: Have I possibly put more trust in religious leaders than in God himself?**

_____

_____

_____

_____

The Chaos of Moral Anarchy

In those days Israel had no king; everyone did as they saw fit.

JUDGES 21:25

As if with bells, whistles, and red flags, somebody's trying to get our attention! In the closing chapters of Judges, we are told no fewer than five times that the idolatry, debauchery, and atrocities recorded there happened during a time when Israel had no king. The implication is that because there was no king, everyone did whatever he wished. Is this somehow meant to justify God giving Israel the very kings he had warned against? Are we about to enter some golden era of national holiness and moral order? Anyone familiar with the history of Israel under its many kings will know that cycles of faithfulness followed by idolatry, rebellion, and abject depravity will persist—king or no king. So just what are these repeated statements telling us?

The point, surely, is to highlight the contrast between the presence of established authority on one hand and moral chaos on the other. Whenever there is an absence of moral authority (personified *by* a king, if not literally embodied *in* a king), a vacuum is created in which nothing but chaos can reign. For either a higher moral authority is in charge, or we are. There is no moral middle ground. This ought to be extremely disturbing for any anti-authoritarian culture. Even a godless totalitarian society with strict rules is better than a free society so liberated from authority that anything goes. But that is all political theory. Truth be told, a society is little more than the sum of its parts. If you want to predict where any society is going, simply look at how parental authority is honored in one family after another. Let enough parents abdicate their role as authority figures, and soon you will have a whole nation running wild!

■ **The confrontive question is: Whenever I am tempted to go a bit wild, have I taken my eyes off the King of kings?**

Falling Not Far from the Tree

Why do you honor your sons more than me by fattening yourselves on the choice parts of every offering made by my people Israel?

1 SAMUEL 2:29

Upset as he was about the notorious sexual sins of his sons, Eli the priest apparently was not fazed in the least when those same sons desecrated the people's sacrifices by using thuggery to make sure they got the finest cuts of meat. Seems Eli enjoyed eating at the sumptuous table of his wicked sons. To condemn one sin while condoning another would be bad enough. But unlike the moral sin he condemned, the grievous sin Eli actually condoned was in direct contempt of God! (Was it not Eli himself who earlier had noted that sins between a man and God leave no one to mediate between them?) The first and most obvious lesson is that we need to take careful inventory of what we condemn and what we condone—and *why*. Yet there also seems to be an important lesson about parents and children. Just how effective did Eli expect his rebuke regarding certain sins to be when he was fully participating with his sons in other sins?

As is true generally, it is not so much what parents *say* as what they *do*. And problems only intensify when there is a glaring disparity between actions and words. Young people are quick to capitalize on such inconsistencies, prompting a discussion concerning why some children turn out bad full circle. If Eli could so easily condone in his adult sons that which he should have condemned, what noticeable character flaw were those sons mimicking as they grew up? While spiritual truancy is not always the parents' fault (countless upright parents have grieved over errant offspring), the fact remains that oftentimes wayward children have not fallen far from the tree.

■ **The disturbing question is: How can I insist "Do as I say, not as I do" without another generation saying, "I'll do as I please!"**

The Art of Divine Conversation

The LORD came and stood there, calling as at the other times, "Samuel! Samuel!"
Then Samuel said, "Speak, for your servant is listening."

1 SAMUEL 3:10

Ever talked to anyone on the phone for what seemed like hours and didn't have to say anything on your end except an occasional "uh-huh"? (If not, is there any chance *you* are the talkative one?) Some folks have an amazing capacity to tap into a stream of consciousness that seems never to quit. You wonder when they ever stop to listen! Then again all of us are pretty good at selective listening. Oh, we *hear,* of course, but when do we truly *listen*? While husbands are notorious for this conjugal flaw, it is not a trait to be cultivated. Quite the opposite, learning to listen is a sign of maturity, especially when the one we are listening to is God. So young Samuel was wise beyond his years to say to God, "Speak to me. I'm all ears." He wasn't simply telling God that he was listening to the sound of his voice, but listening with an eagerness to respond to whatever God wanted him to do.

Good conversations are always two-sided. There's an easy give-and-take going on. You talk, then listen—listen, then talk. As much as wanting the other person to know what's on your mind, you want to know what's on theirs. It's a matter of mutual respect. A good example of a phenomenal conversation occasioned Samuel's birth. As a disconsolate barren woman, Hannah frequently prayed to God that she might have a son, whom she vowed to give over to the Lord. When the text tells us that "the LORD remembered her," it's obvious that God had been listening intently to Hannah's prayers. This is an amazing thought—that the Lord of the universe not only speaks to his creatures, but *listens*!

■ **The question to ponder is: Do I have balanced conversations with God, as eager to be "all ears" as "all mouth"?**

Calling All "Nobodies"

Saul answered, "But am I not a Benjamite, from the smallest tribe of Israel, and is not my clan the least of all the clans of the tribe of Benjamin? Why do you say such a thing to me?"

1 SAMUEL 9:21

How many times have you heard a woman say, "I'm just a housewife"? Or perhaps a man say with a touch of embarrassment, "I'm currently unemployed"? Or maybe someone lament, "I'm a nobody!" Self-esteem is not a universally shared trait, nor is pride in one's station in life guaranteed for all. For every "high flier," there are many more common, ordinary folks in the world who don't have much to brag about. Of what use are they to anyone? To look at them, nothing in particular would suggest they are special. So maybe they are right. Maybe they are like Saul, a nobody among nobodies. But hang on! If they are a "nobody" like Saul, then they are a "nobody" that God could make a king! Or the mother of a king. Or an honored servant of a king.

If perhaps you can identify with Saul's hiding among the baggage when he is named as Israel's first king, take heart. He knew he was no more suited to being a king than the donkeys he had been chasing the day before. What he had not counted on, however, was God's power to transform him into an instrument God could use for his own purposes. Not surprisingly the process began with a change of heart. No, not *Saul* changing his heart, but *God* changing Saul's heart. And then there was that spirit of prophesying with which God miraculously empowered Saul. What a shock that must have been for a former "nobody"! While God never promised to make all "nobodies" kings, of this we can be certain: Nobody's a "nobody" when God is working in their life.

■ **The question for all us ordinary folk is: How can I possibly be a "nobody" if the King himself has made me a child of the King!**

It's Not About Numbers

Nothing can hinder the LORD from saving, whether by many or by few.

1 SAMUEL 14:6

K now what it is like to stand alone for some crucial principle? To be the only one willing to fight some battle needing to be fought? It has to be said that not many people fall into that category—otherwise there would not be those rare individuals who stand out from the crowd. But you don't have to be someone who is consistently out front to know those times when you've been outnumbered in some worthy cause and wondered if you could succeed. It's not exactly true, as is often said, that God and one person make a majority. Even without you or me, God alone is always the majority! Yet it is absolutely true that an individual acting alone cannot fail when God is on his side.

Scripture often records the number of men in the armies on either side of a battle. Often the armies of Israel were nowhere near the size of their enemies' armies, but victory was never dependent on size. Faithfulness and trust in God's power—not numbers—were the keys to Israel's military success. The story of Jonathan and his brave assistant is a vivid reminder that even one or two people trusting in God can overcome overwhelming odds. Whether it be battles in the workplace, conflicts at church, or military engagements on foreign soil, God is always on the side of those who put their trust in his power, not their own. Even if the trusting believer doesn't win every skirmish that comes along, you can be sure that it's not because God was counting the number of combatants. If that mattered, why would we ever need God?

■ **The encouraging question is: What battle will I fight single-handedly today that, by trusting in God, will turn out easier than I ever could have imagined?**

Caving in to Peer Pressure

Then Saul said to Samuel, "I have sinned. I violated the LORD's command and your instructions. I was afraid of men and so I gave in to them."

1 SAMUEL 15:24

Why on earth do teenagers dress the way they do? Forget the trends, fads, and glitzy marketing. Surely it's the need to be like everybody else that cons teens into wearing those silly styles they'll be so embarrassed about one day. The more serious question is: Why do teens smoke, drink, and do drugs? One would have to put peer pressure at the top of a list of reasons. It's not easy resisting temptation when friends are putting pressure on you to conform. And peer pressure is not exclusively a teen problem…or a contemporary problem. When Saul confessed his sin to Samuel, peer pressure was foremost among the lame excuses he offered. Of course it's something of a stretch to think of a king having peers, but the point remains—Saul had caved in to political pressure as much as any teenager ever bowed to pressure from his peers.

So what is the antidote to peer pressure? How do we swim against the tide? The easy answer is: Be your own person. Think for yourself. Be true to yourself. Yet Samuel said that Saul's sin was fundamentally a problem of arrogance, at the heart of which is a self-focus needing incessant affirmation from others. Whether teenager or adult, whether king or commoner, what makes peer pressure so powerful is that it feeds both our deep-seated craving for acceptance and our insatiable egos. However, for those who find their acceptance and sense of self-worth in God alone, peer pressure has little appeal. Why crave acceptance from others when we already have all the approval we could ever need?

■ **The question for young and old is: If I should be tempted to do something simply because of peer pressure, will I remember that the only approval I need is God's?**

Appearances Can Be Discerning

The LORD does not look at the things people look at. People look at the outward appearance, but the LORD looks at the heart.

1 SAMUEL 16:7

They stand out in a crowd, "the beautiful people." They're the ones with the perfect face, perfect hair, perfect skin, and effervescent personalities. Not surprisingly they often marry each other, consequently forming "couple beautiful" and producing perfect children in their own image. Nothing they can do about it really. It's who they are…or at least what they look like. *Who they are* might or might not be a beautiful person. As we know appearances can be deceiving. So why do we keep attaching such importance to a person's physical appearance—and even to our own? Why so much time beautifying our outer packaging and so little effort enhancing our inner selves? What would we be like on the inside if we spent as much time cleaning and primping our souls as we do our bodies? Might we have an altogether different opening paragraph? Such as…

They stand out in a crowd, these "beautiful souls." You know them, the ones with the quiet inner spirit, the gentle grace, and the purity of character that is unmistakable. Not surprisingly they often marry another "beautiful soul," consequently forming a truly spiritual marriage and producing godly children in their own image. Through prayer and spiritual discipline, it's what they've become. And no matter whether ugly, ordinary, or beautiful on the outside, it's really and truly *who they are*. This is good news for all of us not-so-beautiful people. Because God is looking on the inside (what we *can* change), his concern is not what we look like on the outside (something we *can't* change all that much). Perhaps this should prompt some serious soul-searching about our own "soul searching."

■ **The follow-up question is: What surprising beauty might I see in others if I look beyond the visible and search for their inner souls?**

If Jealously Could Kill

And from that time on Saul kept a close eye [or *jealous* eye] on David.

1 SAMUEL 18:9

When we think of the word *jealous,* typically what comes to mind is a jealous lover. Maybe the one they love has given them reason to be jealous. Maybe not. Ever known anyone whose jealousy was born out of a deep sense of insecurity? Saul must have been that type. He simply couldn't stand it when David's popularity began to eclipse his own. So suddenly he is throwing spears at David, then hoping the Philistines will kill his rival, and—when that fails—even sending men to assassinate David. Not exactly *petty* jealousy! Yet perhaps we gain further insight into jealousy when we consider that the word *fear* keeps cropping up alongside Saul's jealousy. What reason would Saul have for fearing David? David wasn't his enemy.

Strangely, the text says that Saul was afraid of David because the Lord was with David. But why should that make Saul jealous…except for the implication that the Lord was *not* with Saul? David's only crime, so it seems, was unwittingly being cast in the role of a messenger delivering bad news to Saul. What's a person to do but kill the messenger—as if without his presence as a constant reminder, the hard truth itself would somehow disappear. Jealousy is not just about suspicious lovers. It's about regarding as a threat anyone who makes you look bad by comparison. Jealously happens when you want to be *them*! So if you've ever had folks throwing spears your way and you can't figure out why, maybe you have given them reason to be jealous. This would put you in good company with David and with all the other people of integrity who are the envy of the world.

■ **The worrying question is: If I have given no one any reason to be jealous of my abundant life in Christ, is it because I am showing them precious little difference?**

A Motley Crew

All those who were in distress or in debt or discontented gathered around him, and he became their commander.

1 SAMUEL 22:2

For a man who was to become Israel's greatest king, it was a dubious beginning. Here was David, on the run from Saul, hiding out in a cave, and having to survive on forbidden, consecrated bread. And who should join him but a ragtag gathering of fearful, indigent, and troubled souls. A band of misfits. Oh, warriors would soon arrive to fight the battles, but the people David first led were a pretty hopeless bunch. Perhaps they were attracted to David because of his reputation as a giant-killer. The down-and-out can always use a giant-killer. But for a hero in exile, surely that reputation would have worn a bit thin. Maybe they sensed in this uncommon man a common bond in the human condition. Someone who, like them, knew what it was like to be fearful and troubled, yet seemed to rise above it all. Had they heard some of his songs—the ones about overcoming fear, being delivered from one's enemies, or being rescued from one's pursuers?

The parallel between David and his descendant in the flesh, Jesus, is uncanny. Each of them would attract the least likely followers. Jesus' disciples would also be a ragtag bunch—the poor, the oppressed, the blind, and the lame—wretched sinners all, desperate for a Savior. In Jesus they saw a man who drank deeply of human suffering and heartache, yet brought hope of deliverance and escape from fear. Ever had times when you've been down-and-out, or experienced mind-numbing fear, or spent sleepless nights confronting seemingly insurmountable problems? No wonder we find such attraction in the One who protects and guides even us misfits!

■ **The challenging question for us is: Are there other hurting, struggling misfits out there today whom I can lead to a loving King?**

Wearing the Ephod

When David learned that Saul was plotting against him, he said to Abiathar the priest, "Bring the ephod." David said, "…Will Saul come down, as your servant has heard? LORD, God of Israel, tell your servant." And the LORD said, "He will."

1 SAMUEL 23:9-11

Mystery surrounds the ephod worn by Aaron the high priest and his successors. The same goes for the linen ephods worn by ordinary priests. It appears that the ephod was worn whenever one wished to inquire of God regarding his will. Repeatedly Israel's leaders sought out a priest wearing his ephod prior to making some crucial decision. If the ephod were part of some heathen religion, we'd likely condemn it as a superstitious talisman more suited to the occult. (Indeed, the golden ephod crafted by Gideon came to be regarded as an idol.) But the text is quite clear that God not only commanded the making of the ephod in the first place but also honored the wearer by communicating his will on the matter in question.

How would you like to have an ephod hanging in *your* closet? Is there anything today that takes its place in the life of a believer? The most obvious answer is prayer. For is it not through prayer that we typically inquire of God? The difference is that God tends not to answer us directly through prayer as he did with the priests wearing their ephods. So if it's directive *words* from God we're after, perhaps today's ephod is God's revealed *Word*. Is there some crucial decision we need to make? Reach for the Bible! Is there uncertainty about what God desires from us? Open up the Scriptures! God's written revelation may not answer every immediate question we might like answered, but wrapping ourselves in the Word is not a bad place to start.

■ **The cautioning question is: When I open my Bible to ascertain God's will, am I reading carefully enough to make sure I truly have his answer?**

The Difficult Virtue of Sharing

Why should I take my bread and water, and the meat I have slaughtered for my shearers, and give it to men coming from who knows where?

1 SAMUEL 25:11

It's not difficult to see why Abigail said her husband lived up to his name—Nabal, *the fool*! Nabal would not be the first to think he shouldn't have to share his hard-earned money or possessions with complete strangers, yet who but a fool would say it out loud! Then again as a matter of moral inquiry, the actual question he poses is not a bad question. Why *should* we share? Just when you think sharing has been so inculcated through child-rearing and cultural values that it is axiomatic, we see not only Nabal questioning the obvious, but also David's warriors. The soldiers who actually went into battle didn't want to share the plunder with those who stayed behind guarding the supplies! Were they not also fools?

If we are brutally honest, hardly a day goes by that you and I don't find ourselves begrudging the moral obligation to have less so that others can have more. Naturally we have less trouble sharing when we know that those with whom we share will reciprocate. We all bring a potluck dish and share our meal together. The more difficult sharing is when the recipients of our bounty are strangers who have neither means nor opportunity to share back. In that instance, what Nabal's question exposes is a fundamentally false assumption—that the water was *his*! Did God create the water just for Nabal? Only when we understand that what we have is not really *ours* can we begin to fully appreciate the virtue of sharing. All that we have is but a trust that God has given us to divide with others as each has need.

■ **The truly painful question is: As I look around at all *my* possessions on every hand, can I really bring myself to think that they are merely on loan until someone else needs them more?**

An Impatient Faith

Saul died because he was unfaithful to the LORD; he did not keep the word of the LORD and even consulted a medium for guidance, and did not inquire of the LORD.

1 CHRONICLES 10:13-14

Were Saul able to read that epilogue regarding his death, he would protest, "But I *did* inquire of God! He wouldn't answer me!" In fairness the text does record that Saul inquired of the Lord. He sought God's guidance through all the usual avenues of dreams, prophets, and the Urim (by which the priest was supernaturally guided). Even Saul's illicit attempt to conjure up Samuel had a measure of justification. At least he was trying to make contact with a man of God. Even so, God was not pleased. That God should fail to provide the answers we seek in the time and manner we choose is no excuse for going outside God's will to find what we are looking for. If patience is a virtue, it is doubly so when it comes to waiting on God. Surely a God who can raise up a dead prophet (the witch didn't do it!) is a God who can determine his own timetable… and whether he even chooses to communicate at all.

Ever wonder why God chose not to answer Saul? Could it be that God was in no mood to humor a leader who had so little faith that he shook in his boots at the very sight of the Philistines? Sometimes our appeals to God expose more lack of faith than faith. Yet Saul's inquiry was also being ignored, says Samuel, because Saul had disobeyed God, particularly regarding the Amalekites. (Samuel might well have mentioned the time when Saul got tired of waiting on Samuel and made the burnt offering himself.) In the most important sense, Saul hadn't truly inquired of God after all. "Inquiring of God" demands a patient faith…and complete obedience.

■ **The question for seekers is: If I grow impatient with God and take spiritual matters into my own hands, can I possibly conjure up anything but trouble?**

Uncivil Civil Wars

Abner called out to Joab, "Must the sword devour forever? Don't you realize that this will end in bitterness? How long before you order your men to stop pursuing their fellow Israelites?"

2 SAMUEL 2:26

Compared with the ongoing civil war between Saul's men and David's, the infamous feud between the Hatfields and McCoys was but a minor scrape. The war between the house of Saul and the house of David lasted a very long time. It can happen between civilizations, nations, tribes, families, neighbors, and friends. Sadly, it can happen between warring factions within the Lord's body—not just long-standing doctrinal disputes but acrimonious personal infighting. *Uncivil* civil war! It's not that some battles don't need to be fought. For every petty dispute, there are other conflicts over principle that cannot, and should not, be avoided. Even then, Abner's question to Joab is a good one, "Must the sword devour forever?" No matter how legendary, the Hatfield-McCoy feud eventually came to an end. So too the Saul-David conflict, though Abner's prophecy of a bitter conclusion proved to be true by his own brutal demise.

Of Abner's three questions, the most compelling is: When is it time to settle the dispute and move on? The less serious the reasons for the feud, the less time need be wasted. Yet in the more principled battles over crucial doctrines or family values, when is it time to end a civil war worth fighting? Surprisingly the answer is *never.* Even centuries of doctrinal error must be challenged in each succeeding generation. And the admonition of right behavior within families is never out of place. The key words in Abner's question have to do, not with pursuing truth, but pursuing brothers. When the battle is against *brothers* instead of *error,* the time to stop is now!

■ **The probing question is: If I have allowed any issue with others to get more personal than principled, what can I do today to bring it to an end?**

Making Sense of Unfairness

When they came to the threshing floor of Kidon, Uzzah reached out his hand to steady the ark, because the oxen stumbled. The LORD's anger burned against Uzzah, and he struck him down because he had put his hand on the ark. So he died there before God.

1 CHRONICLES 13:9-10

Have you ever heard it said that airline accidents are virtually always the result of a combination of factors? What often is labeled as "pilot error" might never have happened were it not for an unexpected delay in departure, bad weather rolling in at just the wrong moment, and that loose engine cowling, which should have been spotted by the mechanics. Had it not been for those factors, the pilot might never have been forced into making the bad decision he eventually made. Perhaps that analogy helps to explain what seems so unfair about God taking Uzzah's life for reaching out to steady the ark. Surely Uzzah acted instinctively and from the best of motives in attempting to save the ark from possible damage. It's likely he feared God's wrath should he have chosen to do nothing and let the ark be destroyed.

When David angrily asked how he could possibly bring the ark to Jerusalem, what he overlooked was the obvious answer to his own question. Was there not another way to carry the ark? God's prescribed way—on the shoulders of the Levites? And was that not precisely why God struck down Uzzah? What, at times, seems so unfair might well be explained by other factors. How many times have we complained to God that something wasn't fair when all along we've been doing something we shouldn't have done in the first place? It's hard to blame God when he has told us to do it another way. Merely consider how often children make some truly innocent mistake while outright disobeying their parents and then howl at the "unfair" consequences!

■ **The cautionary question is: What sin is there in my life that is just waiting for a disaster to happen?**

The Joy of Singing

David told the leaders of the Levites to appoint their fellow Levites as musicians to make a joyful sound with musical instruments: lyres, harps and cymbals.

1 CHRONICLES 15:16

Apart from the metaphors of trees and birds "singing," the human ability to sing is a unique blessing. Instruments of metal or wood can make beautiful music, but which of them can match the melodic emotion of the human voice or the pristine harmony of four tonal parts blended together? Singing is one of those human traits that sets us apart from lower animals. Without a soul, how can one sing? Indeed, what would there be to sing about! One can certainly "sing the blues" when mournful, but more often singing is a natural expression of inner joy. Think about those who go around singing while they work, and you'll likely recognize one person after another whose whole life is a song! No wonder, then, that David called for singing to celebrate the moving of the ark to Jerusalem.

If the many songs David wrote are any indication of the lyrics sung by the Levites on that occasion, their singing had a story to tell about God's grace and goodness in making and fulfilling promises to his people. About battles won and miracles performed. With all that to celebrate, how could anyone *not* sing! Yet have you ever considered that singing does not play a central role in some religions? Perhaps there is an inward-focused chanting, but not joyous, exuberant singing. Why should that be unless they have no story to tell? No story that tracks so intimately with the soul that lips cannot help but proclaim the joy! We may have been created a little lower than the angels, but not when it comes to the gift of singing. Even if we can't carry a tune in a bucket, in song and in story we are downright angelic!

■ **The interesting question is: Among all the songs I might choose today, which will best honor the God who gave me lips to sing?**

A Matter of Priorities

After David was settled in his palace, he said to Nathan the prophet, "Here I am, living in a house of cedar, while the ark of the covenant of the LORD is under a tent."

1 CHRONICLES 17:1

What in the world would the sovereign Creator of the universe need with an earthly dwelling? How, possibly, could an unearthly Spirit inhabit any man-made dwelling! Yet God himself seems not to be bothered by David's idea of building him a special dwelling place. Indeed, God affirms that he has been "dwelling" in a tent ever since the Israelites came out of Egypt. The fact that God is an omnipresent, ethereal Spirit does not preclude his special presence being associated with either a tabernacle or a temple. Although God declares that his "house" is not to be built by David himself, God clearly blesses David's dream of erecting a permanent structure to replace the portable tabernacle. Of course it is not the temple itself, but David's sense of spiritual priorities that God truly is blessing. Who else sits in an elegant palace and feels guilty about God's ark being housed in a tent!

It's an interesting thought, isn't it? If God is to have a "dwelling" of any kind, should the house of any man be grander than the house of God? Think about our own houses, for example. How do they compare with God's house? No, not some familiar "church house." It is not bricks and mortar that matter. What matters is how the time, attention, and money we have spent on our homes compares with the time, attention, and money we have spent on honoring God and furthering his kingdom. Are we living in the lap of luxury (even relatively speaking) while ignoring far greater spiritual priorities? If our homes, in particular, are grander than whatever it is that we do to honor God, how do we expect to be blessed?

■ **The compelling question is: How much of my time each day is devoted to maintaining *my* home and how much to honoring *God's*?**

Grieving Over Sin

For I know my transgressions, and my sin is always before me.

PSALM 51:3

One can read the story of David and Bathsheba a hundred times and still be perplexed and dumbfounded. The surprise is not that David proved himself to be morally flawed. Each of us in our own way can identify with moral failure. If nothing else, Jesus' teaching regarding the inner essence of adultery and murder condemns virtually all of us as adulterers and murderers in a spiritual sense. Even acted-out adultery is not unknown among God's people. But how many fervent believers have premeditatedly killed a person to cover up for some grievous sin! Try as we might to empathize with David, the egregiousness of his sin stretches our moral comprehension to the breaking point. Harder still is figuring out how this cold-blooded killer could be described as a man after God's own heart!

To make any sense of it, we must observe that David's genuine, heart-wrenching repentance was as notorious as his sin. Unlike many of us, David actually *grieved* over his sin. So much that he employed the hyperbole of having been a sinner from birth to lament how thoroughly sinful he was. It was not, of course, some unconscious sinfulness in his mother's womb, nor some misdeed as an infant, that he was lamenting, but rather his all-too-conscious, adult sin with Bathsheba. It was that shameful sin—and the foul murder that followed—that he could never wipe from his mind. Not because he could never feel God's forgiveness, but because—through those two dramatic sins—his sensitivity to all sin was put on high alert. How could God *not* love a heart so attuned to one's own moral failure? For if to sin is human, to bewail one's sin is divine.

■ **The embarrassing question is: Just how much time do I spend truly grieving over my sins?**

_____

_____

_____

_____

Toward Godly Resignation

He answered, "While the child was still alive, I fasted and wept. I thought, 'Who knows? The LORD may be gracious to me and let the child live.' But now that he is dead, why should I go on fasting? Can I bring him back again? I will go to him, but he will not return to me."

2 SAMUEL 12:22-23

Callous? Calculating? Cold? How are we to interpret David's answer to his servants? Had he been putting on a show to win God's favor? If we didn't know David better, we might be tempted to think so. Even giving him the benefit of the doubt regarding the sincerity of his fasting and weeping, what are we to think about David's seemingly matter-of-fact response to his son's death? If the child were ours, could we possibly be so blasé? This brief snippet speaks eloquently of the intimate, trusting relationship between David and God. Whether in joy or in sorrow, David wears his heart on his sleeve. When he's happy, he takes off his kingly robes and dances around as if still a shepherd boy. When he's sad, he weeps unabashedly. Childlike, David is open and vulnerable to God. Does he want something passionately? The little boy in him asks for it passionately! But if he doesn't get what he asks for, the trusting child in him takes it on faith that his Father knows best.

Unless some great tragedy strikes, rarely can any of us ever know for sure just how intimate a relationship we have with God. Superficial relationships rarely survive adversity. Tears of pain and sadness are to be expected, but the real test of our faith is how we handle the aftermath. Can we come to grips with reality? Can we trust that God's eternal plan is bigger than our immediate pain? Being resigned to blind misfortune is frustrating fatalism. Being resigned to God's purposes is turning tragedy into triumph.

■ **The sobering question is: Is there some bitter disappointment in my life that I need to turn completely over to God this very day?**

_____

_____

_____

_____

A God Who Rescues

Like water spilled on the ground, which cannot be recovered, so we must die. But that is not what God desires; rather, he devises ways so that a banished person does not remain banished from him.

2 SAMUEL 14:14

On this side of heaven, death is the ultimate reality. Like taxes, there's no escaping death…and, importantly, no coming back. Apart from the notorious miracles in which the dead were brought back to life, the effects of death cannot be undone. Those reincarnationists and others who think we live more than once on this planet simply do not understand. As David said upon the death of his son by Bathsheba, "I will go to him, but he will not return to me." He might well have added, "in any form, at any time, under any circumstances." Like Nicodemus, we too could ask: Are we to reenter our mother's womb? Heaven is to this life, what living outside the womb is to the womb itself. In terms of this earth, death is irreversible banishment.

That hard reality need not ring of hopelessness. For the God of heaven and earth exists on both sides of death…and, more mystifying still, has personally experienced both sides of death! Considering that God has taken countless lives in punishment for sin, one cannot say that God doesn't take away life. What can be said with certainty is that God has no desire to bring death upon anyone. More yet, that, death or no death, it was never God's wish to banish his creatures forever. That in the ethereal realm of the spirit lying beyond the earthly "birth canal" of physical death, God takes no pleasure in eternal estrangement. So what does he do about it? Marvelously and wondrously, he "devises ways" to rescue us from an eternal banishment. Because of God's love, the finality of death need never be final!

■ **The question having eternal consequences is: Am I dead certain that I have been rescued through the ways God has devised to save me?**

Open to God's Discipline

Leave him alone; let him curse, for the LORD has told him to. It may be that the LORD will look upon my misery and restore to me his covenant blessing instead of his curse today.

2 SAMUEL 16:11-12

Have you ever taken one of those personality tests designed to identify your strengths and weaknesses? From what we know of David's complex personality, we can only imagine how incredibly interesting his test results would be! Perhaps we get some indication from this fascinating incident where Shimei suddenly comes out of the crowd, hurling rocks and insults at David. Yet David suspects that Shimei is not as mad as he appears, for what Shimei says about David's being a man of blood has more than a kernel of truth to it. Whether in battle or in more personal conflicts, David's hands have been covered in blood as have few others. That part of David's personality—the strong, dominant trait—doesn't surprise us. What *does* surprise us is David's gentler side that seems so incongruous for a warrior. Instead of having Shimei's head cut off, David considers the real possibility that Shimei is speaking on behalf of God and lets him go.

The irony, of course, is that David's softer side is not a trait of weakness, as one might assume, but is entirely consistent with his strong, dominant trait. To take taunting of any kind requires great strength of character. To be open to piercing rebuke requires courage and wisdom, indeed. How many of us can discern the difference between taunting and rebuke? And do we ever stop to consider the possibility that it might be God speaking to us through the abusive words and actions of our fellow man? Seeing God through the madness of mortals is, if not inborn, a strong personality trait to be cultivated.

■ **The intriguing question for each of us is: Even if the criticism I receive is not clearly from God, might I be wise to consider that it just *might* be?**

A Father's Love

The king was shaken. He went up to the room over the gateway and wept. As he went, he said: "O my son Absalom! My son, my son Absalom! If only I had died instead of you—O Absalom, my son, my son!"

2 SAMUEL 18:33

What memories or impressions do you have of your father? It's no secret that how we view our own earthly father often shapes our view of the heavenly Father. Had Absalom looked closely enough, he would have seen in his father, not just the fallible man of flesh he knew so well, but also the noble man of God he never fully appreciated. Human that they are, fathers are a mix of good and bad, the admirable and the disappointing. Then again that goes for sons as well, including Absalom. Quite amazingly (perhaps because he was all too aware of his own moral shortcomings) David was willing to look tenderly upon a rebellious son who had conspired to steal his throne, tried to kill him, and openly slept with his concubines!

Most fathers have never had a son that rebellious and evil. Yet countless fathers can relate to David's anguish at the loss of a son—especially one who is still living. Note the line about the forest swallowing up more victims than the sword in 2 Samuel 18:8. Most lost sons don't die by violence, but like Absalom, simply get caught up in the snares of this world. Unable to extricate themselves, they are as lost as if dead. When David cried that, if possible, he would gladly have taken Absalom's place, he expressed the anguished pain of many a grieving father. Beyond even that he foreshadowed yet another son who would come from his lineage—an altogether different, obedient Son who, with the same loving grief in his heart as the Father, willingly died in our place.

■ **The question for all us wayward children is: If I have a doting Father who is willing to forgive my unremitting rebellion, is there someone I myself need to forgive in the same extraordinary way?**

In Praise of Mothers

She continued, "Long ago they used to say, 'Get your answer at Abel,' and that settled it. We are the peaceful and faithful in Israel. You are trying to destroy a city that is a mother in Israel."

2 SAMUEL 20:18-19

Exceptions abound, but there is nothing quite like the wisdom of motherhood. We know almost nothing about the "wise woman" in the town of Abel who saved her city from destruction by her advice, but we wonder if she isn't best described by her own description of the town itself. The city apparently had a long-standing reputation for being a source of wisdom. Have a question? Find the answer at Abel! Need some good counsel? Get it at Abel! And from all accounts, the inhabitants of Abel took their own good advice. The city was a place of peace and faithfulness, but most of all, wisdom. No wonder, then, that the city of Abel was likened to a *mother*. (Remember when Deborah, Israel's woman judge, described herself as "a mother"?) We are on safe ground to assume that this wise woman was, first and foremost, a mother.

Mothers are indeed wise peacemakers. They come by it almost naturally, if not by sheer necessity! Virtually minute by minute, young mothers in particular must play the role of judge, negotiator, and arbitrator. Whose turn is it to play with the toy? Which child was simply being selfish? What is the best way to resolve the dispute so that neither child ends up resentful? No formal education can teach this kind of wisdom. Whatever's not instinctive is quickly learned by experience. Too bad, then, that more civil disputes and world affairs can't be sorted out by mothers! It's also a shame that any men in charge don't inherit more wisdom from the women who rocked their cradles. Were we all as wise as mothers, peace and faithfulness would enshroud the world!

■ **The question for all would-be peacemakers is: What new insight for peace and justice might I glean from some frazzled young mom today?**

The Importance of Silent Protest

But Joab did not include Levi and Benjamin in the numbering, because the king's command was repulsive to him. This command was also evil in the sight of God; so he punished Israel.

1 CHRONICLES 21:6-7

Ever been in one of those situations where you've been asked to do something you don't feel completely right about? Perhaps what you've been asked to do is clearly wrong, yet innocent people might get hurt if you fight that particular battle. In the integrity wars, not all is as cut-and-dried as we might wish. David's general Joab was hardly a paragon of virtue, but even he was repulsed by David's arrogance in numbering Israel's army. Hadn't Joab reminded David that—whatever the number of troops—with God on their side they could win any battle, anytime, anywhere? But Joab also knew that, foibles and all, David was God's anointed leader. And so he dutifully carried out the king's loathsome command…almost.

Maybe it seems contradictory, inconsistent, or even deceptive, but when Joab refused to include the tribes of Levi and Benjamin in the census, apparently it was his small, silent protest for having to do something morally objectionable. Some would argue that Joab was just as guilty as David for having carried through with the census as far as he did, that he should have resigned rather than even begin the process. Perhaps they are right. Then again, to permanently remove himself from being a positive influence on an essentially good king might well have been morally shortsighted. In the complex struggle to maintain ethical integrity, sometimes the best we can do for the moment is to be true in some small way to our own consciences, while hoping for future opportunities to encourage others in their integrity. Winning even the smallest ethical battles can be the prelude to great moral victories.

■ **The question for struggling ethicists is: If for the greater cause I've sometimes protested quietly behind the scenes, do I risk becoming as ethically compromised as those I hope to influence?**

Service, the Great Equalizer

Young and old alike, teacher as well as student, cast lots for their duties.

1 CHRONICLES 25:8

It's not the American way. It doesn't even sound quite…well…*godly*. Turning temple service into nothing more than a game of chance? Throwing dice to decide *who* serves *when?* Why do you suppose we are told over and over that the Levites cast lots to decide the rotation of their priestly duties? What lesson are we to learn from that strange way of doing temple business? Unless, perhaps, it has something to do with its very randomness—a randomness that crosses all boundaries of age, experience, knowledge, and ability. When you think about it, the world rotates on the axis of rank and tenure—and position, power, and prestige. But in God's realm, none of that seems to matter. Sure, some are called to be teachers and some disciples. Some are gifted as administrators and some gifted as worker bees. Some get all the glory while others get none. But in God's kingdom, there isn't any such thing as seniority or rank when it comes to personal importance. Or responsibility. Or reward.

To be chosen by lot is simply to be chosen for service. In the big picture, it hardly matters *what* service. You have your responsibility, I have mine. I have my duties to fulfill, you have yours. And all to the glory of God! What could it possibly matter if your service is more high-profile than mine? When service to God becomes the great equalizer, there's no room for arrogance or humiliation. It is true that we may have been specially called by God in different ways according to his eternal purpose and plan. But as far as *we* are concerned, God might just as well have thrown the dice.

■ **The only question is: If I compare my gifts with those of others, have I not missed the whole point of random service in the kingdom?**

Invasion of Privacy

And you, my son Solomon, acknowledge the God of your father, and serve him with wholehearted devotion and with a willing mind, for the LORD searches every heart and understands every desire and every thought.

1 CHRONICLES 28:9

In today's rights-oriented culture, one breaches the inviolate right of privacy at his peril. Tragically, privacy trumps even the right to life. Of course none of us wishes to give up our privacy. In a world where "Big Brother" is recording every minute detail of our lives, the need for privacy grows daily. If you feel as if you are completely exposed to a hostile world, you are not entirely wrong. Yet that is the least of our concern. Although Scripture affirms that no one knows the mind of a man except the spirit within him, it is speaking only of other human beings. The story is altogether different with a God who can penetrate even the heart.

There's no need to be paranoid about it, but the awesome, sobering truth is that God knows, not just what you and I are doing at this very moment, but what we're thinking! And even *why* we're thinking it, which is more insight than we ourselves have! Consider this: With whom are you close enough to share your most intimate, secret, embarrassing thoughts? No one? Probably not. But the fact is that you are sharing those very thoughts, moment by moment, with the omniscient Judge of the universe before whom one day every knee will bow. If that's not a wake-up call, what is? If there is any reassurance for those of us who could hope for greater privacy from God's penetrating eyes, it is that he sees not only all the bad things, which embarrass even us, but also the good things we might not give ourselves credit for.

■ **The question we need to ask is: If I am too embarrassed to tell even my closest family and friends what I'm thinking about, dare I allow it to enter my mind for an observing God to see?**

A God Who Seems Distant

Why, LORD, do you stand far off? Why do you hide yourself in times of trouble?

PSALM 10:1

Let enough absentee landlords take over, and you can safely predict that the neighborhood will soon be in ruins. For a neighborhood to thrive, owners and landlords need to be on-site and in sight. As with other situations, perception is half the battle. Consider a boss who is never in the office, a parent who is never around, or a coach who never shows up for practice. In those situations, to whom do we complain? What good is it if there's no one to respond? By now you can guess we're talking about one of the most challenging aspects of our relationship with God. Where is God when we need him? Why doesn't he swoop in wearing a red cape and fight off the bad guys? Unseen and unseeable, how do we even know that God is real?

Are you ever bothered by the fact that we pray to a God who never talks back? Does it help that we fervently believe God briefly appeared on earth in flesh and bones, yet went away again? Has he abandoned us? Some get nervous at such a harsh indictment of God, but David certainly pulled no punches. And how can we forget the Son of God himself pleading on the cross, "Why have you forsaken me?" Even if there's more to that question than first meets the eye, it's not as if God hasn't heard all of this before. The easy answer is that we simply need more faith. And, of course, we do. But that doesn't solve the problem of an absentee God. His absence emboldens the bad guys, gives skeptics fodder for their disbelief, and makes even people of faith wonder. But if God truly had abandoned us, how would we explain all the unmistakable evidence of his presence?

■ **The question for doubters is: If I look closely enough at my world today, can I say beyond a doubt that God truly doesn't care?**

Confidence in the Lord

Vindicate me, LORD, for I have led a blameless life; I have trusted in the LORD and have not faltered.

PSALM 26:1

Sorry, David, but something seems terribly amiss with that brash claim! You, the adulterer. You, the murderer. You, so much a man of blood that God would not even let you build his temple! Not that you don't have a great heart for God…but *blameless*? And *trusting without wavering*? Dare we remind you of that time you numbered Israel's forces, as if your trust were in the size of your army and not in God?

It's possible, of course, that David might have written this particular song prior to the events surrounding Bathsheba and long before the offensive census. Even so, is it not the height of presumption for anyone to claim being blameless? Yet this is the same David who talked about his sins being ever before him. So David's claim to be blameless makes no sense…unless, perhaps, by way of relative comparison with his enemies. Compared with *their* wickedness, he was as pure as a newborn infant! While it may be true that he was "a man of blood," unlike his enemies he was not bloodthirsty! Despite his great sins, David had an extraordinary love for God's truth, a fervent desire to serve the Lord, and an unabashed passion for worship. As we think about our own sins, there is danger in making self-serving comparisons with those who may be even greater sinners, as if we could rationalize our "less-serious" sins. On the other hand, because we and they are all sinners, there must be some critical factor separating the righteous from the unrighteous, the "blameworthy" from the "blameless." If that factor isn't a sinner's heart for God like David's, what is?

■ **The question for all of us is: Do I minimize my sins by comparing them with others, or am I reminded of just how much all of us need God's saving grace?**

When Betrayal Hurts Most

If an enemy were insulting me, I could endure it; if a foe were rising against me, I could hide. But it is you, a man like myself, my companion, my close friend, with whom I once enjoyed sweet fellowship at the house of God, as we walked about among the worshipers.

PSALM 55:12-14

One of the most famous lines in all of literature draws deeply from the well of bitter human experience. By legend, "Et tu, Brute?" were the last three words of Julius Caesar when he was being stabbed to death by a group of Roman senators, including his good friend Marcus Brutus. A loose translation of the Latin is, "Even *you*, Brutus?" Caesar wasn't surprised by all the other conspirators, but never could he have imagined his close friend being among them. As Mark Antony put it, that was "the unkindest cut of all." If you have ever been betrayed by a close friend, you know that unique pain—it pierces the heart. It's not just the loss of friendship, but a soul-jarring violation of trust.

One can only imagine how Jesus must have felt when one of his chosen twelve betrayed him. Of course Jesus knew all along that Judas would succumb to kissing away not only a relationship of special trust, but the very life of the Son of God! It's the paltry reasons behind "companion betrayals" that we have such difficulty understanding. (Thirty pieces of silver!) Yet, typically, a major incident of betrayal is but the final act in an ongoing series of deceptions about the true nature of the relationship. When, in the end, a supposed close friendship is exposed for the fraud it has been all along, we suddenly realize that we've foolishly invested years of misplaced trust. Imagine, then, how God must feel when we lay claim to a close relationship but, for plainly unworthy reasons, so willingly betray him.

■ **The haunting question is: If I constantly betray God in little ways, might a day come when I inflict the unkindest cut of all?**

Shame by Association

You, God, know my folly; my guilt is not hidden from you. Lord, the LORD Almighty, may those who hope in you not be disgraced because of me; God of Israel, may those who seek you not be put to shame because of me.

PSALM 69:5-6

Watching hundreds of dominoes falling one after another in a long serpentine line is a fascinating sight. The phenomenon has even given rise to one "domino theory" after another, whether in politics, science, or business. Let one domino factor occur, and before you know it, a second domino factor causes a third one to fall, and so on. The domino theory can also happen in matters of faith. Wherever we go, whatever we do, people are watching. And evaluating. And making their own decisions, influenced in part by what they see in us. That is especially true for those who are seen as spiritual leaders at any level. As much as any of us might prefer it to be otherwise, we do not live unto ourselves alone. How we live invariably influences a myriad of others, for good or for ill.

David's remarkable prayer presents a variation of the typical domino theory. Beyond even the pernicious influence we can have on complete strangers is the danger of bringing undeserved disgrace to others because of our own sin. Right or wrong, people naturally make associations between those of like kind—sometimes laudable, but often contemptuous. If, for example, one Christian brings notorious shame on himself or herself, that individual disgrace can tarnish all who wear the name of Christ. First there is the one, then the others. One, two, three, we all fall down! That David would be concerned not only about his personal sin but about the shame and disgrace it could bring on others is one reason why he was one of the most noble of sinners.

■ **The disturbing question is: Is it possible that some deserved shame I bring on myself might also bring reproach on fellow believers who don't deserve it?**

A Lifetime of Learning

Since my youth, God, you have taught me, and to this day I declare your marvelous deeds. Even when I am old and gray, do not forsake me, my God, till I declare your power to the next generation, your mighty acts to all who are to come.

PSALM 71:17-18

Perhaps you have heard the story of the dying man who was asked what great truth he could impart. To those who were listening in hushed expectation, the man replied, "Jesus loves me, this I know. For the Bible tells me so." After a lifetime of education and experience, the greatest spiritual legacy this man could leave to others was a simple, yet profound truth he had learned as a child! Life has a way of coming full circle. "Second childhood" is not a myth. As with an airline passenger taking off and landing, the familiar landscape one returns to in the descent is usually little changed from what one left behind at take-off.

Between the bookends of our human existence is a lifetime of learning about God and his eternal will for mankind. Given enough time, we all move from being students to teachers. Whether formally or informally, what we learn we transfer to others. Yet what is so amazing about the process is that the more we learn, the more we realize how little we know. And the more we know, the more we find ourselves getting back to the basics we first learned as a child—before all the intellectual clutter inexorably chokes out the essence of childlike faith and trust in the simplest truths. Perhaps the one advantage that the "hoary head" has over the "towhead" is a lifetime of witnessing God's incredible deeds. Combine the profound truths, which even children can grasp, together with the marvelous deeds, to which the more mature can testify, and you have the story of a lifetime!

■ **The question for us older folk is: Have I grown so sophisticated in my knowledge of Scripture that what I teach others is overly complicated?**

Questions at Death's Door

I am overwhelmed with troubles, and my life draws near to death…Do you show your wonders to the dead? Do their spirits rise up and praise you? Is your love declared in the grave, your faithfulness in Destruction? Are your wonders known in the place of darkness, or your righteous deeds in the land of oblivion?

PSALM 88:3,10-12

As is often said, "There are no atheists in foxholes." When bombs start dropping, bullets begin flying, and men are dying all around you, rare is the soldier who does not lift a pleading prayer to God. Rarer still, one suspects, is the mortally wounded soldier who lies conscious on his deathbed and doesn't question what awaits him on the other side. We do not have to be on our deathbeds, of course, to wonder about what lies beyond the grave. Surely even atheists must be more than slightly curious. In their heart of hearts and at death's door, who possibly could *not* wonder?

Those of us who are disciples of Jesus Christ often speak glibly of death, resurrection, judgment, heaven, and hell—as if we knew every detail. The New Testament (principally through the apostle Paul) gives us far more insight into the afterlife than was available to the ancients of David's day. Yet even for us the actual details are scanty, particularly regarding what happens at the moment when the soul separates from the body. If you have ever watched anyone die, you know the profound mystery of that transition. Those "near-death" folks (who speak of seeing lights and hearing voices) try to fill in the blanks, but "near death" is *not* death. And we get no insider information from Lazarus or the many others who were raised miraculously from the dead. Or do we? What does it tell us that none of them tells us! Except for the most important fact of all…that death is not the end!

■ **The question at death's door is: Have I thought seriously enough about the destination that the details don't matter?**

What God Lets Slip

The LORD will keep you from all harm—he will watch over your life; the LORD will watch over your coming and going both now and forevermore.

PSALM 121:7-8

Have you ever walked precariously along a narrow mountain path, wondering if at any moment your foot might slip, causing you to fall to your death? It would be nice to think that every safe return from such danger affirms David's confidence that the Lord keeps us from all harm. But what about those times when the foot has slipped and even some person of great faith has been claimed by the mountain? It is interesting that in this same psalm the writer talks about lifting his eyes to the hills from which his help comes (speaking of God). In point of fact, lifting one's eyes while walking precariously on a mountain isn't the best idea! More troublesome by far is the fact that even fully trusting in God is no guarantee of complete safety, whether we are literally walking on a mountain or facing some other kind of harm.

So is it just poetic license when the writer says that God will not let our foot slip? In a sense, yes. This psalm, like several others, is "a song of ascents," meaning that it was traditionally sung by pilgrims making their way up to Jerusalem for the various festivals and holy days. Apparently it was sung especially to keep the children's attention along the way and teach them something important at the same time. (Perhaps it was not unlike "Onward Christian Soldiers," written by Sabine Baring Gould for a similar purpose.) Yet even children must sense that God doesn't literally keep them from scraping their knees. What *is* true is that, when the potential harm is mostly within our control, looking to God is the only sure way of never slipping.

■ **The crucial question for strugglers is: What spiritual threats might I face that I can confidently escape by keeping my eyes steadfastly on Jesus?**

Getting a Perspective on Evil

Do not fret because of those who are evil or be envious of those who do wrong; for like the grass they will soon wither, like green plants they will soon die away.

PSALM 37:1-2

Night after night you toss and turn, unable to sleep. If it is not an illness you are worried about, or a relationship problem, or some insoluble financial crisis, chances are that you are fretting over a grievous wrong that has been done to you by some seemingly evil person. "Why is this happening to me?" "Why does God allow this creep to exist?" "How can I get back at this pestering person!" From reading David's psalm, at least you know you are not the first person to feel the way you do. There's just a lot of wickedness out there, which means there are a lot of people doing all those wicked things. How do we deal with them? How, by any means, can we get back to sleep?

If you check the footnotes in your Bible, you will see that Psalm 37 is an acrostic poem, each stanza beginning with the successive letters of the Hebrew alphabet. Unless you know Hebrew, that obscure fact is pretty useless. To fully appreciate the acrostic literary device, you would first need the Hebrew text and have some understanding of the language. It is a translation problem. Strangely, so is the problem of understanding people who do wicked things. On our own we have no way to resolve the issue of evil (except to acknowledge that we ourselves are part of the problem). From God's perspective, however, the evil ones from whom we struggle to flee in the night have already been put to rout! Put another way (using successive letters of the alphabet), God hides instant judgment.

■ **The question for those who fret is: If God already has the evildoers secretly under judgment, is there any reason not to have sweet dreams tonight?**

_____

_____

_____

_____

_____

When Sin Comes Home to Roost

For troubles without number surround me; my sins have overtaken me, and I cannot see.
They are more than the hairs of my head, and my heart fails within me.

PSALM 40:12

With one sentence, your whole life changes. "I'm afraid you've tested positive for HIV." "I know it's not what you wanted to hear, but you are definitely pregnant." "I've just learned you've been having an affair." Suddenly your world stops. Those words are right up there with being told of cancer or the death of a loved one. The crucial difference is that some bad news is sin-related, and other bad news is not. When it's sin-related, the words might just as well have been, "You're busted!" Some sins have more devastating consequences than others. More than once David has talked about his *sins* (plural) being ever before him or, as here, overtaking him. Maybe that's where you find yourself so guilt-ridden that you're in a deep spiritual depression, thinking God could never forgive a sinner like you.

Do you remember that line from the apostle Paul who claimed to be the "chief of sinners"? He must have carried around a huge burden of guilt for having put to death followers of Christ before his own conversion. We can all relate to his ongoing struggle with the flesh. Yet Paul still seems such a paragon of virtue that we feel all the worse by comparison. We do ourselves no favors by thinking that sins come in sizes, or that sins are judged by volume. When we come to see that no sin known to man is incapable of God's forgiveness, there's never a time when our moral world need stop. Maybe it's too late to do anything about life-altering consequences, but the sin itself is no cause for heart failure. Merely repentance.

■ **The encouraging question is: If I have been absolutely debilitated by overwhelming guilt, isn't that godly sorrow the very broken heart God is looking for?**

Contentment in God's House

Better is one day in your courts than a thousand elsewhere; I would rather be a doorkeeper in the house of my God than dwell in the tents of the wicked.

PSALM 84:10

Upward mobility—that's the goal. From rags to riches is a story that sells. However good our present position, we are forever looking around at even better positions, despite the fact that some of those "better positions" are associated with people and organizations we would have nothing in common with spiritually. Ever thought about the source of our discontent? Why are we never satisfied with our jobs, our incomes, our marriages, or our homes? Why does the grass always look greener on the other side? Is that grass truly greener or does it only seem so because we can't see how green the grass is under our feet?

The person who says, "I'd rather be a doorkeeper in God's house than live in luxury with the unrighteous," is a person who has his spiritual priorities right. It is the same person who would say, "I'd rather be in poverty and be saved than be unsaved and have all the wealth in the world." Or, "If given a choice between a job and integrity, I'll choose integrity every time!" Of course making those intellectual choices is not the hard part. The hard part is coming to the point where we are so content that we quit looking for greener pastures. Maybe it all depends on whose "house" we see ourselves working in, whatever our present or future position. If we truly see ourselves serving in "God's house" instead of the world's, how could we not be content playing some "lesser role" with his blessing than playing what the world deems a "greater role" without his blessing?

■ **The question for all ladder climbers is: If there is some better position I'd like to have, would it open doors for greater service in God's house?**

A Blurred Cosmology

When I consider your heavens, the work of your fingers, the moon and the stars, which you have set in place, what is mankind that you are mindful of them, human beings that you care for them? You have made them a little lower than the angels and crowned them with glory and honor.

PSALM 8:3-5

The word *awesome* may be the most devalued word in the modern vocabulary. Its original meaning had far more to do with a true sense of wonderment than today's catch-all phrase of giddy excitement used for everything from the latest rock star to one's breakfast bran flakes. Actually, if you want to see something truly awesome, just lift your eyes to the night sky and be awestruck by the countless celestial bodies twinkling from an unfathomable distance. That is *if* you can see them. Given the pervasive light pollution these days, few of us on the planet can catch much of a view of the wondrous cosmos. This is especially true for anyone living in a large metropolis. Cast your eyes heavenward and all you will see is the glare of city lights. The glory of the cosmos is now all but lost, and with it a loss of awe for both the wondrous universe around us and the truly awesome God who created it.

So when the psalmist asks about the significance of lowly man compared with the awe-inspiring heavens above, suddenly the comparison takes on a whole new perspective. In the absence of cosmic wonder, man himself seems larger and more important than he otherwise might. Could this explain why city dwellers are often less religious than folks in the country? In one stroke a blurred cosmos both diminishes the awesomeness of the universe and exaggerates the significance of man. When there is nothing greater to compare with ourselves, how very self-focused we become.

■ **The truly awesome question for most of us is: When was the last time I looked with wonder into the night sky and knew that my significance was in God alone?**

The Ultimate in Giving and Receiving

When you ascended on high, you took many captives; you received gifts from people, even from the rebellious—that you, LORD God, might dwell there.

PSALM 68:18

One of the great things about Scripture is the way every piece fits together. As most readers know, New Testament writers prolifically quote from their Old Testament counterparts, with the primary intent of showing how ancient prophecies are fulfilled in Christ. Yet the writers of the Gospels and Epistles employ a fair amount of literary license when quoting the Scriptures, as does Jesus himself. A passage with one meaning in the Prophets might well be given a rather different application, seemingly without objection from the rabbis (unless, perhaps, the new application ran radically counter to misguided Jewish expectations). In similar fashion the psalms, including this passage from Psalm 68, are often quoted, but with a twist. The "twist" in this case comes in Paul's letter to the Ephesians (chapter 4) where Paul quotes Psalm 68 as follows: "When he ascended on high, he took many captives and gave gifts to his people." Looks virtually the same, but it's not. Spot the crucial one-word difference?

In the days of ancient Israel, it was customary for conquering kings to return from victory leading his people of captured men and booty. As a sign of submission, the defeated forces would give gifts to their new ruler, the conquering king. And rightly so in terms of the analogy with God, our own conquering King. Yet our King is no ordinary king. The picture Paul paints is of Christ ascending into heaven, taking with him a train of those who have submitted to his rule in their hearts. The surprising, marvelous "twist" is that this conquering King not only *receives* rich gifts, but even now *gives* rich gifts to those who will ascend with him.

> ■ **The question for all of God's conquered people is: What rich gift has Christ bestowed upon me, his humble servant, and how can I give it back in honor of my King?**

Faithfulness in the Face of Unfaithfulness

For the Lord is good and his love endures forever; his faithfulness continues through all generations.

PSALM 100:5

Perhaps only those who have experienced the loss or betrayal of a deep love can fully appreciate the constancy of God's love. Of all the characteristics that make God *good,* his unerring faithfulness must surely be near the top of the list. Certainly we give him every reason *not* to love us, so we should hardly be surprised that he might turn his back on us. And yet even when he does, it's as if he has eyes in the back of his head, watching anxiously for any signs of repentance. On this side of Judgment, God never gives up on us. The more unfaithful we are, the more faithful he is. Even when God turns his back on us, it is because he loves us, not because he has rejected us. Not many of us can say that we have turned our backs on others solely out of love!

If God's love endures from one generation to the next, why is it so hard for us to be faithful to him and to each other within a single lifetime? Why does human love evaporate so quickly? For example, why are some folks so eager to end a marital relationship when there has been an "act of unfaithfulness"? What kind of faithfulness is it when the "faithful spouse" is secretly hoping an "unfaithful spouse" will provide a good excuse to leave! Is that what Jesus intended when he taught that divorce and remarriage hinge on acts of unfaithfulness? If God had given up on Israel at the first sign of infidelity, not one of his promises would have been fulfilled. The lesson, surely, is that—compared with God's faithfulness—our notions of "faithful" and "unfaithful" fall far short of divine.

■ **The challenging question for us mortals is: In what way today might God's unrelenting faithfulness prompt greater faithfulness in my own relationships?**

_____

_____

_____

_____

_____

The Compassion of Human Frailty

As a father has compassion on his children, so the LORD has compassion on those who fear him; for he knows how we are formed, he remembers that we are dust.

PSALM 103:13-14

Most great truths are finely balanced between opposite extremes. Not to get overly philosophical, but how we perceive ourselves is one of those high-wire balancing acts best appreciated in the nature of a paradox. Simultaneously we are both god-like (being souls made in God's image) and animal-like (being made of mortal, physical flesh). No one should think we are sinful in flesh but pure in spirit. The fine line between flesh and spirit simply isn't that bright. What we do in the flesh makes an indelible imprint on our souls, and what we are in spirit can dramatically affect our physical bodies. That very complexity is what makes the separation of the soul from the body at death so intriguing.

Only our Creator fully understands our paradoxical nature. Fortunately for us, when God considers his vast universe, including the most far-flung stars and wonderfully complex micro-organisms, he remembers that we are—as in that great verse above—but *dust*. "Frail children of dust," as Sir Robert Grant penned the immortal lines, "and feeble as frail." Little wonder, then, that we sing those wonderful words of assurance: "In thee do we trust, nor find thee to fail. Thy mercies how tender, how firm to the end. Our Maker, Defender, Redeemer, and Friend." To see ourselves as "dust" is not to excuse our sin, but rather to appreciate a God who has every reason to expect more of us, yet wondrously understands our human foibles. Like any loving parent, whenever we fall he dusts us off and calls us higher.

■ **The question for us "frail children" is: If God's compassion comes from seeing *me* as dust, does that give me a clue as to how I can be more compassionate to those around me?**

_____

_____

_____

_____

Having an Inside Track

Your commands are always with me and make me wiser than my enemies. I have more insight than all my teachers, for I meditate on your statutes. I have more understanding than the elders, for I obey your precepts.

PSALM 119:98-100

Nobody likes a wise guy, but everyone wants to be one. At least everyone wants to be "in the know." To have an inside track. As is often said, "Knowledge is power." That is why education gives a child from the inner city a leg up. It is why most young people do whatever it takes to go to a university and why people read, and inquire, and soak up as much information as possible. Yet if all of that is true, why do you suppose so few people spend the time necessary to get the *real* scoop? Is it possibly because the "real scoop" comes packaged in the form of religious instruction? Even in seemingly onerous *commands*? The negative connotation many have attached to reading Scripture has robbed millions of a divine wisdom that could have provided endless solutions for a troubled world.

The writer of this lengthy psalm is a person "in the know." He knows that God's laws contain insight far greater than all human knowledge put together. God's wisdom helps us triumph over our enemies by providing smarter strategies. God's wisdom appreciates whatever knowledge a teacher might impart, but is able to take that knowledge a giant leap beyond what the ordinary teacher knows. And God's wisdom can surpass the accumulated insight of the most-experienced men and women. Because divine law is the vehicle that conveys the insight only God himself can have, to ignore God's law is to foolishly disdain the extraordinary wisdom that brings us the highest possible knowledge and power.

■ **The question is: If I have spent years acquiring earthly knowledge, isn't it time I spent an equal amount of effort drinking in the wisdom from above?**

In Praise of Night Workers

Praise the LORD, all you servants of the LORD who minister by night in the house of the LORD.
Lift up your hands in the sanctuary and praise the LORD.

PSALM 134:1-2

Are you a night-shift person? If so, you have unique insight into a nocturnal world of activity most people rarely see. Custodians, cabbies, bakers, medical staff, policemen and firemen, newspaper deliverers, airport workers, and truckers on the road all play important, often unappreciated, behind-the-scenes roles. The city may sleep, but the night shift works silently on, protecting, providing, maintaining, and healing. If we take that activity for granted, consider that the passage above speaks of those who minister in the Lord's house throughout the night! Perhaps it's hard for us moderns to think of anyone working through the night in a darkened ancient culture—especially priests.

If you have ever walked around at night, you know that it is like being in a shadowy, far-away universe. Few experiences are more suited to deep, contemplative thoughts and fresh perspectives. You—the silent observer and explorer of the night's closely held secrets. So when you encounter the night shift at work behind the scenes, it's reasonable to wonder if that is also how God works behind the scenes. While we sleep, God—who never slumbers—is protecting, providing, maintaining, and healing. Why else have nighttime if not for God to give us fresh starts? To heal the body. To clean up behind us. To prepare spiritual nourishment for the coming day. To deliver insights through the night that we'll "read" as we awake. As much as we want God at our side throughout the busy day, have we lost sight of a God who is with us even when we close our eyes?

Whatever shift we're on, the question is: Have I considered that starting and ending each day with praise in my heart lessens God's need to work during the night?

_____

_____

_____

_____

Fearfully and Wonderfully Made

For you created my inmost being; you knit me together in my mother's womb. I praise you because I am fearfully and wonderfully made; your works are wonderful, I know that full well. My frame was not hidden from you when I was made in the secret place, when I was woven together in the depths of the earth. Your eyes saw my unformed body.

PSALM 139:13-16

Autopsies are not everyone's cup of tea, but for those who have shared that unique experience, it's hard to come away without genuine amazement at the intricacy of the human body. At once the body is a marvelous piece of engineering and a sublime work of art. How all the organs and miles of nerves, arteries, and blood vessels work in harmony to keep a person alive defies imagination. Looking down into the opened cavity of the body (and more so into the exposed brain) is both incomparably fascinating and humbling. Living in a prescientific age, David could not fully have known how "fearfully and wonderfully" made we really are. Nor did he have the benefit of today's medical advances to see the incredible development of the human form from its very earliest stages in the womb.

Yet for all its wonder, the human body doesn't begin to equate with what David described as "my inmost being." If asked where the real "you" resides, what would you answer? Because our thinking process seems closest to who we are, most of us tend to associate our inner self with the brain. But if our souls reside within the brain, what is left of the soul when those gray cells deteriorate in the grave? If there is to be life after death, the soul must be something quite apart from the brain. Compared with my incredible body, how much more fearfully and wonderfully made must be my immortal soul!

■ **The profound question is: In my sentient, thinking mind today, how conscious will I be of my "inmost being," which at death will survive the very brain with which I ask this question?**

Confession Is Good for the Soul

Then I acknowledged my sin to you and did not cover up my iniquity. I said, "I will confess my transgressions to the LORD." And you forgave the guilt of my sin.

PSALM 32:5

Suspects under arrest must be advised by the police that they have a right to remain silent, and that anything they say can be used against them in a court of law. No criminal defense lawyer would permit his client to confess to a crime unless pleading guilty pursuant to a favorable plea bargain. The rules of the criminal justice game weigh heavily against conviction by confession and, to some extent, rightly so. Who feels comfortable where a conviction is *solely* by confession without any shred of corroborating evidence? Too many confessions have been coerced out of unsuspecting innocents. And what's to account for all those crazies who rush to confess having committed notorious crimes they couldn't possibly have done? Yet the most amazing phenomenon is not the crazies who insist on confessing, but the genuinely guilty. Despite repeated police warnings, many suspects can't wait to confess.

There is within each of us a need to deal with whatever moral guilt we are carrying around. Until pent-up guilt is released, there is no rest for the wicked. No peace of mind. No joy of redemption. Did you catch David's lead-up line (verse 3), "When I kept silent, my bones wasted away through my groaning all day long"? It may sound heretical, but the criminal justice system does criminals no favors to discourage confessions. How else is the offender ever to be rehabilitated? It may sound equally heretical to some cheap-grace churches these days, but without genuine, hard-core confession of sin, how can any of us expect to know either God's forgiveness or our own?

■ **The question for us guilty souls is: What debilitating guilt is silently eating away at me because I have yet to *truly* confess my sin?**

Longing for God

As the deer pants for streams of water, so my soul pants for you, my God. My soul thirsts for God, for the living God. When can I go and meet with God?

PSALM 42:1-2

Those words have become a standard fixture in contemporary Christian music. Week after week, worshippers sing about that mythic deer panting for water and their own soul's panting and thirsting for God. Sometimes we sing perfunctorily, sometimes with great passion. But one does wonder how often even the well-intentioned worshipper really and truly *pants* for God. Can you remember such a moment in your life? A moment of spiritual desperation for God? Try to imagine someone who has been without water so long that a genuinely life-threatening thirst drives his desperate quest for water. Can we even conceive what that would be like—or more importantly—its spiritual counterpart?

Twice the psalmist speaks of his soul being downcast, and twice he refers to his enemies asking where his God is. The picture being painted is of a person of faith falling on such hard times that onlookers taunt him with the thought that God has abandoned him. Have you ever felt *abandoned* by God? If so, perhaps you can identify with the soul that despairingly yearns for God. For those who have never known such feelings of abandonment, perhaps the greater loss is in never having had that experience. Imagine how exhilarating it must be to know that God is still there after having every reason to think he's not! For those of us who blithely sing about our souls panting for God without knowing what it means to truly thirst, the deer we sing about seems far too pampered.

■ **The question for introspection is: Am I content merely to sing about panting and thirsting when God calls me to pant for him on a more desperate level?**

Knowing the Limits of Knowing

My heart is not proud, LORD, my eyes are not haughty; I do not concern myself with great matters or things too wonderful for me.

PSALM 131:1

Ever noticed how many scientific books written by atheists have "God" in their titles? It seems that God can best be debunked by redefinition. Denying the concept of God altogether would be too obvious. But by postulating some godless theory of the cosmos and then calling that explanation "God," it receives critical acclaim! Adding irony to irony, associating their theories with "God" is thought to gain these skeptics added respectability. That such respectability could only exist if God himself existed is apparently lost on them. Yet the real problem is the object of the exercise—to come up with "a theory of everything." Even atheists understand that our complex universe is so interrelated that no explanation short of *everything* will ultimately suffice. But what human dares to discover the undiscoverable?

Both by definition and in reality, the explanation for *everything* is...God! He is the first cause and sustaining power of all that exists. While searching for alternatives to God is the height of human foolishness, the height of human wisdom is searching for how the creator God of heaven has ordered his universe—physically, spiritually, and morally. God invites us to search, question, and reap the benefits of such discoveries. Yet we are foolish to think that we humans could ever unravel the mystery of God himself. Speculative theologians who speak glibly of the Incarnation or God's divine sovereignty are only slightly less arrogant than atheistic scientists. This serves as a warning to us average believers, that all we truly need to know about God is what he has given us to know. Beyond that, it's not *knowing* that counts, but *doing*!

■ **The question for inquiring minds is: How can I more humbly respond to whatever great insights I might think I have about God?**

_____

_____

_____

_____

_____

Hope in the Midst of Despair

My God, my God, why have you forsaken me? Why are you so far from saving me, so far from my cries of anguish?

PSALM 22:1

How many sermons have been dedicated to the thorny problem of the Father abandoning the Son on the cross, based upon Jesus' cry: "My God, my God, why have you forsaken me?" At face value it sure looks like Jesus was being forsaken. How could a holy God *not* forsake a Son who was taking upon himself the sins of the world? Yet it's also possible that Jesus was signaling quite the opposite—that in the midst of despair there is always hope. This rather different understanding is suggested by the fact that Jesus is clearly quoting the opening line of Psalm 22. Surely David's prophetic words were playing on his mind. Consider, for example, those verses which were even then being fulfilled, "Dogs surround me, a pack of villains encircles me; they pierce my hands and my feet" (verse 16). And again, "They divide my clothes among them and cast lots for my garments" (verse 18).

By quoting the psalm's opening words, it is as if Jesus were saying, "If ever you think God has forsaken you, read Psalm 22!" Why? Because it begins with the obvious question countless sufferers have asked, yet ends on a sublime note of reassurance. "For he has not despised or scorned the suffering of the afflicted one; he has not hidden his face from him but has listened to his cry for help." And when future generations are told about the Lord's mercies, "They will proclaim his righteousness…He has done it!" Far from turning his back on us, God has already answered our every need.

■ **The question for sufferers is: Should I find myself groaning in agony of flesh or spirit, will I seek reassurance in the same comforting psalm as Jesus?**

Finding Your Theme

My heart is stirred by a noble theme as I recite my verses for the king; my tongue is the pen of a skillful writer.

PSALM 45:1

Everyone wants to be a writer, so it seems, yet relatively few have that gift. Even for the gifted, good writing is a daunting task. To begin with, there is the difficult craft itself, then the challenge of knowing one's audience, and always those menacing editors waiting in the wings. As suggested in today's verse, the songwriter's tongue, like the writer's pen, must be honed and sharpened to accomplish its intended effect. Yet the skill of any writer is useless without a story to tell. Say you want to write? What do you have to say? What story or lyric is desperately trying to get out of you? What new and different message do you have for a world that has seen and heard it all? What passion to share? What irrepressible dream? Just how inspired are you by some irresistible idea? As love covers a multitude of sins, so too one's passion put to paper covers a multitude of inept compositions. While a good editor can fix the mechanics, you must first find a theme that stirs your blood. A *noble* theme.

Even for those who never aspire to write, the crucial question remains: By what noble theme are *you* stirred? In what grand story do you play a part? What transcendent dream keeps you alive? What unbridled passion drives you? What lofty ideal demands your utmost? Perhaps you are thinking you have no noble theme or, at best, have little idea how to express it. Yet if you are a true believer in the passionately loving Author of life, you cannot help but have a story to tell! A grand vision! A reason to live! And you needn't worry about the details. For he is both "the author and perfecter [read *editor*!] of our faith."

■ **The stirring question is: In what tangible way might that noble theme bring renewed passion to my life this very day!**

The Mystery of Beauty

Then they searched throughout Israel for a beautiful young woman and found Abishag, a Shunammite, and brought her to the king. The woman was very beautiful; she took care of the king and waited on him, but the king had no sexual relations with her.

1 KINGS 1:3-4

Something's not right here. To begin with, did David really need someone lying next to him in order to stay warm? Even if he did, does this unusual "remedy" actually merit being mentioned in Scripture? And why didn't one of David's wives sleep next to him? (Bathsheba, for instance, who apparently wasn't bothered in the least by the curious arrangement!) However strange it may seem to us, let's assume that there is nothing unconventional going on. Is there anything else that strikes you as odd? What about the perceived need to find a *beautiful* young woman as David's companion? If David was so infirm as not to be sexually attracted to Abishag, what difference would beauty make?

Besides, beauty is in the eye of the beholder. Who is to say who's beautiful and who's not? Well, actually, the Bible says it! But doesn't the Bible itself warn against putting emphasis on one's outward beauty, knowing how deceptive it can be of one's inner beauty and even (as with Bathsheba) lead to unwarranted lust? And how are less-than-beautiful women supposed to feel when such an emphasis is placed on good looks? Perhaps the only way to make sense of this unusual passage is to consider David's position as king and to recognize that only the best (or what was considered best) was suitable for a king. And the lesson? Surely it is that the King of kings deserves to be attended by only that which is beautiful. No, it's not what you or I might look like in the mirror, but the beauty we offer him from within.

■ **The question for all of us is: Do I put too much emphasis on how I look to others and give too little thought to what beauty God sees in me?**

Praying for Wisdom

So give your servant a discerning heart to govern your people and to distinguish between right and wrong. For who is able to govern this great people of yours?

1 KINGS 3:9

Anyone can tell the difference between black and white. It's gray that confuses us. Is it *dark* gray or *light* gray? If black and white were *knowledge,* gray would be *wisdom.* Knowledge can be learned from lectures and books. Wisdom is only acquired through experience, thought, and reflection. Solomon's exceptional wisdom was a gift from God. Who can forget that stroke of genius and keen insight into human nature when Solomon dramatically resolved the dispute as to whose baby it was? Don't you find it intriguing that in order to resolve the "gray" issue, Solomon wisely reverted to couching the controversy in stark black and white? ("Cut the living child in two!") Both definitive "black and white" and the more uncertain "gray" have their place. The trick is having the wisdom to discern between them.

Yet take a close second look at Solomon's prayer for discernment to distinguish between right and wrong. Do any of us really need wisdom to understand what's right and what's wrong? If given a stark choice, probably not. But normally our most difficult choices are between two conflicting "rights" or two conflicting "wrongs." In these cases how do we decide? We can't exactly call for a sword and threaten to cut up some innocent baby! No, but the Bible does speak of "the sword of the Spirit," which is able to deftly divide even bone from marrow if necessary. So if you find yourself having to make a Solomon-like decision, pray that God will give you an extraordinary spirit of discernment.

■ **The black and white question is: If God answered Solomon's prayer for wisdom, is there any reason why he couldn't answer my own for discernment?**

_____

_____

_____

_____

The Importance of Quiet Times

In building the temple, only blocks dressed at the quarry were used, and no hammer, chisel or any other iron tool was heard at the temple site while it was being built.

1 KINGS 6:7

Noise has all but taken over the world. Where can we possibly escape the blaring sounds of televisions, phones, screeching autos, and jet engines? By contrast what absolute peace there must have been in the pre-media world of the pioneer! Not that virgin forests were silent, but "blaring" hardly describes the rich cacophony of sounds emanating from birds, animals, and the wind whistling through the trees. Of course not all the nostalgia in the world could ever resurrect that glorious silence. What gets crowded out by all the invasive sounds is not just blissful silence but, more to be pitied, a deeper communion with nature and nature's God. If there is a time for making a joyful noise before the Lord, there is also a time to stop and listen to that still, small voice.

Once built, the temple itself would become a hubbub of activity and noise. (Just imagine all those bleating sheep and roaring bulls being sacrificed!) But how eerie—even surreal—it must have been during the temple's construction to see it rise spirit-like from the ground with not a sound to be heard. Ever wonder why no tools were to be used on-site? Not only does it picture how God himself puts all the pieces together, but it suggests a connection between silence and reverence. Between quietness and holiness. Many believers would not trade anything for their morning or evening "quiet time" ritual of shutting out the world and communing with God. Reading. Praying. Reflecting. If you want a closer walk with God, switch off and switch on.

■ **The ominous question to be asked above the noise is: Can I bear to have silence in my life, or am I afraid that God just might speak to me in the stillness?**

The Best Laid Plans

But the LORD said to my father David, "You did well to have it in your heart to build a temple for my Name. Nevertheless, you are not the one to build the temple, but your son, your own flesh and blood—he is the one who will build the temple for my Name."

2 CHRONICLES 6:8-9

Have you ever had a wonderful, exciting dream that never came true? Some grand idea that seemed so perfect, but came to nothing? Why couldn't others catch the vision? And because it was intended for God's glory, why did he not give it his full, divine backing? Many a godly dreamer has been sorely disappointed. It doesn't mean that God was displeased with the vision. Perhaps God just had a different builder in mind. Or a different time and place. From what Solomon says about his father's dream, God was thrilled that David had it in his heart to build a temple. Yet for his own reasons, God had reserved that task for Solomon.

One wonders if Solomon didn't learn some valuable lessons from his father's experience. Solomon would later write a number of proverbs addressing this very issue. On one hand the wise king urges, "Commit to the LORD whatever you do, and he will establish your plans" (Proverbs 16:3). Yet that advice is tempered by the perspective that, "Many are the plans in a person's heart, but it is the LORD's purpose that prevails" (Proverbs 19:21). Between those bookends is the balanced truth that what plans we commit to God will succeed, *unless* God has a particular plan of his own. Indeed (as with David's design for the temple) one's "failed" dream might eventually become reality, right down to the last detail, only perhaps a lifetime later and by someone else. So here's to dreaming big dreams for the Lord!

■ **The crucial question is: Do I have great dreams worthy of God's glory, even if I never see the trees that grow from the seeds I plant?**

Not a Wise Move

Solomon brought Pharaoh's daughter up from the City of David to the palace he had built for her, for he said, "My wife must not live in the palace of David king of Israel, because the places the ark of the LORD has entered are holy."

2 CHRONICLES 8:11

There's no fool like an old fool," so the saying goes. And changing that only slightly, "There's no fool like a wise fool." Normally a "wise fool" would be an oxymoron, but in Solomon's case it's simply a fact. Even at the height of his glory, the world's wisest man makes some uncharacteristically foolish decisions that one day will come home to roost. Consider, for example, Solomon's choice of wives. In worldly terms it might have been thought wise for Solomon to marry the daughter of Egypt's pharaoh. That felicitous political union would certainly help ensure peace for Israel along its southern border. But what in the world is Solomon thinking when he chooses his wife from a pagan culture? Has it been so long since God dragged Israel kicking and screaming out of Egypt's pagan clutches? One needn't give away the story's ending to see where this is headed!

Being wise, of course, Solomon is not oblivious to the problem. Why else did he go to the trouble of building a palace for his heathen wife outside of the City of David so that she doesn't bring the ark of the Lord into disrepute? But does Solomon really think he is honoring God by taking a commendable course of action only made necessary by his own foolish decision? In an odd kind of way, of course, it's almost reassuring for us to know that even the wisest of the wise made foolish mistakes. Yet it also serves as a dire warning against taking whatever measure of godly insight we have for granted. No matter how wise we are, it takes but one dumb decision to act the fool.

■ **The disturbing question is: What seemingly smart move have I made lately that has every potential for spiritual disaster?**

Calling All Nincompoops

Folly is an unruly woman; she is simple and knows nothing. She sits at the door of her house…calling out to those who pass by…"Let all who are simple come to my house!" To those who have no sense she says, "Stolen water is sweet; food eaten in secret is delicious!"

PROVERBS 9:13-17

They both cry out to all who pass by, these personified characters, Wisdom and Folly. It's like a slugfest between two women battling over a crowd of simpletons. The one—Wisdom—wants to make wise men out of the simpletons. The other—Folly—wants merely to deceive them and take advantage of their naiveté. Wisdom speaks the truth straight up, lauding the virtues of knowledge and understanding. Folly, by sharp contrast, is a cunning liar. She makes wrong seem like right and right seem like wrong, knowing that if simpletons fall for that ridiculous ploy, they will fall for anything. It is the classic battle of life: truth versus falsehood; good versus evil; right versus wrong. Wisdom always wears the white hat, and Folly the black one. Why anyone would side with Folly is a mystery.

So much for Wisdom and Folly, but what about those simpletons? (Or should we say *us* simpletons?) To be thought of as simpleminded isn't exactly the description of choice for any of us. Were someone to refer to us as "simple," they might just as well call us a dimwit, dunce, dumbbell, ignoramus, moron, or nincompoop! And yet it sure looks like the collection of wise sayings known as the Proverbs is directed at just such knuckleheads. That would be you and me! Unless, that is, we wise up. Unless, that is, we *quit* being knuckleheads. If perhaps some folks cannot help being simple, the rest of us can claim to be innocent and naive only for so long. After that (to cite a wise simpleton of our time), "Stupid is as stupid does."

■ **The simple question for us simpletons is: If I'm no dumbbell, but often act as if I am, who have I been listening to lately—Wisdom or Folly?**

_____

_____

_____

_____

Wising Up the Hard Way

The fear of the LORD is the beginning of knowledge, but fools despise wisdom and instruction [or discipline].

PROVERBS 1:7

No wonder there are so many fools around. If to be wise we must be afraid of God and sit in the corner all day for being naughty, not many are going to choose that option! Nor is the connection between fear and discipline lost on most folks. How many times have parents disciplined a child and then said, "I put the fear of the Lord in him"? Yet there is no reason why fear or discipline need have negative connotations. Consider how we use the word *discipline* in any number of positive ways. Athletes, for instance, willingly discipline their bodies, hoping to win medals. And scholars discipline their minds to learn how to think more sharply. By definition, discipline is never easy or terribly exciting, but only a fool would rob himself of its proven benefits.

Fear can actually be our friend. It keeps us from crossing busy streets to our peril or jumping from a plane without a parachute. Fear also has various connotations. The fright we experience when watching a horror film is different from fearing an approaching tornado or fearing the demise of our nation. So to fear the Lord doesn't mean we must quake in our boots with dread. By contrast, the fear of God that begets knowledge is a fear which manifests such profound respect for God's authority that one dare not question his word on any matter. Because God's word is true without exception, only a fool would prefer to be deceived. So if you really want to be wise, discipline yourself to hang onto God's every word!

■ **The question for all potential fools is: Do I boldly claim to fear the Lord, yet listen only superficially to his Word and avoid spiritual discipline if at all possible?**

Disciplining for Eternity

Do not withhold discipline from a child; if you punish them with the rod, they will not die.
Punish them with the rod and save them from death.

PROVERBS 23:13-14

"Spare the rod, and spoil the child" goes the adage drawn from biblical proverbs like the one above. By now the degree to which that adage has fallen into disrepute is no secret, even among many believers. Unfortunately the evil of excessive force belies the time-tested value of corporeal punishment when used with loving restraint. While it is possible to discipline a child without slapping the hand or spanking the bottom, it is hard to deny the close correlation between physical punishment and well-disciplined children. Nor is there any evidence suggesting that adults spanked as children suffer long-term physical or psychological damage from such punishment.

What's important is that, while the stinging bottom is quickly forgotten, the object of the exercise has a long-lasting, character-forming effect. This goes a long way toward explaining the play on words between "die" and "death." The first speaks of physical death, the second of spiritual death. Make no mistake, says God, discipline or the lack of it is a matter of life and death. Sparing the rod altogether can result in a soul being destroyed eternally in "the second death." Like parents, churches would do well to remember the crucial role of discipline. The apostle Paul enjoined discipline to snatch the wayward soul from hell. Church discipline needs to be taken far more seriously! No wonder our heavenly Father himself can often be heavy-handed. Sometimes the only way to get our attention is not through our heads but on the other end.

■ **The question for us disobedient children is: Do I truly welcome God's harsh discipline as a means to preserving my eternal soul?**

_____

_____

_____

_____

_____

Of Hidden Motives

All a person's ways seem pure to them, but motives are weighed by the LORD.

PROVERBS 16:2

Ever watch a dramatic presentation of a police investigation or trial? Everybody wants to know who had a motive and who didn't. Of course detective mysteries supply virtually every character with some kind of motive just to throw us off track. Yet you might find it surprising that motives need never be proved in a prosecution. Although the jury may find motive important to identify the killer, the motivation behind an unlawful killing does not matter. So-called "mercy killings" are still murder, despite the compassionate intent to end a loved one's suffering. By contrast, having the right motive might completely justify what otherwise would be murder, as when a killing is done in self-defense. As with all of life, sometimes motive is important, sometimes not.

When it comes to moral and spiritual actions, motives are equally complex. One can act from the purest of motives, yet violate God's commands. As Samuel reminded Saul, where there is outright disobedience, an act of sacrifice is worthless before God. The more difficult situation is suggested by today's featured verse, where we are doing all the right things for all the wrong reasons. Consider, for example, regular participation at times of worship, contributing generously to good causes, or personally helping the poor and oppressed. All good things, yet there is potential for wrong or mixed motives that never occur to us because we underestimate our own capacity for impure motives, or we overvalue our nobility of character. Rarely do we give others that same benefit of the doubt, so why should we think we are somehow exempt? Whatever our own view of ourselves, in God's eyes it's not just *what* we do that counts, but *why*.

■ **The obvious question is: When was the last time I double-checked my motives for doing even the good things I do?**

The Virtue of Patience

Whoever is patient has great understanding, but one who is quick-tempered displays folly.

PROVERBS 14:29

You know those people, don't you? People who fly off the handle when you least expect it? People who flare up when something goes wrong that needs putting right. Depending on who you are, some of those people are very much like…well you and me! Certainly you and I are not the worst offenders—not us people of faith who write and read daily devotionals. Must be those *other* folks! Actually, many of those other folks do have the same problem with impatience and quick tempers, but it does not excuse our own, or make us feel any better about it. Unlike some sins, a quick temper often surprises even ourselves. *Where did that come from!* And embarrasses even ourselves. *I just hate it when I do that!*

Of course these occasional flare-ups are really not our fault. The people on the other end *deserve* our raised voices and clinched fists. Idiots on the highway. Robotic clerks who refuse to deviate from ludicrous regulations. Pestering telemarketers who dare to invade our privacy. Even religious zealots on our doorsteps who insult our intelligence with their programmed answers to any question. Since they all need instant correcting, who better than us? Solomon didn't have to put up with any of this outrageous nonsense, so why should we? Unless it is because we ourselves have been idiots on the highway and done all sorts of maddening things that have made others want to scream at us. With advancing age we ought to be more self-controlled, not less. More aware of our capacity to snap. More resolved to rise above the maddening crowd.

■ **The question for embarrassed idiots is: Even when someone truly deserves to be screamed at, might I not make a renewed effort to give them *less* than they deserve?**

Bad Timing, or Blind Self?

If anyone loudly blesses their neighbor early in the morning, it will be taken as a curse.

PROVERBS 27:14

It is a picture worth a thousand words—a man enjoying the luxury of sleeping in longer than usual, only to be awakened by his eager-beaver neighbor loudly calling out some pious blessing at the break of dawn! But for the honor, our man in bed would rather have passed up the blessing, thank you very much! Even when it comes to blessings, timing is everything. It's not *what* we do, but *when* and *how* we do it. Like courts ruling on inappropriate speech, the wise consider not simply the act, but the factors of time, place, and manner. The exact same words expressed under one set of circumstances might take on a completely different hue if expressed under other circumstances. As with so many things in life, it's context, context, context.

The intriguing question is: Why didn't the eager-beaver neighbor consider the possibility that his blessing might not be appreciated at such an unearthly hour? Maybe he could be excused if the two neighbors regularly exchanged morning blessings at that early hour. But because the proverb seems not to cut him any slack, neither will we. More likely we are dealing with one of those people who genuinely believe that "others" is their motto, but are really thinking only of themselves. Whatever *they* want to do has a funny way of turning out to be what *we* must want. The "favor" they do for us invariably furthers their own selfish interest. And if they are blessing us, it is only because there's some reward in it for them. When the context is always *me*, time, place, and manner rarely get the time of day.

■ **The question for do-gooders is: Have I developed a habit of fulfilling my own needs and desires by pretending it's really what others want?**

A Better Way of Seeing the Light

In a lawsuit the first to speak seems right, until someone comes forward and cross-examines.

PROVERBS 18:17

You've just testified, Mr. Jones, that you saw my client turn through the intersection on a red light, is that right?" "Yes." "Any doubt about that?" "No." "Tell us again where you were and what you saw." "I was sitting in my car, stopped at the intersection opposite your client. I saw him approach the intersection and come to a halt. Moments later, he turned left and, in just about the middle of the intersection, collided with the other car." "Mr. Jones, how familiar are you with that particular intersection?" "Not very." "Did you happen to notice anything unusual about the size of the traffic signal?" "I can't recall." "Would it surprise you to learn that the signal had a separate green-arrow light for left turns?" "Well…" "So might it be possible that my client turned left on a green arrow and was hit by the other guy who was running a red light?" "I suppose so…" "Thank you, Mr. Jones!"

Without cross-examination, even an honest witness might be telling the truth as he knows it, but perhaps not the *whole* truth—because he doesn't know it. The search for truth in any arena demands careful scrutiny and an open mind. You have to ask the right questions, and coming up with those questions requires thinking through all the possibilities. Is what you've learned about the Scriptures from your parents or preacher the *whole* truth? Have you accepted the doctrines you hold dear without ever really asking hard questions? When you study the Bible, do you dig behind the obvious, looking at the passage from every possible angle? For those with truly open minds, traditional red lights have a way of becoming enlightening green arrows.

■ **The question for honest searchers is: Is my truth really as true as I believe it to be?**

Securities and Trust

The wealth of the rich is their fortified city; they imagine it a wall too high to scale.

PROVERBS 18:11

Stocks and bonds are often called "securities." What irony that anyone takes security in something as unpredictable as the Dow Jones. Just as our featured proverb describes the rich imagining their wealth as a secure, unscalable *wall,* many of today's modern investors similarly imagine their portfolios as another unscalable wall… *Wall Street*! Need we be reminded of Jericho and all the other cities over the centuries whose walls—whether literal or figurative—have come tumbling down? Nobody foresaw the devastating financial losses suffered on Black Tuesday in the crash of '29. Up to the last minute, brokers were claiming that stocks had reached a permanently high plateau. With their trust woefully misplaced, millions of investors lost it all, in large part triggering the Great Depression.

The depression was not just economic. It was also psychological, leading to high levels of suicide. Sadly, the crash was a breach of trust of a different kind. Although the words "In God We Trust" had appeared on coins from the late 1860s, it's clear that people's trust was in the money, not in God. When the money was gone, there was nothing left to trust and nothing left to live for. In the wake of the crash, a "depression generation" became notoriously cautious, saving every penny, every piece of string, and every brown paper bag. *Mounds* of string and paper bags, as high as walls. New walls, but still walls all thought to be unscalable. Even with the hard lessons learned about investments, the most important lesson of all seems as yet unlearned. Apart from utter trust in God, no form of "security" brings real security.

■ **The hard question is: If I'm being completely honest, in what seemingly unscalable walls do I trust for my security?**

_____

_____

_____

_____

Wearing Blindfolds to Please

If a ruler listens to lies, all his officials become wicked.

PROVERBS 29:12

In Hans Christian Andersen's story *The Emperor's New Clothes,* a vain ruler is convinced by unscrupulous tailors that the finest clothes could be made from special cloth invisible to anyone who is stupid or unworthy. Fearful of appearing stupid, the emperor's advisors rave about the beautiful (invisible) cloth. Not wishing to be thought stupid himself, the emperor dons the invisible clothes and parades himself before all the townspeople, who, in turn, pretend that nothing is amiss. It's not until a boy in the crowd cries out, "But he has nothing on," that the bubble of denial bursts. "The Emperor has no clothes" has become a metaphor used to describe any situation where observers feign ignorance in disclaiming the obvious, no matter how absurd.

Today's proverb concisely states how evil is introduced when a king, CEO, politician, president, or church leader surrounds himself with "yes-men." When a leader prefers a glowing image over dubious reality, those who wish his favor must go along with the game. In time their pretense can no longer be justified as love covering a multitude of sins or well-intentioned naiveté. Eventually some honest soul will blow the whistle on the entire farce. While many proverbs counsel the wisdom of having advisors, the unstated assumption is that those advisors will speak honestly and courageously. As many imprisoned leaders have realized too late, uncritical support for unethical conduct is not the hallmark of a loyal staff, but is an act of betrayal. Want to do your bosses—and yourself—a favor? Speak the truth in love, even if they are so self-deceived they prefer to hear lies.

■ **The compelling question is: Am I willing to speak the truth, no matter the risk of devastating consequences?**

Man, Woman, and Mystery

There are three things that are too amazing for me, four that I do not understand: the way of an eagle in the sky, the way of a snake on a rock, the way of a ship on the high seas, and the way of a man with a young woman.

PROVERBS 30:18-19

Why can't a woman be more like a man?" wonders Henry Higgins when dumbfounded by the intriguing Eliza Doolittle in *My Fair Lady*. Higgins proceeds to extol the superior virtues of the masculine soul: "Men are so honest, so thoroughly square; Eternally noble, historically fair." Higgins might have been "thoroughly square," but he was also thoroughly hooked! With but a glance, Eliza had him twisted around her cute little finger. It's what makes women so endearing. A man with seven hundred wives and three hundred concubines ought to know something about that! Yet maybe the mystery behind the battle of the sexes is underscored by the fact that not even Solomon could understand the enigmatic relationship between men and women.

It is not just the obvious gender differences, seemingly planets apart. For opposites to attract, they have to be…well, *opposite*! To put it more biblically, each was created to supply what was missing in the other. It is a wonderful ideal, of course, but the moment-by-moment dynamics are so incredibly complex that, at best, it's a wonder. Why, then, are we so quick to pass judgment on couples having domestic problems? What can we know of their unique intricacies when the odds are that *they themselves* don't fully understand? The amazing thing is not that committed couples occasionally have trouble getting along, but that couples who have trouble getting along remain committed. Next time you help celebrate a golden anniversary, praise God for a man and woman who resolutely defied all the odds.

■ **The question for couples is: When frustrating moments inevitably come along, can I remember that it is the mystery that makes the journey worthwhile?**

_____

_____

_____

_____

_____

Pure Passion

Daughters of Jerusalem, I charge you by the gazelles and by the does of the field: Do not arouse or awaken love until it so desires.

SONG OF SONGS 3:5

The two most frequent explanations for the surprising appearance in Scripture of the sensuous Song of Songs are either that it is an allegory of Christ and the church or that it describes the beauty of marital intimacy. But in the rush to drape this sexually candid work of art with a more acceptable modesty, have we actually missed the intended meaning of this remarkable love song? The song's traditional placement, following Proverbs and Ecclesiastes, could be a clue because wisdom literature was often written as advice for young people. The Song of Songs is a fantasy of intimacy being played out in the mind of the beloved as she contemplates her desire for her lover. Yet in the midst of all the sensuous longing and anticipation, there appears—three times—the wise caution found in our featured verse: *Don't jump the gun!* Looking on anxiously, her friends ask if she will be a determined *wall* or a willing *door*. As our beloved weighs the pleasure she desires against the sexual purity to which she is committed, she resolutely replies, "I am a *wall*!"

If the importance of sexual purity truly is the theme of this song, the lesson is that a rush to physical intimacy kills the goose of emotional and spiritual intimacy that lays the golden egg of sexual fulfillment. Against all instinct, abstinence from pleasure is the surprising gateway to enhanced pleasure. With sex, as with so much of life, good things come to those who wait. In the meantime be extra careful with your feelings. True love waits for *pure* love…and pure passion.

■ **The question for young people is: Do I really think I can go right up to the edge without falling, or remain sexually pure as long as I don't go all the way?**

Turning Our Backs on God

As Solomon grew old, his wives turned his heart after other gods, and his heart was not fully devoted to the LORD his God, as the heart of David his father had been.

1 KINGS 11:4

How does this happen? In his final years, the world's wisest man—who has been more richly blessed than any of us can imagine, and to whom God has personally appeared twice—actually turns his back on God! (Can you imagine following Christ throughout your lifetime, then one day worshipping at Hindu shrines?) How does a person so specially chosen and gifted end up in such a state? There were his wives, of course, whom he should never have married in the first place. Yet the more important reason is seen in the comparison made between Solomon's heart and his father's. The diagnosis of Scripture is that, in spiritual terms, Solomon died of heart failure.

In describing Solomon's downfall, the text tells us "he did not follow the LORD completely, as David his father had done." But hang on! David was hardly perfect! True, but for all his sin, David never once gave up on God, so God didn't give up on him. Unlike his father, Solomon did not have a heart *fully devoted* to God. Surely only that crucial difference can explain how Solomon possibly could have turned to other gods! Yet one would think that the wisest man ever would know to guard his heart more closely because all of the issues of life flow from the heart—such as who to marry and especially who to worship. It's hard for us to imagine ourselves ever renouncing Christ and turning to, say, Buddha. But that might only mean we're stuck in a traditional faith. It doesn't mean our hearts are fully devoted. In fact hearts that are not fully devoted are merely that—*stuck in a traditional faith.*

■ **The question for "faithful Christians" is: Being brutally honest about it, just how fully devoted am I?**

When Vanity Is Meaningless

The words of the Teacher, son of David, king in Jerusalem: "Meaningless! Meaningless!"
says the Teacher. "Utterly meaningless! Everything is meaningless."

ECCLESIASTES 1:1-2

Vanity plates. Vanity mirrors. Vanity press. *Vanity Fair.* "Vanity of vanities, all is vanity." Or so reads the King James Version and most others. But we have lost the Scripture's meaning of "vanity" today if we think of ego, arrogance, narcissism, or merely excessive preening in front of a mirror. That kind of vanity belies the intended meaning. Unfortunately the NIV's more updated rendering is not helpful. The writer is not saying this life has no meaning, only that if not seen in the context of man's mortality and things eternal, this life is empty. A close look will reveal that the author finds rich meaning in life, just not the excessive value we normally attribute to such temporal matters as pleasure, achievement, politics, and wealth.

Over the years, Ecclesiastes has acquired an undeserved reputation as a depressing book. Far from being despondent about life, the writer speaks of the simple joys of everyday eating and drinking—and God having made everything beautiful in its time. "The conclusion of the matter" is certainly sobering, but hopeful. Even when we are pointed to the awesome Day of Judgment as the ultimate touchstone of life's meaning, implicit within that is an optimistic expectancy of life beyond the grave. The grand irony of the writing is that it so moves us into an otherworldly reality that it condemns the vainglorious vanity we immediately think about. In the face of eternity, indulging ourselves only in self-vaunting, temporal pursuits is not just unworthy conceit, but a sad, depressing emptiness.

■ **The question of Ecclesiastes is: If I am looking for meaning in my life, am I looking in all the wrong places?**

A Cord of Three Strands

Also, if two lie down together, they will keep warm. But how can one keep warm alone? Though one may be overpowered, two can defend themselves. A cord of three strands is not quickly broken.

ECCLESIASTES 4:11-12

Have you wondered about the origin of the unity cord which many brides and grooms tie as part of the wedding ceremony? The "cord of three strands" comes directly from this passage, though it slips in unnoticed like a last-minute arrival at a wedding. As brides and grooms intuitively sense, there is great advantage to two over one. The text suggests that keeping warm is one obvious advantage, along with ganging up on burglars in the night! Practically speaking, household chores can be divided, bank accounts merged, and backup provided for times of sickness or injury. Romantically speaking, sunsets are more beautiful when shared by two, and candlelight dinners and Christmases each take on a new glow.

Sadly, not every couple anticipating marriage has considered the invaluable advantage of that "third strand," which surely is God. Just as one person takes on added strength when joined with another, so too a couple (the two having become one) takes on added strength when God is intertwined with them. If it is "not good for man to be alone," neither is it good for the husband and wife to be without a divine companion. Who else will keep them warm should their love grow cold? Who else will come to their rescue when they are being overpowered by debilitating illnesses, financial difficulties, family problems, or the weight of the world? With God on their side, they are more than the sum of their parts. With God intertwined in their lives, they are less likely to be worn to a frazzle and break apart. If you didn't have a cord of three strands at your wedding, it is never too late.

■ **The question for couples is: Can my marriage possibly find true fulfillment without the extra binding of this third strand?**

Avoiding the Extremes

Do not be overrighteous, neither be overwise—why destroy yourself? Do not be overwicked, and do not be a fool—why die before your time? It is good to grasp the one and not let go of the other. Whoever fears God will avoid all extremes.

ECCLESIASTES 7:16-18

Have you ever considered the possibility that you might actually be "overrighteous"? And is it good to be *somewhat* wicked as long as you're not "overwicked"? Perhaps you have wondered about that old chestnut, "Moderation in all things." You mean it is okay to lie, cheat, and steal, as long as it's done in moderation? Surely in both sayings is an implied assumption that the activity being done in moderation is not inherently sinful. Yet even that clarification does not completely eliminate the problem. Is it really possible, for example, to be overly enthusiastic in our praise to God, or excessively generous toward the poor, or inordinately dedicated to Bible study? Are acts of worship and service ever meant to be moderated?

If there is any firm starting point, perhaps it is the obvious truth that we have all sinned and fallen short of God's glory. To that extent, we are all "wicked," so it's no surprise that we should be cautioned against being "over-wicked." The less sinful the better, naturally. It is the other side of the coin that is more troublesome. When Jesus admonished his disciples to "be perfect, therefore, as your heavenly Father is perfect," he obviously was talking about the ideal of sinlessness. In that sense, we could never be excessively sinless! But being overly righteous is another matter. Ever know any insecure soul who was exhausted from soul-numbing efforts to be righteous? For whom being good was never good enough? *That*, surely, is the graceless extreme to be avoided. The believer without a balanced sense of sin and forgiveness is an extremist headed for meltdown!

■ **The question of balance is: From what I honestly know of myself, do I need to be far more harsh with myself, or perhaps far more gentle?**

The Seasons of Life

There is a time for everything, and a season for every activity under the heavens.

ECCLESIASTES 3:1

If you are reading these devotionals on their appropriate dates, all you have to do is look out the window to appreciate the beauty of early summer. Back at the beginning of spring, daffodils, tulips, and a chorus of blooming flowers all warmed up for the main performance. Spring is all about anticipation, renewal, and fresh starts. In spring we're glad to have survived another gloomy winter! But just listen to us complain when the winter was too mild to kill off the beastly creatures we have to deal with in the summer. And as we glance at the leaf rake propped in the corner of the garage, we're reminded that it won't be long before we'll be raking up after the exhilarating fall colors fade. We fickle folks seem to have a love-hate relationship with the seasons! But what would we do without them? "There's a *reason* for the season" is not just a Christmastime sentiment.

As with nature itself, all the many seasons of life also play a role. From the joyous season of birth to the culminating season of death, each season has its place. If perhaps the season of Jesus' birth was more rapturous, the season of his awful crucifixion was indispensable. How can we expect seasons of happiness without seasons of pain? Or seasons of growth without seasons of plantings? Or seasons of excitement without seasons of calm? To wish that our "winters of distress" could be milder is to risk missing the strength of perseverance harsh winters produce. To dread the fast-fading autumn of our lives is to miss its unique beauty. For the wise, no season is to be feared or avoided. We learn from the seasons of nature that, while no season of life lasts forever, every season is important.

■ **The question worth asking is: Have I learned to welcome whatever season comes my way?**

Identifying with the Righteous

After burying him, he said to his sons, "When I die, bury me in the grave where the man of God is buried; lay my bones beside his bones."

1 KINGS 13:31

The bizarre story of the older prophet lying to the younger prophet raises seemingly endless questions. What prompted the older prophet to interfere with the younger prophet's mission? What motive did he have to lie to him? Why did God sic a lion on the dedicated young prophet for acting in good faith? And why did the older prophet want to be buried in the same grave? We can only speculate, unless perhaps God was setting up a teachable moment. At least the third question has a plausible answer, suggested by the apostle Paul's warning against accepting another gospel, even if it comes from an angel. If that's the intended message, it was a hard lesson indeed for the well-intentioned young prophet!

The fourth question reveals a redeeming aspect to the story that is both reassuring and inspiring. First, there is the remorse felt by the older prophet for having led the young man to his death. Such genuine grief suggests that the strange scenario might have been a test from God. Then comes that unusual request, "lay my bones beside his bones." It's as if the prophet is saying that he would be proud to be associated with anyone who takes God's instructions as seriously as he did. If the young man made a grave error in judgment, it wasn't for lack of fervently desiring to do God's will as he understood it. How many people do you know who have a passion for obeying God? They may not always get it right, but give them credit for a fully committed heart. And when you're choosing your closest friends, give careful thought to whose bones you want to be around!

■ **The question of association is: Among my acquaintances, who has the kind of commitment to God's leading that I would most benefit from emulating?**

When Death Is an Honor

When you set foot in your city, the boy will die…He is the only one belonging to Jeroboam who will be buried, because he is the only one in the house of Jeroboam in whom the LORD, the God of Israel, has found anything good.

1 KINGS 14:12-13

Who can know the grief of a parent who has lost a child? Who, then, can't sympathize with Jeroboam in the death of his son? If we are tempted to think that Jeroboam deserved his grief since it was his sin that caused the death, Jeroboam himself must have been all the more conflicted by that very thought. He would not be the only parent to know the unimaginable pain of having contributed to a child's death. Which leads to an interesting discussion. Having condemned Jeroboam's entire family to a brutal and ignominious end, God determines that Abijah alone would have an honorable burial because he was the only good person in Jeroboam's household. But wait! If Abijah was *good,* why did God let him die?

Although God clearly has power over life and death, it doesn't appear that he providentially pulls the plug on each and every life. Remember what Ecclesiastes said about time and chance happening to us all? So much, then, for all those grasping words heard at funerals: "It was just his time." Or, "God called him home." That God knows when and how we will die says nothing about whether God personally flips the switch. Felicitously, the fact that God chose to make that call in Abijah's case might well give renewed comfort to those who grieve. Maybe our loved ones have died merely as the result of time and chance. But it's also possible that God has taken them from this cruel world because they are "good." For some death might be a special honor.

■ **The question for the grieving is: If I'm struggling to cope with the loss of a loved one, might it bring comfort to think they could be one of God's special honorees?**

Too Little Faith from the Faithful

In the thirty-ninth year of his reign Asa was afflicted with a disease in his feet. Though his disease was severe, even in his illness he did not seek help from the LORD, but only from the physicians.

2 CHRONICLES 16:12

Asa was one of the rare "good kings" whose heart was fully committed to the Lord. Yet we are given this account of his lack of faith. When he discovers that his feet are diseased, he does what any of us would do—he goes to his doctor. Seems that no matter how many specialists are brought in, there's no resolution to either cause or cure. Whether his team of physicians brought Asa any relief is not known, though his death two years later seems more than coincidence. Might Asa have lived longer if the problem with his feet had been resolved? The suggestion seems to be that he might have, if only he had sought God's help, either in addition to his physicians or instead of them.

As you know the Bible never speaks badly of physicians, as if they have no legitimate role to play. Indeed Luke was widely known as "the beloved physician," and Jesus even makes reference to himself as the Physician. The difference is that, whereas physicians use both skilled knowledge and the natural healing agents found in God's creation to bring about cures, Jesus healed miraculously. The point, surely, is that there are two distinct avenues of healing—one valuable and the other far more effective. To pray simply that God "guide the hand of the physician" is to make only a feeble attempt at enhancing one avenue while making no real appeal to the other. It is amazing how many people of faith like Asa minimize the power of God to work directly in the healing process. If perhaps "faith healing" can be a sham, healing by faith must never be ruled out.

■ **The medical question is: When illness comes my way, do I ever make an appointment with the Great Physician?**

Time to Decide

Elijah went before the people and said, "How long will you waver between two opinions? If the LORD is God, follow him; but if Baal is God, follow him."

1 KINGS 18:21

Make up your mind! Don't you hate it when the driver in front of you can't decide which lane to stay in? Or when the person ahead of you in line for ice cream can't choose a flavor? Or when your college junior still can't settle on a major? No wonder Elijah was perturbed with Israel's fickle faith. One day they bowed to God—the next they bowed to Baal. One day the temple was a place of honor—the next any ol' "high place" was good enough. It was as if the people of Israel were hedging their bets, trying to hold hands with both God and paganism. Call it wishy-washy religion. Lots of folks still practice it.

The literal translation of "wavering between two opinions" paints a wonderful picture of a bird hopping between two branches, unable to decide where to land. Like that bird, Israel could never feel completely comfortable on either branch. Having every reason to fear God, they still could not bring themselves to fully reject idolatry. God offered them joy through faithfulness. Idolatry promised them pleasure through indulgence. As much as they might desire the joy of the spirit, they weren't about to give up the pleasures of the flesh. If that ambivalence doesn't wreak misery, what does? And what irony. Unable to rid themselves completely of the fear of God, they could never completely enjoy their fleshly pleasures! It was back and forth, back and forth. Sort of like you and me, huh? God's person one moment—the world's person a moment later. The next time you can't quite seem to land, remind yourself that spiritual schizophrenia is for the birds!

■ **The question for branch-hoppers is: Is my attempt to keep one foot in the world while keeping the other on higher ground robbing me of an inner peace I've never known?**

Lord of Hills and Valleys

The man of God came up and told the king of Israel, "This is what the LORD says: 'Because the Arameans think the LORD is a god of the hills and not a god of the valleys, I will deliver this vast army into your hands, and you will know that I am the LORD.'"

1 KINGS 20:28

Ben-Hadad's advisors had it all figured out. The reason Israel defeated the Arameans the first time around was because the battle had been fought in the hills, and (obviously) Israel's gods must be hill gods! So here's what Ben-Hadad should do next time—bring Israel down out of the hills so the Arameans can fight them in the valleys where (obviously) Israel's gods are powerless. Right! In today's more sophisticated age, we tend to forget the superstitious notions of earlier civilizations. Without any concept of a transcendent God, it was hard for them to think beyond localized deities such as "gods of the hills" or "gods of the valleys." Yet Israel's subsequent victory in the valleys was not alone a message for the pagan Arameans. Fickle, flirtatious Israel needed to be reminded that their God—the true God of heaven and earth—could bring victory under any and all circumstances.

Even for us today, it's hard not to think that God is more a "God of the hills" than a "God of the valleys." When everything's going great, isn't God good! But when nothing is going right, we begin to lament, "Where is God when we need him!" When you think about it, it is not all that far removed from what the Arameans had surmised—that "hill gods" have the easier task. What makes our God great is not so much his prowess on the mountaintops, but how he brings unexpected victories in the valleys of difficulty and despair. It is in the most serious battles that God reveals himself most clearly.

■ **The encouraging question for the discouraged is: With a God who brings victory in the valleys, how can I possibly not prevail?**

When Prayers Get Desperate

For we have no power to face this vast army that is attacking us. We do not know what to do,
but our eyes are upon you.

2 CHRONICLES 20:12

We've all been there. Somewhere along the line everybody experiences those desperate moments when we have run out of ideas. Whatever problem we are facing is far too big for us. There's simply no way out, so now what? Prayer comes to mind, of course, but how are we to pray? In times of distress, we could do worse than echo the prayer of Jehoshaphat when Judah was being invaded by the marauding Moabites. Jehoshaphat's prayer is a model of trust, humility, and hope. First comes an acknowledgment of who God is. *Are you not* the omnipotent God of the universe whom no one can withstand? Next comes a reminder of what God has already done. *Did you not* by force and power bring your people into this land and place your temple in its midst? And finally comes the desperate plea. *Will you not* judge the Ammonites for their sins and save us from destruction?

If the words seem simple enough, it is the attitude behind the words that really counts. One can't pray a desperate prayer without first confessing complete helplessness and total dependence. In a self-sufficient world, that's not always easy to do. Nor is it easy to keep our eyes fixed on God in moments of crisis. Oh, we may *talk* to God more when the situation is dire, but often we get so transfixed by our fear that we look away from God and focus on the apparent hopelessness of our situation. At times like that, we need to remember how God answered Jehoshaphat's prayer. "Take up your positions…do not be discouraged," said God, "for the battle is not yours, but God's!"

■ **The question for desperate souls is: The next time I find myself in a hopeless situation, will I trust God enough to praise him for the victory he is about to achieve?**

Believing the Bald Truth

From there Elisha went up to Bethel. As he was walking along the road, some boys came out of the town and jeered at him. "Get out of here, baldy!" they said…He turned around, looked at them and called down a curse on them in the name of the LORD. Then two bears came out of the woods and mauled forty-two of the boys.

2 KINGS 2:23-24

Today's passage simply has to be a favorite of all who are follicly challenged. It is sweet revenge indeed for all those "bald" jokes. Yet isn't the revenge in this case rather excessive? Was Elisha so sensitive about the state of his scalp that he would invoke God's power to get back at those little bullies? Not a chance. It wasn't about Elisha's bald head. It was about his mentor, Elijah, having been taken up into the heavens in a chariot of fire…or so Elisha had claimed. Likely story! Undoubtedly taking a cue from the skeptical prophets who insisted on searching for Elijah's body, these young scoffers had nothing better to do than vent their irreverent cynicism. Elisha was an easy target, but he wasn't the *real* target.

For unbelieving skeptics the realm of the miraculous is always ripe for taunts and jeers. Better that than having to seriously face a spiritual dimension which might end up making demands on them or even mauling them for their blasphemy! Perhaps you have heard similar taunts. "Go on up to your make-believe heaven when you die, you silly fool!" "Are you so naive as to believe Jesus really rose from the dead?" There will always be plenty of fodder for jeering skeptics. The greater mystery is why professed believers who intellectually acknowledge the miraculous do not take their own faith more seriously. It's one thing to believe the biblical story of Elijah and the chariot. It's another thing altogether to believe that God can work a miracle in *my* life!

■ **The taunting question is: Am I just a "believer," or am I a *true* believer?**

Music to Soothe the Soul

"But now bring me a harpist." While the harpist was playing, the hand of the LORD came on Elisha.

2 KINGS 3:15

If asked to put on some relaxing music, would you choose rock 'n' roll or something more classical? Why is dreamy "mood music" often heard in dentists' offices and fancy restaurants? And what is the connection between lullabies and sleeping babies? The common thread in these questions must surely help us make sense of that ever-so-curious reference to the harp. If you recall, Elisha is more than a little miffed at King Joram of Israel for hoping to receive God's blessing for the battle, when normally Joram would be inquiring of false prophets. Incensed as he was, Elisha needed to calm down considerably before being in any state to receive a word from the Lord. Hence the harp. Its dulcet tones would quickly soothe Elisha's troubled soul like David playing the harp when Saul was in one of his bedeviled moods.

Not all music soothes the soul. If you want to see how particular music moves the inner spirit, just play two radically different kinds of music in the presence of a small child and observe the reactions. We would do well to consider how the music we listen to either enhances or detracts from a spirit that is receptive to God's leading. Is a "heavy metal" world open to God? For the word of God to softly alight on the heart of a believer, that heart must be serene—listening with full attention without distraction from anger, commotion, or the jarring noise of a raucous world. Maybe you think harp music nauseates more than soothes. Maybe a quiet walk in the woods is what you need, or perhaps even a power nap on the couch. Whatever it is, if you want to hear from God, call for your "harp" of choice.

■ **The soothing question is: How best can I prepare my heart today to hear God's comforting voice?**

Dysfunctional Gloating

You should not gloat over your brother in the day of his misfortune, nor rejoice over the people of Judah in the day of their destruction, nor boast so much in the day of their trouble.

OBADIAH 1:12

Sibling rivalry is not limited to the first generation of children. For example, no end of trouble has resulted from the rule of primogeniture, whereby the oldest male child receives the lion's share of the estate. Resentful family attitudes can linger for generations. Despite the fact that Jacob and Esau reconciled after their disputes, their descendants were embittered against each other. Descending from Esau (who foolishly sold his birthright), the Edomites seemed to have a particular grudge against Israel, as if they were the ugly stepchild. When anyone in the extended family begins to think of themselves as second-class compared with all the others, there's trouble ahead. Low self-esteem perpetuates itself and can actually give way to false pride and inverse snobbery. Interestingly, the haughty Edomites lived high up in the rocks, as if symbolizing how they looked down on everybody else!

When our pride comes from deep-seated insecurities rather than genuine achievement, there is heightened danger of gloating. Even the slightest misfortune befalling those who are envied has a perverse way of confirming for the insecure that they're not so distanced from their hoity-toity relatives after all. Rather than share their pain, they exult in their pain! There doesn't even need to be actual pain for gloating to kick in. Family underdogs are sometimes so anxious to see their favored cousins fail, they're actually *hoping* for a fall from grace! Dysfunctional families are illustrative of the wider problem of gloating. Family or no family, you don't actually have to consider yourself second-class to gloat. But if you *do* gloat, you're definitely second-class!

■ **The question for would-be gloaters is: If I would be thrilled should a particular person fail, might someone else gloat over my bad attitude?**

_____

_____

_____

_____

_____

When God's Way Is Offensive

But Naaman went away angry and said, "I thought that he would surely come out to me and stand and call on the name of the LORD his God, wave his hand over the spot and cure me of my leprosy."

2 KINGS 5:11

Naaman's leprosy was only slightly less a problem than his elevated ego. All his pompous self had to do was snap his fingers and some lowly private would hurry off to do whatever he had been commanded to do, trivial or great. Yet here Naaman was, desperate for a cure and willing to do whatever onerous mission this mystery God might demand. But Naaman could hardly have been more surprised…or offended. For openers Elisha didn't even do him the honor of a personal greeting. No one snubs this army commander! Then as if rubbing salt into the wound, the prophet's instruction to dip seven times in the (muddy!) Jordan was an insult to his intelligence! Was he to be treated like a private? As it happens…yes!

Like Naaman we'd rather God come to us on our own terms rather than ask the simplest thing from us before he delivers us from some predicament no amount of human initiative could possibly resolve. Downright leprous with sin, we would be willing to do almost anything to be forgiven. Go on a long pilgrimage. Give all our money to the poor. You name it. But when we're told to simply get ourselves soaking wet, suddenly we think God is kidding. What does getting wet in some slimy baptistry have to do with God's curing my spiritual leprosy? As a soaking wet Naaman could tell you—*everything*! Being a commander of thousands, Naaman should have recognized the principle immediately. There is nothing magic about the water or, in Naaman's case, dipping *seven* times. The only thing that matters is a willingness to do whatever it is our Commander orders us to do.

■ **The question of spiritual healing is: Do I expect God to forgive me on his terms or mine?**

Masking the Real You

Then Jehu went to Jezreel. When Jezebel heard about it, she put on eye makeup, arranged her hair and looked out of a window.

2 KINGS 9:30

She's a real Jezebel if I ever saw one!" When that is said, virtually everyone knows what kind of character is being described. Referring to Ahab's sinister wife, the term "Jezebel" has become synonymous with an evil woman. It was Jezebel who championed idolatry and witchcraft in Israel—and Jezebel who cold-bloodedly devised to kill Naboth just to get his vineyard. As the moment finally arrives for her comeuppance, what do we find her doing? Putting on her makeup! That little detail should not be overlooked. No offense, ladies, but are you aware of the etymology of the word *cosmetics*? It comes from the same Greek word as *cosmos*, meaning order out of chaos! What could be more ironic than that? In her last moments on earth, Jezebel was engaged in a cover-up. It's not likely she would have admitted it, but the spiritual chaos in Jezebel's life must have been extraordinary. Was she subliminally attempting to mask that chaos?

In terms of beautifying the body, makeup is an artificial preparation used to cover defects or to apply more color to the skin. When a character defect needs covering, we use all sorts of means to hide and disguise, attempting to fool even ourselves that sophistication, good deeds, drugs, or intoxication can mask what's so wrong inside. Superficial "cosmetic changes" can never adequately address the fundamental problem. Bringing order out of spiritual chaos requires conformity to God's own moral order. Oblivious to that moral order, Jezebel was reduced to painting her eyes. She's not alone, of course. We're all pretty adept at putting on masks to hide the truth.

■ **The more-than-cosmetic question is: Is the superficial mask I wear for others fooling even myself?**

Being Honest About God

The LORD said to Jehu, "Because you have done well in accomplishing what is right in my eyes and have done to the house of Ahab all I had in mind to do, your descendants will sit on the throne of Israel to the fourth generation."

2 KINGS 10:30

Have we read the Bible so many times that we just gloss over the disturbing parts that normally would shock our moral sensibilities? We've already struggled with this conundrum, but for anyone not jaded by all the dead bodies strewn among the pages of the Old Testament, the wholesale slaughter of Ahab's extended family seems particularly gruesome. Though Hosea will cast doubt about Jehu's acting for God, it certainly looks like this bloodletting is at God's command, including those seventy, innocent young princes whose heads ended up in baskets! As if to underscore God's hand in the massacre, Jehu consoles the people who had done the killing, saying, "You're innocent. This was the Lord's doing!" And here we have God commending Jehu for the mass murder of those unwitting ministers of Baal who had fallen victim to Jehu's cunning deception. If all this doesn't disturb us, that's disturbing!

It seems we have managed to rationalize a Jekyll-and-Hyde God by supposing that the vengeful God of the Old Testament mysteriously transforms into the loving God of the New Testament. Never mind that God wouldn't suddenly morph simply by our turning a page. Of course we can always fall back on God's unassailable sovereignty or perhaps soothe our qualms by acknowledging the obvious—that God is beyond human understanding. Yet being brutally honest about God continues to leave us uncomfortable. Until we get more answers, maybe the best we can do is be brutally honest about how we somehow manage to forgive in ourselves what we are not quite willing to forgive in God.

■ **The nagging question is: What glaring inconsistencies in my life do others find difficult to reconcile with what they expect of me?**

The Day of the Lord

Blow the trumpet in Zion; sound the alarm on my holy hill. Let all who live in the land tremble, for the day of the LORD is coming. It is close at hand.

JOEL 2:1

D o you know when the end of time will be? Or when the great Day of Judgment will commence? Lots of people have believed that both would happen in their lifetime. You can't blame them for thinking that. First, there is the oft-repeated promise: *The day of the Lord is coming!* And invariably there's that tagline: *And soon!* But so far "soon" hasn't yet happened. Or has it? It depends on which "day of the Lord" we are talking about. Because "the day of the Lord" always refers to God's judgment, the prophets often speak of that "day" in more than one sense. So when Joel refers to the coming "day of the Lord," he is talking out of both sides of his mouth…but telling the absolute truth. Unless Judah repented, God was prepared to bring a catastrophic national judgment against her. And soon! Time and again!

Yet the people of Judah individually would also face a potentially more destructive "day of the Lord" at the Great Judgment of all mankind. You rightly ask, "How could that great day come *soon,* given that we all die at different times?" Actually our more personal "day of the Lord" is far easier to predict than some future national judgment. For the Day of Judgment is near—and very near—for all of us. As the Hebrew writer puts it (Hebrews 9:27): We are all going to die, "and after that…face judgment." On the scale of time, Judgment Day for mankind must await Christ's return. But unless the Lord comes while we are still alive, death will forever close the door to our preparation for Judgment. And for even the youngest among us, that death is just around the corner.

■ **The compelling question is: Would I be ready for the Lord if the Day of Judgment were to come this very day?**

The Excitement of Restoration

They did not require an accounting from those to whom they gave the money to pay the workers, because they acted with complete honesty.

2 KINGS 12:15

Imagine a world in which everyone is so honest no accounting of funds would ever be needed! In the euphoric days when the temple was being refurbished under Joash, seemingly everyone was on a rare spiritual high. People were so excited about contributing to the project that the money chest repeatedly had to be emptied! And did you notice what the money was being spent on—or *not* spent on? Initially it was not for items of silver and gold to be used in the temple, but for repairing the temple itself. Where there is a genuine revival of faith, aesthetics don't matter. What got people excited was not stained glass and steeples but recapturing an ancient vision of worship.

Maybe we can never reproduce those euphoric days immediately following Jesus' resurrection and ascension, or relive that incomparable day of Pentecost when 3000 were saved, or personally experience the thrilling aftermath when the Spirit-filled disciples joyfully fellowshipped with each other daily. But just imagine being one of those very first Christians, so on fire for the Lord that you would actually sell your possessions in order to share with fellow believers! The irony is that, instead of refurbishing some magnificent edifice, they left all the pomp and circumstance behind and celebrated the Lord around simple tables in humble homes. The excitement was not in external trappings, but in the vision of having intimate fellowship with God and each other. What could be more exciting? What could move us to greater generosity? What could make us so openly and obviously honest about our faith that no one would need an accounting!

■ **The reviving question is: What restored vision of faith today might prompt me to become euphorically spiritual?**

Grave Humor

Once while some Israelites were burying a man, suddenly they saw a band of raiders; so they threw the man's body into Elisha's tomb. When the body touched Elisha's bones, the man came to life and stood up on his feet.

2 KINGS 13:21

Funny stuff, this guy bouncing back to life! It's high time we got some comic relief from all the bloody fighting, political intrigue, and depressing spiritual depravity of Israel. Also nice to know that God has a sense of humor. Better yet it's nice to know that there is hope for the future. What can this story possibly be telling us, if not that a time is coming when Israel will bounce back to life! Then again the bad news is that God's people will have to completely "die" first and that this death will occur when God uses the surrounding nations as "raiders" to cart his people away into captivity. The "bouncing back" will come when God restores the Israelites to their land. Although it is a long way off for the people of the present generation, God is foretelling this to a future generation so that when it happens, they won't forget who did it.

Tying this story to Elisha's bones undoubtedly was intended not only to highlight the prophet's many warnings about the deadness of idolatry, but also to provide assurance of God's power to bring Israel back to life. Had not Elisha revived the Shunammite's son? For God, nothing was too difficult, whether making an axhead float, or feeding a hundred men with only twenty loaves, or purifying poison stew, or miraculously increasing a widow's oil. Of course there would be another miracle worker whose tomb would be far more important than Elisha's. For those of us who are spiritually dead and in need of bouncing back, identifying with the death of Jesus—lying bone to bone, as it were—is our one and only hope!

■ **The grave question is: If I want to overcome death, am I willing to jump into an open tomb for that to happen?**

Something Fishy About Obedience

And the LORD commanded the fish, and it vomited Jonah onto dry land.

JONAH 2:10

Virtually every child knows the story of Jonah and "the whale." Because whales aren't actually fish, maybe it wasn't the gray, blue, or killer whale we see spouting off in all the drawings. But it's still the biggest fish tale ever told and—despite defying credibility—still the truest. As for the details, don't ask. It's God's job to sort out how Jonah could be inside that mammoth creature with both of them surviving. What's far more interesting is that God somehow commanded a fish to vomit! And the fish obviously obeyed! As did the superstitious sailors who threw Jonah into the tumultuous sea at his direction. And as did the heathen Ninevites when told to repent. The odds of a whole city of idolaters obeying a command to repent must surely be a bigger fish story than the "whale"!

Did you notice who is left out of the list of the obedient? Jonah! Swarthy pagan sailors, unlikely heathen worshippers, and even a fish in the sea, all did what they were told to do. Only God's prophet had to be dragged kicking and screaming to obedience! Even then he resented the Ninevites for having followed God's command more eagerly than himself. Is there not a lesson or two here for those of us who consider ourselves to be God's people? The most obvious is that we should never ignore a call of God when we sense it, no matter how far-fetched it may seem. The second lesson is that God often calls us far outside of our comfort zones to reach people we tend to dismiss. Why waste time on them? But if God can fashion a fish big enough to swallow a prophet, he can create hearts big enough to accept a Savior!

■ **The reluctant question is: What is God calling me to do that I would rather not do…but will?**

_____

_____

_____

_____

What's in a Name?

I will show my love to the one I called "Not my loved one." I will say to those called "Not my people," "You are my people"; and they will say, "You are my God."

HOSEA 2:23

From the beginning, names have had special meaning. Adam, having been formed from the ground, was aptly named for the word denoting *earth*. And Eve, the mother of all the living, had the perfect name, which means *life*. Then there was the *princess* Sarai whose name was changed to Sarah, *the mother of many*. And it's easy to see why Peter's name, the *rock,* was eventually appropriate—though it easily could have been whatever the Greek is for wet noodle! Even many modern names represent pleasant characterizations, such as Margaret (*a pearl*), Amy (*beloved*), Emily (*trying to excel*), Tyler (*tailor*), and Randy (*wolf* or *shield*). It's no surprise that God would make meaningful use of names in the Scriptures.

The names divinely chosen for Hosea's children bore a stinging message. Jezreel's name foretold a punishing *dispersal* of Israel because of her unfaithfulness. Lo-Ruhamah, meaning *not loved,* and Lo-Ammi, meaning *not my people,* were hardly terms of endearment. So when today's verse reveals that surprising promise of a name change from *not my people* and *not loved* to the Hebrew equivalent of today's "Amy" (*beloved*), an extraordinary change in relationship is being foretold. Consider how that parallels the radical change of relationship inherent within the name "Christian." Before we claim that name, we are *not God's people.* When we proudly take on that name, we proclaim to an unbelieving world that we *are God's people*! What a tremendous responsibility we assume in the name that we wear—not simply *claiming* the name of Christ but *honoring* it.

■ **The interesting question is: What spiritually descriptive name might be given me by those who know me best?**

_____

_____

_____

_____

Destroyed by Lack of Knowledge

The more priests there were, the more they sinned against me; they exchanged their glorious God for something disgraceful. They feed on the sins of my people and relish their wickedness. And it will be: Like people, like priests. I will punish both of them for their ways and repay them for their deeds.

HOSEA 4:7-9

The priest, a wanderer from the narrow way; the silly sheep, no wonder they stray," goes the pithy ditty. Throughout the centuries the formula remains the same: fallen shepherds, scattered sheep. When spiritual leadership drops the ball, it's never long before God's people are headed in the wrong direction. The immediate target of Hosea's prophecy was a scripturally illiterate nation. "My people are destroyed from lack of knowledge," comes the ringing rebuke appropriate for any generation that doesn't know its Bible. In Hosea's day it was the priests' fault for not teaching God's Word. Today it is not only the fault of those who would presume to be spiritual leaders but the fault of individual believers. For all of God's people are "priests" serving under Christ, our High Priest.

Little has changed since Hosea's time. In sermon after dumbed-down sermon these days, it is not difficult to recognize that the glory of the revealed Word of God is regularly exchanged for disgraceful showmanship, psychologizing, and politicizing. The sins of the people no longer elicit priestly rebuke, but priestly redefinition. Wouldn't want to bite the hand that feeds you, would you? But who can we really blame if we are now the "priests"? Bibles are no longer chained to pulpits. You and I probably have several Bibles around the house collecting dust…or being skimmed, but not being read reflectively, carefully, or critically. In whatever Bible reading we do, is it possible we have exchanged the glory of God's Word for unworthy, self-affirming meanderings?

■ **The priestly question is: If I don't know my Bible by heart, whose fault is it?**

Good Cop, Bad Cop

"How can I give you up, Ephraim? How can I hand you over, Israel?…My heart is changed within me; all my compassion is aroused. I will not carry out my fierce anger, nor will I devastate Ephraim again. For I am God, and not a man—the Holy One among you. I will not come against their cities."

HOSEA 11:8-9

In the movies we often see the police playing "good cop, bad cop" to weasel confessions out of reluctant criminals. First, the "bad cop" threatens the prisoner with all sorts of undesirable scenarios before leaving in a huff. Then comes the "good cop," all smiles. Sympathizing with the prisoner about his bad treatment, the gentle cop promises to keep the mean cop at bay if the prisoner will merely confess. This classic police tactic is a variation on theme from the more acceptable practice of employing "carrots and sticks," used by everyone from loving parents to economic planners. Call it promises and threats. Incentives and disincentives. Like heaven and hell. Seems we need both the positive and the negative to respond appropriately. Indeed in the absence of a proper balance, there is great risk. Too much grace or too much law, and we're distorted. Too little fear or too little love, and we're warped.

Perhaps this explains why—only a few sentences apart within a single prophecy—Israel is equally exposed to both ends of the continuum. At one moment it's all about God's wrath and his lack of compassion. The next moment (as in today's featured passage) God is the reassuring "good cop"—all compassion and no wrath. The truth is, of course, that God is both the "good cop" by intention and the "bad cop" when we force him to be. Even then (as Israel would learn) the "bad cop" in God is still the "good cop," lovingly bringing us back to our senses.

■ **The question for us prisoners of sin is: Because I know God wants to be the "good cop," why do I so often force him to be the "bad cop"?**

The Moment of Truth

Therefore this is what I will do to you, Israel, and because I will do this to you, Israel, prepare to meet your God.

AMOS 4:12

Along rural roads, particularly in the South, one used to see billboards bearing the words: "Prepare to meet thy God." Given the hazardous two-lane highways in those days, the signs had particular relevance! Whatever the circumstances, meeting our Maker is no trivial matter. The thought of being asked by the Lord of the universe to give an account of our lives is daunting to say the least. Not that *he* doesn't already know, but *we* haven't yet owned up to it. No matter how certain we are that there will come a moment when we must look God in the eye and tell him what we have done with the great potential he has imbued within us, that moment seems comfortingly distant. Yet what if we knew with equal certainty that the moment of truth would come at the end of this very day? What would we be thinking about right now? How would we prepare to meet God face-to-face?

The problem is that few of us have reason to believe today's the day. Sure, someone will die before midnight, but not me. I can always put off the moment of truth to another time. Maybe I'll even clean up my act by then. Surely that is what the people of Israel must have thought despite all the warnings coming from Amos. In fairness, Israel's accounting to God did await another day. But it didn't wait forever. On a particular day—a day not unlike this very day—the judgment God had threatened finally happened. Which can only mean that the delay we take such comfort in is a delay we must take no comfort in. The only reason for God's patience is to give us more time to prepare.

■ **So the urgent question remains: If the close of this day should find me unexpectedly in eternity, am I ready for my ultimate moment of truth?**

The Faith Roots of Social Justice

Away with the noise of your songs! I will not listen to the music of your harps. But let justice roll on like a river, righteousness like a never-failing stream!

AMOS 5:23-24

In recognition of his inestimable contribution to the cause of civil rights for those of color, countless tributes have been made in memory of Dr. Martin Luther King, Jr., giving him due honor. Along with his famous "I Have A Dream" speech and "Letter from Birmingham Jail," one of the most memorable phrases associated with King's plea for civil liberties is the expression, "Let justice roll like a river." A man of deep faith, King purposefully drew those words from today's focus passage. By using Amos' imagery of justice flowing like a river, King was evoking Amos' many exhortations to Israel about overcoming such social injustices as oppression of the poor, partiality in the courts, and economic inequality. Racial injustice was (and remains) clearly bound up with all of that and much more.

Few people make the connection between this classic biblical imperative to "let justice roll" and the immediately preceding verse, which addresses the evil of empty religious ceremony. Where religious ritual is void of meaning and commitment, social injustice is bound to follow. What does it say about organized religion when, historically, most of the racial injustice took place in traditionally religious areas, except that such religion was mostly just that—*traditional*. Where there is genuine worship, the relationship with God that it engenders compels a greater responsibility toward our fellow man. To the contrary, if we think we can honor God by going through the motions of worship ritual while dishonoring our fellow man, we've missed the boat. When that happens, justice is never like a river, but only a stagnant pool.

■ **The thought-provoking question is: If I have done nothing to promote social justice lately, what kind of meaningless religion am I practicing?**

Prophets, Priests, and Kings

Then Amaziah the priest of Bethel sent a message to Jeroboam king of Israel: "Amos [the prophet] is raising a conspiracy against you in the very heart of Israel. The land cannot bear all his words."

AMOS 7:10

What degree of credibility do you give to all those personality charts purporting to identify you by such things as temperament, blood type, or date of birth? Is it not highly improbable that *everyone* could be so easily pigeonholed? Besides, what good would it be to know our category? Can a leopard change his spots? Even if we could better concentrate on our characteristic foibles as a "phlegmatic" or "Type A," we also risk overly psychologizing ourselves and others. Yet if you're fascinated by such pigeonholing, might our featured verse provide a more spiritual approach? Glance up for a moment and see if you can spot three categories into which most folks could fit.

If you guessed priest, king, and prophet, you're right. Most of us tend to be more like one than the other two. "Priests," for example, typically maintain the status quo and uphold tradition and the establishment. They seldom rock the boat, preferring to go with the flow. "Kings" are into management and most often see themselves as movers and shakers. They tend to climb ladders toward positions of authority. "Prophets," by contrast, are just plain troublemakers! They're always challenging tradition and authority by calling everyone to a higher standard. No wonder they're the least loved of the three! So which role best describes you? Intriguingly, Christ himself is Prophet, Priest, and King in equal measure—which might have something important to say to us about being spiritually well-rounded. While being faithful to our unique callings, might we do well to consider strengthening our less dominant sides?

■ **The challenging question is: If I see myself predominantly playing one of these three classic roles, am I aware of its strengths and drawbacks?**

Dressed for Disaster

In that day the Lord will snatch away their finery: the bangles and headbands and crescent necklaces, the earrings and bracelets and veils, the headdresses and anklets and sashes, the perfume bottles and charms, the signet rings and nose rings, the fine robes and the capes and cloaks, the purses and mirrors, and the linen garments and tiaras and shawls.

ISAIAH 3:18-23

D ress for success" is standard advice for anyone climbing the corporate ladder. Entire books have been written on the premise "Clothes make the man." Maybe, but Isaiah is not so sure about that, especially regarding the women of Judah. His scathing rebuke was not just for the haughty way the women strolled along the streets of Jerusalem, to see and be seen. At the heart of his concern was the time and attention spent on fancying themselves up in the finest apparel the brand-name stores had to offer. It's not so much *how* they dressed that concerned Isaiah, but *why* they dressed as they did. Seems the women of Judah were all about image. "Clothes make the *woman*" was as much in vogue then as now. But what would be left of them as a *person* when invading armies would literally strip them of their finery? Beneath all the expensive dresses, jewelry, and perfumes, what virtue remained of their threadbare souls?

In their own way, of course, men can be just as image conscious as women. So whatever caution here is good for the gander is also good for the goose. Still it has to be said that apparel and accessory stores for women far outnumber clothing shops for men. When it comes to strictly personal appearance, women typically spend far more time and attention thinking about how they look. Why that is true should give women of faith pause. Does a woman with a godly soul really need as large a closet as her spiritually weaker neighbor?

■ **The question for both men and women is: The next time I go shopping, will it be all about pretentious image or tastefully meeting basic needs?**

Unworthy but Chosen

"Woe to me!" I cried. "I am ruined! For I am a man of unclean lips, and I live among a people of unclean lips, and my eyes have seen the King, the LORD Almighty."

ISAIAH 6:5

To be called to special duty as a prophet of God must have been ineffably mystifying. You'll recall Amos saying that he was neither a prophet nor the son of a prophet before being tapped for duty. One day he is a simple backwater shepherd in Tekoa, the next day he's commissioned to speak out in judgment against the king of Israel. Must have taken some faith to accept that assignment! Indeed all of God's prophets must have been stupefied, if not horrified, by their dubious appointments, especially knowing that prophets were almost always hated and often killed for heralding bad news. But Isaiah is especially mystified and humbled, being acutely aware that he is unworthy of the task. If righteousness was a prerequisite for the job, he of all people wasn't qualified!

Sounds like the apostle Paul, doesn't it—that "chief of sinners" so unworthy to be chosen. And what about that petulant hothead Peter? In fact what about all those swarthy fishermen-turned-apostles, not to mention Matthew Levi, the presumably corrupt tax collector? Whoever would have chosen any of them for kingdom service? For that matter the choice of rebellious Israel as God's special people runs counter to all logic. If there is any logic at all in Isaiah's appointment, maybe it is that a nation of unclean lips needed a prophet of unclean lips to effectively communicate the message. Perhaps that's where you and I come in—we of unclean lips, hearts, and minds. Could God ever use unworthy rubbish like us? If his track record is anything to go by, the answer is yes. Sometimes it takes one hopeless sinner to reach another.

■ **The question for broken vessels is: If God uses sinners just like myself, with which fellow sinners might he be calling me to share the gospel?**

When True Religion Becomes Idolatrous

All this is because of Jacob's transgression, because of the sins of the people of Israel. What is Jacob's transgression? Is it not Samaria? What is Judah's high place? Is it not Jerusalem?

MICAH 1:5

We should not be surprised at the association between Samaria and idolatry. Ever since the ten northern tribes seceded under Jeroboam, idolatry had flourished in Samaria. So it was natural to pair Samaria with idolatry. Yet we tend not to think of Jerusalem that same way. Didn't Jesus confirm to the Samaritan woman that Jerusalem, not Samaria, was the seat of true worship? Paraphrasing Jesus, "The mixed-race Samaritans no longer know the true God of Israel as do the Jews in Jerusalem." However, because Jerusalem was not immune from idolatry during Micah's time, he was right to condemn Jerusalem for being as equally odious a "high place" as Samaria.

By the time of Jesus, pagan idolatry was no longer being practiced in Jerusalem. Yet it doesn't mean that the Jews' worship of God was void of idolatry. Otherwise, why did Jesus speak about a time to come when true worshippers would worship neither in Jerusalem nor in Samaria but in spirit and in truth? For first-century Jews, *Jerusalem itself* had become virtually sacred. As was the temple. As was the Jewish religion generally and its sacrosanct traditions in particular. Even the Torah scrolls were often revered in the same manner as objects of pagan worship. All of which raises important questions about our own religious practices. Is it possible that even true religion can turn into an object of idolatrous worship? When do we cross the line between venerating God and venerating his church? Between joyously singing sacred music and the music itself becoming sacred? Between doctrine that leads us to God and doctrine that becomes God?

■ **The question for true worshippers is: Without my realizing it, has my religious practice itself become the greater object of my fervor?**

Hope You Can Count On

But you, Bethlehem Ephrathah, though you are small among the clans of Judah, out of
you will come for me one who will be ruler over Israel, whose origins are from of old, from
ancient times.

MICAH 5:2

O little town of Bethlehem, how still we see thee lie!" Who in Micah's time could possibly have guessed we would be singing those words today in celebration of the events Micah foretold seven centuries before they happened? If God doesn't have a plan for man right down to the last detail, nothing is certain! How any prophecy that specific could be revealed centuries before its fulfillment defies comprehension. Yet the more intriguing question is *why* that detail is given so far in advance. Knowing the Messiah's birthplace would have been of no possible benefit to those in Micah's generation, and apparently even first-century Jews were largely oblivious to its significance. So what was the point?

God has repeatedly explained why he foretells coming events. It is so that when those events finally occur, we know who did it and why it was done. It is a divine version of man's more spiteful "I told you so!" Such prophecy is at its best when what's predicted is future punishment. But Micah's prophesy of a coming Messiah sounds more like: "Didn't I tell you? Isn't it great!" Which explains the story line formed from the conclusion to each stanza of Phillips Brooks' glorious carol:

> The hopes and fears of all the years are met in thee tonight.
> And praises sing to God the King, and peace to men on earth!
> Where meek souls will receive Him still, the dear Christ enters in.
> O come to us, abide with us, our Lord Emmanuel!

When you consider that *Bethlehem* is a picture of hope fulfilled, how about that celestial Jerusalem to come? If for our generation a prophesied *heaven* seems a long way off, is it any less certain?

■ **The question today is: Is heaven truly a daily hope for me, or is it too remote to think about?**

Words to Live By

He has showed you, O mortal, what is good. And what does the LORD require of you? To act justly and to love mercy and to walk humbly with your God.

MICAH 6:8

How does one possibly appease God? What is required to win his favor? How much time spent in church? How much fasting and prayer? How many oblations, confessions, tithes, and offerings? Just how many mission trips, youth rallies, and inner-city ministries does it take to make God happy? From the way we act, it seems many of us believe we can never do enough. And don't forget the obvious importance of getting all our doctrinal ducks in a row. Surely our theology and doctrine have to be correct! If our worship ritual and doctrine count for nothing, why has God commanded the ritual and stressed the importance of right doctrine? Perhaps he intended for them to produce a result far less complicated than either the ritual or doctrine itself, as a necessary means to the desired end. Both are crucial but not, in themselves, the object of the exercise.

Our featured verse today is a classic summary of what God expects of us. Look closely. There is not a hint of *appeasing* God. To the contrary, when we *act justly* and *love mercy* the focus is not on God, but on our fellow man. Add that last phrase about *walking humbly with God* and what you have, in a nutshell, is all of the law and the prophets—love God, love your neighbor. Why the mysterious doctrine of the Godhead? To instill a deeper love for God. Why the acts of service in Christian worship? To encourage better service to each other. So if you think ritual and doctrine are important, they are! But think again about why.

■ **The question for religious folks is: Am I so focused on doing and understanding everything correctly that I've missed the simplicity of result?**

_____

_____

_____

_____

Creeping Incrementalism

In the time of Pekah king of Israel, Tiglath-Pileser king of Assyria came and took Ijon, Abel Beth Maakah, Janoah, Kedesh and Hazor. He took Gilead and Galilee, including all the land of Naphtali, and deported the people to Assyria.

2 KINGS 15:29

It begins. Throughout the two centuries since Israel became a divided nation, both Israel and Judah have received repeated warnings about a coming time when they would be taken captive. Who could have believed it? "Surely not *us*! Not God's chosen people! Not the people to whom God has given the land promised to Abraham!" But here it is, the time has finally come. Well, almost. Today's terse passage records merely the beginning of the end for Israel. But that's enough. It is the first tiny crack in a badly weakened dike that will lead inexorably to a complete collapse. That is how God's punishment often works—slowly, gradually, incrementally, as if to give one final chance for repentance. As if the first taste of being taken captive will sound the alarm and set red lights flashing. But, of course, it won't.

There is grand irony in the incrementalism of Israel's captivity. The gradualism of the punishment was but a reflection of the gradualism of Israel's sin that made that very punishment necessary. For breakaway Israel, at first it was just a couple of golden calves. Seemed innocent enough because it was Israel's true God supposedly being worshiped. But once the door was cracked open even the slightest, it was no time before Baal himself walked through! It's the same with us really. Instead of being captured in a sudden ambush, we're typically lured into a situation where sin ensnares us over time. Once even slightly seduced by sin, we are increasingly vulnerable to its charms. Why, then, are we so surprised when we finally wake up as slave to that with which we only intended to flirt?

■ **The question for gradualists is: Do I really think I can go just a little way down the slippery slope without suddenly sliding to the bottom?**

Knowing What to Fear

Do not call conspiracy everything this people calls a conspiracy; do not fear what they fear, and do not dread it. The LORD Almighty is the one you are to regard as holy, he is the one you are to fear, he is the one you are to dread.

ISAIAH 8:12-13

Who do you think killed John F. Kennedy? If Lee Harvey Oswald, was he acting alone? It hardly matters that the Warren Commission reached that conclusion. That was just adding fuel to the fire for conspiracy theorists. But the stakes of that unwinnable debate are penny-ante compared with larger conspiracy theories. Consider, for example, the claim by some that "New World Order" conspiracies lie behind the United Nations, or that there was government complicity in the 9/11 tragedy, or that conspiracies exist to bring about Jewish global domination. If any of those are true, we're not exactly talking about folks who believe the lunar landings were a figment of some conspiratorial imagination. Grand conspiracies can have far-reaching social, political, and spiritual implications.

Conspiracies do exist, whether to rob the local bank, murder a crucial witness, or ally one country with another. But that is hardly the concern of our featured passage. The problem it addresses is the fear on which most hardcore conspiracy theories thrive. Especially for those who are more fearful by nature, a conspiracy theory is a simple way to channel their fears. It's an easy target to shoot at. In Israel's case, rampant conspiracy theories purporting to explain why the nation was headed for destruction were fed by all the wrong fears. If Israel had feared God and kept his commandments, none of this would be happening. It was not some grand conspiracy that was bringing them down, but a fearsome God they refused to fear. To give a slight twist to FDR's famous line—We have nothing to fear but God himself!

◼ **The crucial question is: Among a checklist of all my fears, where does my fear of God rank?**

When Ends Justify the Means

Woe to the Assyrian, the rod of my anger, in whose hand is the club of my wrath!

ISAIAH 10:5

The classic conundrum of God's providence interplaying with human action is rarely seen in sharper relief. Repeatedly now we have seen that what man intends for evil, God (working in the background) may intend for good. So once again we see God working behind the scenes, dispatching Assyria to bring divine punishment against Israel. But God is not happy with Assyria for relishing the assignment! Once her commissioned task is complete, Assyria will be punished for her own evil motives, which have nothing to do with righteous judgment, only selfish national imperialism. We are vividly reminded here that God can take man's sinful actions and turn them into forces for good. The question is: How can God ethically justify using human evil to achieve some well-intended result? Would God be pleased if we took a similar approach?

To put the question in its usual format: Do the ends ever justify the means? The less-than-reassuring answer is sometimes yes, and sometimes no. For instance would anyone object on ethical grounds to the deliberate razing of a single house to save an entire neighborhood from a raging fire? Or (to raise the stakes) to the brutal torture of a terrorist in aid of locating a nuclear bomb set to explode in New York City? Not all ethicists agree on this one. What do you suppose Jesus would do in such an instance? If answers to thorny ethical questions are not always readily forthcoming, we might at least give serious consideration to the thought that God himself seems at times to cross normal ethical boundaries in aid of a spiritually higher cause.

■ **The unsettling question is: Since I am not God, dare I rush to judgment as to when some spiritual priority trumps an ethical imperative?**

Global Sovereignty

This is the plan determined for the whole world; this is the hand stretched out over all nations. For the LORD Almighty has purposed, and who can thwart him? His hand is stretched out, and who can turn it back?

ISAIAH 14:26-27

National sovereignty is a huge issue for the world's nations. To give up national sovereignty is a cardinal sin, and invasion of one's borders is tantamount to a declaration of war. So when we read that God has his hand stretched out over every nation, we're talking about a global sovereignty superceding the authority of all nations and their political leaders. The thought of God providentially working in national and international affairs to bring about a plan he has devised from eternity boggles the mind. Yet reading about how God dealt with nations in biblical times gives us some sense that God actually stepped into history to bring about history. Specific history. With specific nations and specific borders either being invaded or defended. (Merely consider the taking of the Promised Land itself.)

All of that is well and good until we consider whether God is still working among nations in the same way even today. If Americans would adamantly contend that God was behind the establishment of the United States, was God also responsible for the slaughter of the American Indian? Was God's hand in Germany's invasion of Poland, France, and Norway, or in either of the world wars? If so, how did that global conflagration, ending in the atomic devastation of Hiroshima and Nagasaki, fit into God's eternal plan? More to the point, what does God have to do with tonight's six o'clock news? Whatever the latest national or international crisis, have we stopped to consider that the events being reported may actually have been orchestrated by a sovereign God?

■ **The disquieting question is: When I vehemently disagree with how political affairs are being handled, am I ever railing against God's will?**

_____

_____

_____

_____

Keep Asking the Important Question

Someone calls to me from Seir, "Watchman, what is left of the night? Watchman, what is left of the night?" The watchman replies, "Morning is coming, but also the night. If you would ask, then ask; and come back yet again."

ISAIAH 21:11-12

Any parent who has traveled with young children will remember those same two questions being asked a zillion times: "Are we there yet?" and "How much longer is it?" For youngsters time and distance are frustratingly elusive concepts. And how confusing it must be when the answer to the second question is always different, depending on how far we've driven. In Isaiah's prophecy the question being put to the night watchman is always the same…as is the answer. But it is not as if the same answer doesn't calculate a significant difference from the time before. In the repetitious sequence of unfaithfulness, punishment, and restoration, to ask where Israel was in the sequence was only to be told, "It doesn't matter when you ask. If the morning of restoration is near, so too is the unfaithfulness and punishment soon to follow." Yet each round of rebellion and restoration was leading inexorably to a time when the punishment would be catastrophic.

For us today the question asked by youngsters is still the right question: "How long, O Lord?" And when we are in our darker moments, the question asked of the watchman still makes good sense: "Watchman, what is left of the night?" Along the way through life's journey, we need constantly to be reminded of where we are in relation to God's time and ours. Journeys don't last forever, not even the one we're making on this earth. *Not* to ask where we are along the way is to lose sight of the destination. So keep asking the question, even if the answer is different every time.

■ **The question for weary travelers is: Is the watchman's answer an indication of progress, or a reminder that I'm bogged down in a senseless cycle?**

The Harsh Reality of Death

They will all respond, they will say to you, "You also have become weak, as we are; you have become like us." All your pomp has been brought down to the grave, along with the noise of your harps; maggots are spread out beneath you and worms cover you.

ISAIAH 14:10-11

When we think of a cemetery, our mind's eye typically envisions marble tombstones and bronze vases full of flowers, all in a beautiful park-like setting. Want to know who was successful in life? The larger and more ornate the tombstone, the more prominent the deceased. Then again we all know that cemeteries are mostly window dressings, perhaps reflecting one's position in society, but telling us little about a person's character. Even when scripture verses or pious phrases adorn the tombstone, the person being remembered might not have been particularly religious or even virtuous. However beautiful, cemeteries are deceptively beguiling.

Who wants to contemplate the harsh reality beneath the gravestones, especially after the loss of a loved one? Yet it has to be said that the tranquil beauty of the cemetery belies the ghastly decomposition taking place within the grave. For no matter how carefully bodies are sealed in coffins and crypts, they inevitably decay. Though we shudder to think of maggots and worms, the fact remains that (if not cremated) our flesh inexorably will deteriorate into nothing. If the Lord tarries, we are all going to disintegrate. At which point the hard truth emerges: when the process of putrefaction is complete, the body no longer counts, only the soul. The mystery is—why doesn't this truth have a far more meaningful impact on us than it does? Out of sight, out of mind might work well for flower-bedecked cemeteries, but not for souls serious about what happens when there is nothing left but rotting bones.

■ **The macabre question is: Do I ever dwell long enough on the prospect of my decomposing body to be prompted for good by that gruesome thought?**

_____

_____

_____

_____

_____

A Heart for Seekers

But Hezekiah prayed for them, saying, "May the LORD, who is good, pardon everyone who sets their heart on seeking God—the LORD, the God of their ancestors—even if they are not clean according to the rules of the sanctuary." And the LORD heard Hezekiah and healed the people.

2 CHRONICLES 30:18-20

God is notorious for rule making and rule breaking. Just when we think we know how God will react in any given situation, he surprises us. When he's a stickler for rules, it is always for the good. When he makes or condones exceptions to the rule, that too is good. Not unexpectedly, God's wisdom in knowing *when* to do *what* is far beyond our ability to do the same, but that doesn't mean we don't have our own part to play in the process. Imitating God is the goal. Incorporating his ways into our ways is a mark of spiritual maturity. And so we spend the first years of our lives being taught the rules, and the rest of our lives learning how to judge between strict obedience and discerning noncompliance.

It gets even more interesting when we move to the next level, involving those other than ourselves. Hezekiah's prayer exposes a heart gracious toward those who desire to seek God, but in imperfect ways. There is no plea for God to permanently change the rules. Hezekiah is praying that God recognize the obvious—that sometimes, as here, there is only a temporary glitch, where something normally unauthorized is done to get back on track. At other times, seekers may even be badly mistaken about the rules but would obey them completely if they were simply taught the way of the Lord more perfectly. Whatever the problem, it is Hezekiah's heart for seekers that comes ringing through loud and clear. Instead of being quick to condemn, the heart that consciously prays on behalf of well-intentioned seekers is a heart able to bring them closer to God.

■ **The question for concerned hearts is: What struggling seekers come to mind on whose behalf I should be praying?**

Walking on a Holy Road

And a highway will be there; it will be called the Way of Holiness; it will be for those who walk on that Way. The unclean will not journey on it; wicked fools will not go about on it.

ISAIAH 35:8

Have you ever wondered why the first converts to Christ were initially known, not as Christians, but as followers of "the Way"? Perhaps these controversial disciples of Jesus were the "third way," in addition to the two established Jewish sects, the Pharisees and Sadducees. Or perhaps there is some connection with Jesus' own self-description as "*the way,* the truth, and the life" (John 14:6). Yet could it be that "the Way" became a designation of choice by the first Jewish converts because they identified so closely with Isaiah's words in today's text? It certainly would have been a marvelous means of calling attention to Isaiah 35, which has Jesus' name written all over it. In Jesus of Nazareth, "they will see the glory of the LORD" (verse 2). As the miracle worker, "then will the eyes of the blind be opened and the ears of the deaf unstopped" (verse 5). As the Savior of the world, "he will come to save you" (verse 4). It's as if Isaiah were saying to first-century Jews, "This Jesus is the very 'Way of Holiness' I'm talking about—the one who alone is the way *to* holiness!"

Is it possible that we have lost something valuable in not thinking of ourselves as followers of "the Way"? While it is true that becoming a child of God is a one-time change in relationship with God, the long road to holiness is an ongoing process. How, except through Jesus, are we to be transformed into God's own holiness? Jesus not only *pointed* the way to holiness, but *explained* the way and personally *modeled* the way. So if we truly want to be holy, we must be—not just "Christians"—but followers of him who is the Way.

■ **The question for Jesus' disciples is: Do I think of my holiness as an accomplished fact or a lifelong spiritual odyssey?**

Give the Rules a Rest!

For it is: Do this, do that, a rule for this, a rule for that; a little here, a little there. Very well then, with foreign lips and strange tongues God will speak to this people, to whom he said, "This is the resting place, let the weary rest."

ISAIAH 28:10-12

Examine any highly bureaucratic political system, and you will see a close correlation between its extreme orientation to rules and a fundamental lack of spiritual underpinnings. Consider how tightly controlled officially atheist nations have been and how increasingly regulated secularist societies have become. Moral and spiritual vacuums always beg to be filled. And what better way to take up the slack than with laws, rules, and regulations. *Onerous* laws, rules, and regulations! Despite all the frenetic religious exercise visible on the surface in Israel, inwardly the nation was spiritually dead. God's people were caught between two mirroring forces—a spiritual sterility that invited an escalation of rule making; an escalation of rule making that inexorably led to even more sterility. The more burdensome the rules, the more the people suffered from spiritual fatigue. Rules are laborious, not liberating. Exhausting, not exhilarating.

For Israel's control-freak religious leaders, the word from Isaiah was to give the people a rest! God has given us enough rules. The last thing we need is more—especially *man-made*! The pretense was that more rules fostered greater righteousness. But that is always a sham. Notice in the follow-up verses how God threatened to punish the rule makers by subjecting them to captivity where there would be *nothing but rules* imposed on them. It should stand as a warning to us today. If our religious life is mostly about rule keeping, our spiritually vacuous lives will be further emasculated by those very rules.

■ **The question for weary worshippers is: If I'm suffering from spiritual fatigue, is it time that I examined just how rule-oriented my faith life is?**

Running a Tight Ship

Your rigging hangs loose: The mast is not held secure, the sail is not spread.

ISAIAH 33:23

Have you seen pictures of sailboats leaning so far over they seem to be on the brink of overturning? Only those who have experienced the exhilaration of speeding over the waves as the wind cuts through tightly trimmed sails can appreciate the seemingly precarious way a boat sails at its optimum potential. Of course even the finest yachts will be useless if not skillfully sailed. It's easy to see how Isaiah would describe God's wayward people as a floundering boat. In their relationship to God, they were fearful at the sight of the first threatening wave, lackadaisical when the winds of fortune were calm, and ceaselessly careless when dangers lurked just beneath the surface. They seemed always to be lost at sea—on course, then off; off course, then on. Given their lack of seaworthiness, it is amazing they stayed afloat at all!

Even now, those who are fearful of committing themselves to God will often abandon crucial spiritual "rigging" at the first sign of the boat tipping. It takes trust and faith to believe that God's boat actually sails best when this world's values are almost upside down! The lazy mariner will not bother to unfurl the written Word. But without biblical knowledge to catch the fair breezes of the Holy Spirit, this ship is going nowhere! Most critical of all—careless sailors won't even notice dangerous doctrinal defects in the mast of faith on which all else hangs. This powerful nautical imagery intended as a rebuke to Israel is a call for us to reexamine our own state of spiritual seaworthiness.

■ **The question for sailors on life's sea is: Am I leaning in trust with my sails trimmed tightly into the wind or drifting aimlessly for lack of faith?**

Pledging Undivided Allegiance

They worshiped the LORD, but they also served their own gods in accordance with the customs of the nations from which they had been brought…Even while these people were worshiping the LORD, they were serving their idols.

2 KINGS 17:33,41

Previous examples of fickle faith have focused on Israel herself. For Israel, having mixed religious loyalties was a perennial problem. But our featured passage today is talking instead about foreigners brought into the land of promise to fill the vacuum created when the people of Israel were carted off into Assyrian captivity. Responding to lion attacks on the new settlers, it was the king of Assyria himself who ordered that these new immigrants be taught how to worship the God of Israel. But because mere appeasement rather than genuine conversion was the object of the exercise, there was never an exclusive exchange of spiritual loyalties. The immigrants were more than happy to mix and match Israel's God with their own national gods. Never having known the *true* God, it is understandable that they would think all "gods" were pretty much the same.

Even now new converts coming to Christ from diverse religious backgrounds often exhibit residual thought patterns and habits from their former ways of thinking and acting. Their past requires patience on our part to mentor them, helping them develop a more mature faith. In that regard, of course, our own values demand closer scrutiny. What we teach most is not how we *believe,* but how we *behave.* In most religious circles today, there is no explicit intermingling of Christian and pagan gods. However, idolatry abounds even in "Christian nations"—from the obsessive cult of self, to the insatiable gods of materialism, to the unabashed gods of sexual erotica. Submerged as we are in such a godless culture, it is *we* who might most need the lessons we have prepared for others.

■ **The probing question is: Am I myself serving this world's idols even while worshipping the Lord?**

Basking in Illusions

Give us no more visions of what is right! Tell us pleasant things, prophesy illusions. Leave this way, get off this path, and stop confronting us with the Holy One of Israel!

ISAIAH 30:10-11

Psychiatrists must surely have a word to describe folks who insist on being self-deceived. But truth avoidance is not peculiar to the peculiar. There are times most of us would prefer self-deception. For example, who wants to hear the doctor tell us we have cancer? Wouldn't some of us wish to be told a lie and be blissfully ignorant of the truth? When there is bad news ahead, our first instinct is to shy away from it. If only that quirk in human nature were the extent of the problem being addressed in our featured passage! Isaiah is not talking about *knowledge* avoidance, but *responsibility* avoidance. The people knew very well what the score was. Their problem was wanting to avoid following God's commands. So please just don't mention them. Let's pretend God never spoke about that. Whatever it takes, distract us. Tell us lies!

It is not likely that many of us would ever hear those exact words coming out of our mouths. But there are more ways than one to express denial. Could this explain why some people never read their Bibles? Are they are afraid to hear God telling them explicitly what he expects of them? And could this explain a person's choice of a church? It is no secret that some churches are altogether happy to sugarcoat the stringent demands of the gospel. Week in and week out, pulpits are filled with only pleasant things and comforting psychobabble. Rarely is the listener confronted with God's call to holiness. The problem is: If all we want to glean from a conversation about God is self-affirmation, then of all people we are most delusional.

■ **The disturbing question is: Are there any ways in which I've subconsciously avoided being confronted by God?**

_____

_____

_____

_____

The Confidence Game

On what are you basing this confidence of yours? You say you have the counsel and the might for war—but you speak only empty words.

2 KINGS 18:19-20

Mention the name "Titanic" and false confidence immediately springs to mind. "Unsinkable," you say? Apparently not! Yet given the technology of her time, there was every reason for the extraordinary confidence in that grand lady of the seas. However, there was also a significant amount of arrogance involved. Seen more clearly in persons than in ships, there is a fine line between confidence and arrogance. But there is no fine line between confidence and lack of confidence. How often do we hear someone described either as "exuding confidence" or "lacking confidence"? How would you describe yourself? Are you by nature a confident person or one who is never quite sure of yourself?

Strangely enough, the key to a healthy self-confidence is not having self-confidence! At least not having an overabundance of self-reliance. The reason Hezekiah could be so confident of victory over the more powerful forces of Assyria was that his reliance was not in himself, nor in his troops or weapons, but in God. And it was that supra-human confidence that Sennacherib didn't understand. Had he not conquered every other nation he'd attacked without the least resistance from their gods? So when he taunted Hezekiah for having false confidence, the irony is that it was Sennacherib himself whose confidence lacked foundation. The key to genuine confidence is not subjective, but objective. No matter how confident I might feel, there remains the possibility that I cannot withstand whatever lurking "icebergs" float into my life. But with God as my protector, there is no "iceberg" big enough to sink my ship. In that I have complete confidence!

■ **The titanic question is: Do I have a good reason for my self-confidence (or perhaps a bad reason for my lack of it)?**

Toeing the Line

Therefore this is what the LORD, the God of Israel, says: I am going to bring such disaster on Jerusalem and Judah that the ears of everyone who hears of it will tingle. I will stretch out over Jerusalem the measuring line used against Samaria and the plumb line used against the house of Ahab.

2 KINGS 21:12-13

Whether for masons or carpenters, being "plumb" is a weighty matter. That goes as well for sailors on the sea "plumbing the depths." In water, a lead weight must be used to sink the end of a line to the bottom. In construction work, a lead weight on the end of a string assures a straight, vertical line from which a true perpendicular can be determined. Fortunately for masons and carpenters, gravity is always straight down! Perhaps you've heard someone talk about a wall being "out of plumb," which is not good. When one wall is wrong, all the other walls and floors that tie into it are also likely to be out of alignment. No wonder we have seen repeated references to God stretching out a plumb line over his people to see how they measure up.

For the people of Judah, there was a crucial lesson to be learned about how God had cast his plumb line over Samaria and Ahab's household—who, quite misguidedly, had thought any ol' measuring string would do, weighted or unweighted. But strings without weights tend to wiggle and curl in all directions. Once they had removed the weight of God's Word from the plumb line, they may have measured up to their own expectations, but not to God's "true vertical" by which they were to be judged. The lesson Judah refused to learn is not a lesson we can afford to ignore. When it comes to our own lives, have we given God's revealed Word enough weight? If not, walls torn down for being "out of plumb" ought to give us pause.

■ **The aligning question is: If I'm feeling all out of sorts, could it be because I am "out of plumb"?**

The Strength of Eternal Youth

Even youths grow tired and weary, and young men stumble and fall; but those who hope in the LORD will renew their strength. They will soar on wings like eagles; they will run and not grow weary, they will walk and not be faint.

ISAIAH 40:30-31

Myth that it is, the so-called "fountain of youth" is a relentless pursuit for those who seek a magical elixir to stave off the onslaught of age. Despite all the magical potions, healing waters, curative diets, and latest injections, the fountain of youth has yet to be discovered. The aging process is inexorable and irreversible. It is no mystery, of course, why dreams of eternal youth remain. Not only would it be the ultimate escape from death, but eternal youth would mean no more aches and pains from the aging process, no more tottering falls for the elderly, and no more naps or nighttime trips to the bathroom. Of course none of this means much to healthy, invincible young people. Little wonder we say that youth is wasted on the young! But for those who are advancing in years, a fountain of youth would look mighty good at times.

Perhaps all this explains why today's featured passage is such a favorite. Its promises are the closest we will ever get to a true fountain of youth. Just imagine no more fatigue! And no more wrinkles! Naturally, the passage is not telling us that the righteous will be running endless marathons while the wicked fall in an exhausted heap. The point is that the *weary soul* finds endless strength and renewal in the Lord. That God alone is the hope of the aging. That faith in God makes us soar over all that would bind our tiring frames to this mortal coil, including advancing age. If staying young is mostly mind over matter, the mind that is focused on God is a mind for which nothing else matters!

■ **The question for any age is: If I'm feeling particularly weary, have I imbibed sufficiently from the fountain of faith?**

The Importance of Tone

He will not shout or cry out, or raise his voice in the streets. A bruised reed he will not break, and a smoldering wick he will not snuff out.

ISAIAH 42:2-3

Throughout Isaiah's many prophecies, God takes great pains to say that he is predicting future events so that everyone will know it wasn't just chance but the unfolding of a divine plan. As the supreme object lesson making that very point, prophecy after prophecy describes in detail the coming Messiah, Jesus of Nazareth. After his death and resurrection, Jesus' disciples would point back to Isaiah's prophecies, among others, to show how Jesus perfectly matched the descriptions divinely revealed centuries before. Taken alone, that fulfillment of prophecy would be worth all the space devoted to Jesus in the Old Testament. But what we learn about Jesus even before his miraculous birth in the first century is also worth the price of admission.

Those who are familiar with Jesus' life and ministry will know that he was no pious wimp. He spoke straightforwardly and minced no words—especially when confronting the religious establishment. ("You snakes—you brood of vipers!" comes readily to mind!) And then there were those two occasions on which Jesus drove the money changers and merchants out of the temple for making a mockery of God's house. So Isaiah's description of Jesus as one who would not raise his voice or hurt a fly, as it were, has to be carefully understood. Isaiah seems to be telling us that, unlike many religious leaders even today, Jesus was not shrill in his teaching and preaching. For all his harsh rebukes, Jesus never presented the gospel in strident tones. Rather he allowed the power of the gospel to speak for itself. How refreshing that would be today—to hear the gospel presented without all the dramatic histrionics, acrimonious debate, and political polarization. When it comes to sharing the gospel, the idea is *zeal*, not *shrill*.

■ **The question for Jesus' disciples is: If I have difficulty sharing the gospel with others, have I taken inventory of my tone lately?**

The Present Presence of God

Forget the former things; do not dwell on the past. See, I am doing a new thing! Now it springs up; do you not perceive it?

ISAIAH 43:18-19

When we think of dwelling on the past, we might first think of Lot's wife looking back toward Sodom and turning into a pillar of salt. That kind of "living in the past" is simply not healthy. (Not to say that we should "live only for the moment" as many do today.) But here Isaiah does not seem to have in mind that kind of "living in the past." Although at times God counsels the wisdom of specifically remembering the powerful deeds he has done in the past, the present context advises against our dwelling on those events. Though God delivered Israel out of Egypt in a mighty and spectacular way, he is not a God who disappeared centuries ago. He is a here-and-now *living* God!

One of the traps we often fall victim to is studying the Scriptures as if they were dry history, concentrating on times, places, people, and events. Over a lifetime, for example, many mature believers have studied the history and geography of Paul's three missionary journeys *ad nauseam* while making precious little effort to recognize and apply the spiritual principles crying for attention. And all because we are dwelling on the past rather than the present presence of God. Is this because the works of God are clearer when reduced to ink on a page? Or because we can always talk about the rebellious people in the Bible without having to confront our own rebellion? Or could it be because we have grown accustomed to studying with the mindset of detached historians rather than opening ourselves to the way in which, even at this very moment, God is "doing a new thing!"

■ **The contemporary question is: If I'm not really sure God is actively working in my life today, is it possible that I have thoughtlessly relegated God to the pages of a dusty history book?**

Of Horoscopes and Other Nonsense

All the counsel you have received has only worn you out! Let your astrologers come forward, those stargazers who make predictions month by month, let them save you from what is coming upon you.

ISAIAH 47:13

What's your sign? Sagittarius? Virgo? And how often do you check the daily horoscopes to see what the future holds for you? Today's verse strongly suggests that any serious reliance on astrologers to predict the future is both worthless and an act of misdirected faith. Anyone with an ounce of sense recognizes that horoscopes are vague, generic predictions that have a statistical chance of coming true for a fair number of folks. Why, then, do so many of us take an occasional glance…just for fun? It's the same fortune-cookie curiosity that takes hold of us in Chinese restaurants. Something down deep in all of us craves special insight into ourselves and our future.

What may be playful curiosity for some is serious business for others. Catering to those who wish to consult the occult has itself become a serious (and lucrative!) business. Increasingly, the occult has become the option of choice for those seeking spirituality apart from traditional faith systems—or indeed as an eclectic New Age blending with normative religious expression. The promise of *at-one-ment* with God without the *atonement* of Christ appeals to those who want all the benefits of spirituality without spiritual accountability. It's not surprising that secularists would think they could put as much stock in horoscopes, palm readers, seances, and psychic mediums as in the gospel of Christ. What's truly surprising is how so many of us calling ourselves Christians are quick to condemn horoscopes and the occult but personally have little trust in the one true God who knows the future like the back of his hand.

■ **The crucial astrological question is: What did the star over Bethlehem have to say about not only *his* life, but *mine*?**

The Hard Lesson of Submission

I offered my back to those who beat me, my cheeks to those who pulled out my beard; I did not hide my face from mocking and spitting. Because the Sovereign LORD helps me, I will not be disgraced. Therefore have I set my face like flint, and I know I will not be put to shame.

ISAIAH 50:6-7

Three layers of teaching are embedded within today's passage. In the first layer, Isaiah is preparing the people of Judah for the attitude they will need when the disgrace and punishment they deserve finally comes upon them. If they are to come away from the process any the wiser, these prideful people must do what they have not been willing to do before—learn to submit with humility. Unknown to them the day was coming when one of their descendants would perfectly personify humility in the face of humiliation, which brings us to the second layer of Isaiah's teaching. That descendant, of course, was Jesus Christ, who, although deserving none of the taunting abuse hurled his way, would model an attitude of restrained submission. He, the sovereign Lord of the universe!

The third layer of Isaiah's prophecy pertains to us, who often deserve whatever humiliation comes our way but just as often *don't* deserve the abuse we get. We have lessons to learn both from the people of Judah and from Jesus—the easier lesson being from Judah. For when we *deserve* humiliation, we usually know it. It's hard to resent punishment we have brought on ourselves. So the more difficult lesson is from Jesus. Turning the other cheek to our enemies may be the hardest lesson we ever have to learn. "It's just not right!" "They shouldn't be allowed to get away with it!" "Surely I don't have to take this!" And do we think none of those thoughts went through the suffering Savior's mind on the cross?

> ■ **The humbling question is: When I have every reason to strike back, just how far have I come in taking on the restrained humility of Christ?**

Blessings for the Barren

"Sing, barren woman, you who never bore a child; burst into song, shout for joy, you who were never in labor; because more are the children of the desolate woman than of her who has a husband," says the LORD.

ISAIAH 54:1

How cruel to play games with the emotions of women who have never had children or who are barren! Indeed, suggesting they will have even more offspring than women with children! For many women this passage seems to rub salt into the wound. Should we believe that all those childless women will be as miraculously blessed as Mary? Which calls to mind Jesus. Which directs us to the preceding verses alluding to the crucified Christ who "will see his offspring." Wasn't Jesus "cut off" from his descendants? Did he have children or grandchildren? How, possibly, could he have! In the answer to *that* question perhaps lies the answer to the earlier question. Because Jesus was willing to die (childless), he had more "spiritual offspring" than he ever would have had otherwise. Righteous barrenness is a fruitful womb.

Isaiah is not speaking directly to or about barren women in this passage. This is one of several analogies Isaiah uses to predict Israel's fruitful restoration following the barrenness of exile. In the midst of her banishment, Israel will feel like a barren woman—with no hope of fulfillment or progeny. But the Lord already knows the "offspring" he will bring forth from that barren womb, including—first and foremost—Jesus, the Messiah, through whom countless millions will be given a spiritual birth they otherwise could not have had. There is more than mere analogy here. It truly is about all those whose lives, in whatever way, seem barren and unfulfilled. Whatever personal loss we feel may yet be God's way of replenishing righteousness on the earth!

■ **The fulfilling question is: Am I willing to allow my greatest disappointment to become a precious, fruitful gift?**

No Wasted Words

As the rain and the snow come down from heaven, and do not return to it without watering the earth…so is my word that goes out from my mouth: It will not return to me empty, but will accomplish what I desire and achieve the purpose for which I sent it.

ISAIAH 55:10-11

Do you know that singular frustration of trying to teach the gospel to those who don't seem to care? Have you spent hours telling the story of Jesus or having Bible studies with friends and neighbors without apparent result? Countless sermons, religious tracts, and pleading conversations have simply gone unheeded. And for what? Has it all been a waste of time? Few, if any, true believers would actually say they had wasted their time unsuccessfully teaching others, but—as with any enterprise—there is a temptation to give up. Call it the law of diminishing returns. Butting our heads against the wall certainly gets old. And yet if we believe anything at all, it is that God's Word itself tells us God's Word is never wasted!

For one thing, we might wrongly assume we've gotten no results. Who knows whether those we have taught might yet turn to God—perhaps after we are long gone? Or maybe the fruits of our efforts will even skip a generation, with the children being converted to Christ because of something we have said to their parents. Testimonies of believers often speak of just a brief word of encouragement—perhaps by a complete stranger—that put them on the road to faith. "Who converted you?" "I don't even know her name!" The obvious moral of the story is that we should never give up for lack of obvious results. As Scripture tells us, our job is simply to plant the Word along the way or to water seeds already planted. Of course there's not much pride in merely planting and watering…which might just be the whole point!

■ **The frustrating question is: Have I been more focused on "winning souls" than simply sharing the good news with everyone I meet?**

Double-checking Our Spiritual Genealogy

But you—come here, you children of a sorceress, you offspring of adulterers and prostitutes!

ISAIAH 57:3

In today's parlance we'd almost have to leave blanks for several of the words in our featured verse. Certainly we would be uncomfortable using some of the slang epithets in a book such as this. The shock of having a respected prophet of God basically calling wicked idolaters "bastards" is made all the more troublesome by its usual implication for those who are said to be "illegitimate children." Of course it is not the children who are "illegitimate," but the forbidden relationships which brought them into the world. ("Illegitimate parents" is a much more accurate term!) Yet there is an element of truth to Isaiah's use of such pointed language. Given Judah's idolatry, those to whom Isaiah is speaking might literally be the children of sorceresses or cult prostitutes. But because Isaiah is rebuking them directly, it is clear that they are not simply the innocent offspring of pagan parents—they are practicing idolaters! So what does that make them in the eyes of God but illegitimate children of a lesser god?

To be a child of God is to have a legacy of legitimacy that others simply cannot have. Once when Jesus was in a heated conversation with some of the Jews who rejected him, the question of spiritual lineage became a testy point of contention. When Jesus dared to suggest that they were not children of Abraham, but rather children of their father the devil, they were outraged. "We are not illegitimate children," they protested. "The only Father we have is God himself." Which ought to sound a warning even for us. Is it possible that we might sincerely believe we are children of God but live in such a way that suggests a less noble parentage?

> ■ **The potentially shocking question is: If Isaiah and Jesus pulled no punches, what kind of explicit language might they use to describe me?**

_____

_____

_____

_____

Beauty for Ashes

He has sent me to bind up the brokenhearted…to comfort all who mourn…to bestow on them a crown of beauty instead of ashes…and a garment of praise instead of a spirit of despair.

ISAIAH 61:1-3

One of the lesser known hymns, inspired by this passage, perfectly captures Isaiah's comforting words. Grant Colfax Tullar's "Beauty for Ashes" (1948) is simple in melody, but powerful in imagery. "Beauty for ashes, God hath decreed! Help He provideth for every need. What is unlovely, He will restore; grace all sufficient: what need we more?" What indeed! "God gives for sadness 'garments of praise'; stars for our twilight, strength for our days; hope for tomorrow, care for today, light for our footsteps all of life's way." And finally come the comforting contrasts: "Beauty for ashes, gladness for tears, sunshine for darkness, faith for our fears; peace for our turmoil, concord for strife, heaven at evening—then endless life!"

To be crowned with beauty is a familiar concept. But to fully appreciate Isaiah's portrait, we must recall the Eastern custom of mourning with sackcloth and ashes. This would be the manner in which Judah would mourn its captivity. The promise, then, of beauty replacing ashes conjured a truly comforting vision. For us there is little prospect of being taken captive and hauled off to some foreign country. Even so, we can all relate to being brokenhearted and despondent—and never more so than at the death of a loved one. In those dark hours, need we despair? When all seems lost, is there no hope? When fear robs us of joy, is there no peace? Whether at this very moment or at some future hour of tragedy, God's gracious promise of beauty for ashes is the exquisite vision to see us through.

■ **The hopeful question is: When I'm covered with the disconsolate ashes of mourning and sadness, do I not always have the promise of beauty rising through the gloom?**

A Snapshot of Repentance

In his distress he sought the favor of the LORD his God and humbled himself greatly before the God of his ancestors. And when he prayed to him, the LORD was moved by his entreaty and listened to his plea; so he brought him back to Jerusalem and to his kingdom.

2 CHRONICLES 33:12-13

Lest we think the exile was all about a *nation* that was punished for her transgressions and then restored, God points to a single individual whose life needed to be turned around. And it was! After all that King Hezekiah had done to bring Judah closer to the Lord, his son Manasseh defiantly led Judah back into idolatry. For that callous rebellion, God punished Manasseh by having him dragged off to Babylon with a hook in his nose. If anything can get someone's attention, that certainly should! And to his eternal credit, Manasseh genuinely and truly repented—so much so that God heard his prayers and restored him to the leadership of his kingdom. It is a wonderful story of brokenness and redemption. But more than that, it is a close-up snapshot, not of an entire nation, but the individual people and personalities who comprised that nation. Nations (as nations) do not repent. It is people who repent.

Were someone to say to us today that the church needs to repent of its materialism, its inattention to social justice, and its moral laxity, they could not be more right—or wrong depending on how we understand that reference to "the church." Some churches (as churches) do indeed need to repent for having adopted official doctrines that debase the holiness of Christ and the clear moral standards promulgated by God. Yet we miss the whole point when we look at churches as institutions we can hide behind. To say that "the church" needs to repent is merely to say that *you and I* need to repent—one by one, person by person.

■ **The discomforting question is: What "hook in my nose" would it take for *me* to repent of the sins of "my church"?**

_____

_____

_____

_____

Shame on You!

"I am against you," declares the LORD Almighty. "I will lift your skirts over your face. I will show the nations your nakedness and the kingdoms your shame."

NAHUM 3:5

Jonah surely would be saying, "I told you so!" To be fair, it has been over a century since the people of Ninevah sincerely repented in response to God's gracious overture. By the time of Nahum's prophecy, there has been a lot of water under the bridge. Even so, it seems that Ninevah is far more wicked than ever—not only turning again to idolatry, but developing a taste for barbaric atrocities. All this after God had shown them extraordinary mercy! No wonder God vows to shame them as if they were lewd prostitutes—raising their skirts over their heads to expose their shamelessness! Or rather, expose their *shame* as our featured verse puts it. *Shamelessness* is the ultimate *shame*! It's bad enough that people engage in reprehensible conduct, but when that sin is committed without the slightest moral compunction, the offense of the sin is greater still.

The shame of it all is that we too live in such a shameless culture. Certainly we're not to be compared with the depraved Ninevites, but a quick inventory of our national sins reveals that we now have little shame about practices which only a short time ago would have been considered utterly shameful. Like the proverbial frog in the kettle that gets cooked because it doesn't sense the water being gradually heated, society's moral conscience has deteriorated incrementally until it has become altogether desensitized. Of course the greater concern ought to be the attitude we personally have about our own sins. If we have learned to sin without shame, then shame on us!

■ **The embarrassing question is: Can I recognize any sin in my life that I've become far too blasé about?**

The Highest Praise

Neither before nor after Josiah was there a king like him who turned to the LORD as he did—with all his heart and with all his soul and with all his strength, in accordance with all the Law of Moses.

2 KINGS 23:25

If you could have anything at all said about you, what would you most want to hear? One would be hard-pressed to hope for a greater tribute than the one given to Josiah. Not even David, who also loved God with all his heart, received such a high accolade. The phraseology describing Josiah mirrors Jesus' famous pronouncement of *the greatest command*: "Love the Lord your God with all your heart and with all your soul and with all your mind and with all your strength" (Mark 12:30), which tracks the original formulation in Deuteronomy. If those criteria are so vital, how do *we* stack up, especially when that word "all" is used? *All* of the heart. *All* of the soul. *All* of the mind. And *all* of one's strength. Who among us can say that *all of us* is fully dedicated to doing the will of God?

The most intriguing question is why full devotion to God is subdivided into the subcategories of heart, soul, strength, and mind? Typically we are more comfortable talking about the heart (our emotional side), or the mind (our intellectual side), or perhaps our strength (the physical side of us). Far more difficult to express is how our whole *soul* can be dedicated to the Lord. Yet because the *soul* is that part of us which survives death, loving God with all of our *soul* is the most eternally significant task we face. Some of us have hearts for God, but not minds. Or minds devoted to God, but not hearts. And how about our *souls*? Having a specific checklist to double-check assures that no part of us is left without room for scrutiny.

■ **The challenging question is: What part of my emotions, intellect, strength, or soul has yet to be *fully* devoted to God?**

On the Threshold of Superstition

On that day I will punish all who avoid stepping on the threshold.

ZEPHANIAH 1:9

Knock on wood, no black cats will cross your path on Friday the thirteenth while you're trying to avoid walking under a ladder. And heaven help you if you break a mirror while opening up your umbrella inside the house! We're a superstitious bunch, aren't we? Fortunately for believers, common superstitions are mostly playful. For many folks, however, Zephaniah's rebuke of those who avoid stepping on the threshold hits closer to home. Undoubtedly Zephaniah was referring to what happened when the Philistines captured the ark of God and placed it beside their carved god Dagon. From the day that Dagon's broken head and hands were discovered lying in the doorway of his temple, the Philistines superstitiously avoided stepping on the threshold.

It is bad enough to indulge in cause-and-effect fantasies, as if stepping on a threshold might bring down the wrath of some phony god. But it is all the worse when superstitions reduce sublime spiritual reality to powerless substitutes. Take "knocking on wood," for example. When nature itself is worshipped as a god, it's not such a stretch to believe that touching a piece of wood could invoke mystical powers. But the Christianization of that superstition—"touching the wood of the cross"—begs belief. It is not the wood of the cross we need to touch, but the Son of God who died on it! If for that reason you and I don't "knock on wood," it doesn't necessarily mean we are not superstitious. Do we, for example, ever entertain the thought that we experience misfortune just because we've quit going to church lately? Or perhaps we are more protected when wearing a cross around our neck? Even for believers, superstitions can slip up on us like a black cat!

■ **The curious question is: In what subtle ways might I be more superstitious than I'd care to admit?**

Toying with God

"If a man divorces his wife and she leaves him and marries another man, should he return to her again? Would not the land be completely defiled? But you have lived as a prostitute with many lovers—would you now return to me?" declares the LORD.

JEREMIAH 3:1

God hates divorce. And no one knows why that is true better than those who have experienced divorce. The incomparable intimacy of marriage is not to be toyed with. It's no wonder that when God reluctantly permitted certificates of divorce (in Deuteronomy 24), he stipulated a "no return" policy. Once a man put away his wife, he could not remarry her if subsequently she had married another man. A spouse is not a plaything to be casually tossed aside one day and picked back up another according to one's whims. In our featured passage, God employs that very analogy to rebuke Israel's persistent unfaithfulness. Considering the rules pertaining to certificates of divorce, should Israel expect God to take her back after she had run off and "married" other gods?

The curious irony is that God is going to do just that—take back his unfaithful wife! We see this in the very next reading where God gives his bride a certificate of divorce but promises to restore her again into his good graces. The difference is that, unlike skirt-chasing, roving-eyed husbands, God himself never desired a divorce. Over and over again, he pleaded with Israel not to leave him, but she would not listen. Reluctantly and tearfully giving her the divorce for which her actions begged, God nevertheless promised to bring her back into his loving arms. God never toys with his people's love. It is we who toy with God's love—faithful today, unfaithful tomorrow, faithful again the following day. If the tables were turned, how would we feel if God kept defiling himself with others, then wanted back in our bed?

■ **The question for unfaithful lovers is: If I would never want God acting that way toward me, why do I keep acting that way toward him?**

The Unfaithfulness of the Faithful

The LORD said to me, "Faithless Israel is more righteous than unfaithful Judah."

JEREMIAH 3:11

There may be no more poignant line in the Scriptures than God's agonizing lament over Israel: "I thought you would call me 'Father'" (verse 19). Who could've imagined the sovereign God of the universe to be as vulnerable to emotional wounding as any parent whose heart has been broken by a rebellious child? Then again who *wouldn't* be pained by unfaithfulness and betrayal? But today's verse seems to make a far more sophisticated distinction between *faithlessness* and *unfaithfulness*. Perhaps the correct sense (as many translations suggest) is that, while Israel may have been guilty of *backsliding*, Judah was downright *treacherous*. Yet the ten northern tribes (Israel) and the two remaining tribes (Judah) have repeatedly turned to idolatry. If that is not both backsliding and treachery, what is? So we are left with the intriguing distinction between *faithlessness* and *unfaithfulness*.

Given the uncertainty of translation, it's worth considering whether we have paid enough attention to the crucial distinction between these two similar-appearing words. To speak of a person as *faithless* is to suggest a lack of faith altogether. Whether that person is a "nonbeliever," or maybe even a confirmed atheist, there is no question in our minds about their eternal destiny. Who could be more lost? Surprisingly, *we* could be! Are we ourselves faithful to God? "Well no," we admit, "but at least we have faith!" So which is better? To have no faith whatsoever, or to have a faith to which we are not faithful? Granting the many advantages of faith compared to no faith, the obvious point of the distinction is to drive home the importance of being faithful to the faith that we have. Unfaithfulness is not just backsliding, but sheer treachery.

■ **The question for believers is: Do I censure my own unfaithfulness as strongly as I condemn the faithlessness of unbelievers?**

Losing a Sense of the Serious

From the least to the greatest, all are greedy for gain; prophets and priests alike, all practice deceit. They dress the wound of my people as though it were not serious. "Peace, peace," they say, when there is no peace.

JEREMIAH 6:13-14

New York, New York, so good they named it twice," goes the popular song by Gerard Kenny. Maybe that explains why today's featured passage is repeated almost verbatim only two chapters later. As we sometimes say, "It's well worth repeating," particularly when something alarming is in the air. Kenny's tribute to his hometown mentions all the scandal and vice of the big city—and why he loves it! In both the song and in Jeremiah's prophecy, the scandal is not so scandalous that folks don't love it. In fact they can't get enough of it! It is easy to see how crazy New Yorkers would revel in the city's reputation for scandal and vice, but why would anyone ever choose to be blithe about sin? More to the point, why would those directly responsible for a nation's moral fabric deliberately abdicate that grave responsibility? Was it really just the money as our text suggests? Or the popularity that comes from telling people the lies they want to hear?

One wonders if the heart of the problem isn't found in that woeful line: "They dress the wound of my people as though it were not serious." Today we would sue them for medical malpractice! But it was not just a matter of negligent conduct. The problem was that the leaders of God's people had lost a sense of the serious. Had they recognized the *seriousness* of sin, the *seriousness* of faithfulness, and the *seriousness* of God's impending judgment, no amount of money could have bribed them, or any amount of popularity swayed them. In light of eternal judgment to come, it's time we all got serious. Really serious!

■ **The question worth asking twice is: Just how seriously do I address my own scandal and vice?**

The Ins and Outs of Faith

"The days are coming," declares the LORD, "when I will punish all who are circumcised only in the flesh…For all these nations are really uncircumcised, and even the whole house of Israel is uncircumcised in heart."

JEREMIAH 9:25-26

Why do children find bellybuttons so fascinating? And who even bothered to come up with the terms "innie" and "outtie"? After all, whether it is one or the other is only the random result of cutting and tying the umbilical cord. Sometimes the knot turns inward, sometimes outward. But when it comes to another "surgical procedure," it seems that God himself cares very much. No, it's no longer about whether a man is circumcised in the flesh, but whether a person is circumcised in the heart. Under Jewish law the outward, physical cutting away of the male foreskin was crucial to covenant identity. As a top priority, every male born into a Jewish family was to be circumcised on the eighth day. Not to be circumcised was equivalent to not being Jewish! As any Jewish rabbi, priest, or common citizen would be quick to tell us, circumcision was absolutely and positively indispensable.

So what is this "circumcision of the heart" that God seems to care so much about? It is the inner commitment to God that the outer fleshly circumcision was meant to represent. Of course the newborn who was circumcised had no personal inner commitment. That was to come later as he matured spiritually. This is why the initiating rite of Christian baptism is not merely symbolic of one's spiritual death, burial, and resurrection (like Christ's), but is a response to the believer's own personal faith commitment to God. For Jewish men (and the women they represented) the problem was that they were outwardly circumcised, but inwardly uncommitted. Today's variation on theme, sadly, is that many who wear the name *Christian* are soaking wet on the outside, but unconverted on the inside.

■ **The obvious question is: When it comes to faith, am I truly an "innie" or just a dunked "outtie"?**

Beyond the Point of No Return

Do not pray for this people or offer any plea or petition for them, because I will not listen when they call to me in the time of their distress.

JEREMIAH 11:14

Do you know that gut-wrenching feeling when you are late for an important appointment and there is absolutely nothing you can do to make up for lost time? Or the agony of having made a terrible mistake that you simply can't undo? When it's too late, it's just too late! Surely, only this can explain what otherwise is a strange verse indeed. Can we ever be so far down the wrong road that God refuses to hear our prayers? Isn't Jesus' story of the prodigal son a promise that the Father is always awaiting our penitent return? Or is that really the issue? Two factors seem to be at work here. One is that God's integrity will not permit him to listen to prayers when he knows he is not the only one to whom people are praying in their distress. How could God possibly listen when he hears prayers that are only hedged bets?

More important, Jeremiah is wasting his breath pleading on their behalf because God has already "pulled the trigger" on their promised punishment. The child who might have escaped a spanking with timely expressions of remorse cannot stop the hand already in motion simply with last-minute cries of woe! A people under judgment of God's wrath cannot thwart God's avengers once they are already at the city gates. The idea here is not that we are to stop praying that those who are unrepentant will yet repent. The point is that, as long as sinners (including us) are unrepentant, prayers to God are voiced in vain. Worse still, there comes a point in every life (if only at death) when it's just too late to avoid the consequences.

■ **The timely question is: Have I fooled myself into thinking that I've got all the time in the world—when actually my time on earth is running out fast?**

When Even Prophets Doubt

But I said, "Alas, Sovereign LORD! The prophets keep telling them, 'You will not see the sword or suffer famine. Indeed, I will give you lasting peace in this place.' "

JEREMIAH 14:13

Political campaign ads are surely the most maddening commercials on television. In a world of competing claims, it's almost impossible to know who or what to believe. Do the politicians themselves ever begin to doubt the truth of their own statements? Maybe not. But consider prophets of God like Jeremiah. After all, he was but one prophet among many…and seemingly the only one out of step with the others. Makes a person wonder if he was the only sane inmate in the asylum or crazier than he would like to admit. It would be nice to think that God's true prophets had a special way of knowing it was God speaking through them at all times. But if it were that simple, Jeremiah likely wouldn't be asking God such questions.

One does not have to be a prophet today to experience similar doubts. You and I obviously believe we have the truth, otherwise we wouldn't believe what we believe! Yet even true believers disagree among themselves about various moral, spiritual, and doctrinal issues. Honesty surely demands that we constantly reassess what we believe. Holding fast to our beliefs is even more difficult when we find ourselves virtually alone in what we hold to be true. The more people there are who believe otherwise, the more sane it is to question one's own sanity! Or at least one's understanding. And yet as Jeremiah's own ministry proves, God is more likely to speak truth through a lone, unpopular prophet than all the other pretenders put together.

■ **The question for honest believers is: Whether I see myself as a lone prophet crying in the wind or as part of a more orthodox mainstream, have I had a heart-to-heart with God lately about where his truth really lies?**

Who Is Influencing Whom?

Therefore this is what the LORD says…"Let this people turn to you, but you must not turn to them."

JEREMIAH 15:19

One often hears a gifted actor, entertainer, or perhaps politician express a passion for sharing their faith with the world through their profession. Praise God when that special salt and light happens! Sadly, there are more cases where, instead of their influencing the world, the world ends up influencing them. One prominent career after another has washed up on the shores of good intentions—sometimes even ending up in public disgrace. In light of today's featured verse, that shouldn't be surprising. If even a prominent prophet of God is vulnerable to that phenomenon, what chance do the rest of us have? Even for the prophets of old, as we have seen, the subtle charms of popularity and monetary gain that often accompany notoriety can be seductive beyond all resistance.

Of course most of us will never have to face the unique dilemma of stardom versus faith. Yet there is a sense in which all of us must fight the same battle. Merely trying our best not to be "of the world" while we're "in the world" is daunting enough. God-fearing celebrities face a larger, more obvious challenge to their faith, yet we are no less vulnerable to this world's seduction. While we're out there spreading salt and light, the reality is that we can easily (and unwittingly) be seduced instead by this world's dazzling lights and imitation salt. Never is that more true than when we intentionally rub up against people of the world in order to bring them to Christ. As noble as that goal is, it's hard not to get our hands dirty when lifting people out of the mud.

■ **The cautionary question is: Which has been greater, my influence on the world or the world's influence on me?**

I Can't Help Myself!

So the word of the LORD has brought me insult and reproach all day long. But if I say, "I will not mention his word or speak anymore in his name," his word is in my heart like a fire, a fire shut up in my bones. I am weary of holding it in; indeed, I cannot.

JEREMIAH 20:8-9

Dietrich Bonhoeffer, the German theologian who courageously spoke out against the unspeakable horrors perpetrated by Hitler and the Nazis, must surely have had second thoughts about blowing the whistle on the Third Reich's twisted faith. Like Jeremiah, Bonhoeffer too was ridiculed and thrown into prison. Unlike Jeremiah, Bonhoeffer eventually was executed for acting from his conscience. So what made him speak out? Why did he put his life on the line when silence would have kept him safe? Undoubtedly there was a fire in his bones that simply could not be contained. No matter the potential consequences, he couldn't help himself!

Yet the more difficult side of our featured passage is how Jeremiah felt *apart from* the fire in his bones. The larger context reveals that Jeremiah is sorely miffed at being called to such a degrading mission. Quite frankly he feels assaulted and bullied by God, who has forced him to be a prophet of doom smack-dab in the middle of a national spiritual renewal. Why wouldn't people think he's crazy! Yet despite every instinct urging him to shut up and go away, Jeremiah knows deep down that he has no choice but to speak the truth. If ever you have felt like God was asking too much of you or forcing you to be an embarrassing minority of one, you can certainly identify with Jeremiah's pique. But the odds are you also know exactly what Jeremiah meant about that "fire in his bones." When the Spirit is truly within us, sometimes we just can't help ourselves!

■ **The frustrating question is: How am I to feel about those times when there was definitely fire in my bones, but I conveniently managed to snuff it out?**

Just Sick About It!

When the king heard the words of the Law, he tore his robes.

2 CHRONICLES 34:19

No wonder Judah had gone off the rails! Without the Book of the Law to guide them, what else could have been expected? Yet there is more to this story than meets the eye. The fact that the Book of the Law had been *allowed* to be lost among the rubble raises interesting questions about Judah's spiritual apathy. Which came first—the decay of the temple or the decay of the people? Assuming the latter, then at one time the Book of the Law would have been safely ensconced in an intact temple, yet apparently ignored by the people and priests alike. More intriguing is the fact that the Book of the Law was discovered when the temple was in the process of renovation. So it is not as if Josiah, at least, wasn't already conscience-stricken about how far the people had departed from the religious practices contained in the Book of the Law. The Book may have been covered with layers of dust and rubble, but its truths still spoke powerfully to righteous hearts.

Why then should Josiah be so grieved that in anguish and remorse he tears his robes? Has he not inherited from his ancestors the basic teachings of the Book of the Law and absorbed its fundamental moral standards virtually by osmosis? Maybe Josiah's anguish is prompted by physically holding such a tangible reminder of just how far Judah has fallen spiritually. Or maybe he realizes it is not enough merely to have some vague idea about God's revealed Word. One wonders what Josiah would think about all the Bibles today that sit unopened and covered with dust in home after home of those who claim to be God's people. Would he not tear his robes all over again?

■ **The heart-rending question is: If my Bible, or any part of it, remains largely unread, why am I not just sick about it?**

Truth: A Crime Worthy of Death

Then the priests and the prophets said to the officials and all the people, "This man should be sentenced to death because he has prophesied against this city. You have heard it with your own ears!"

JEREMIAH 26:11

Who ever would have believed it—false prophets condemning a true prophet! Don't they know that by impugning Jeremiah they are bringing their own prophetic office into disrepute? When you can't trust one prophet, inevitably all prophets become suspect. More important, these popular prophets seem wholly uninterested in the truth, only the perceived disparagement of all they hold sacred. So what kind of prophecies do they bring? Only good news? Always something flattering? Hardly worthy of the title *prophet*! And then there is the shrillness of their condemnation. They will not be content until Jeremiah is dead and buried! Wow, what's going on here?

Whatever it is, it is a graphic preview of the Sanhedrin's strident demands for Jesus' death. When Jesus dared challenge the religious establishment of his day, the chief priests considered it an attack on the Jewish nation and bayed like wolves for Jesus' condemnation. Truth was irrelevant. They wanted only to maintain the system which assured their positions of authority. Incredibly, they were willing to take the life of an innocent man rather than consider the truth. But suppose for a moment that Jeremiah and Jesus were only teasing folks for a laugh. Would that have evoked calls for the death sentence? Not a chance. Or suppose what they said was merely offensive in style or tone. Still not a chance. If ever we wondered how important truth itself is, now we know. As even reprobates intuitively recognize, truth is a matter of life and death. And when truth is worth killing for, it must also mean that truth is worth dying for.

◼ **The true question is: Short of the unlikely prospect of being killed, what am I willing to forfeit in defense of truth?**

The Matchless Balm of Gilead

Go up to Gilead and get balm, Virgin Daughter Egypt. But you try many medicines in vain; there is no healing for you.

JEREMIAH 46:11

Merely mention Johns Hopkins Hospital or the Mayo Clinic and immediately people think of world-renowned medical centers. Absent a miracle from God, if you can't get cured there you're not likely to be cured. In biblical times Gilead had a similar reputation. Perhaps you recall that young Joseph was sold by his brothers to a caravan of Ishmaelite traders headed to Egypt, carrying spices, myrrh, and balm from Gilead. Even in Jeremiah's day, Gilead's reputation for its healing balms and physicians was still strong. So strong, in fact, that in an earlier chapter Jeremiah had rebuked the people of Judah saying that not even Gilead could cure their sinfulness. Here once again Jeremiah says virtually the same thing to Egypt—being all the more significant since Egypt itself had quite a reputation for its medicine and healing.

To be told by a doctor that your disease is incurable must be devastating. Unfortunately one gets the feeling that neither Judah nor Egypt ever gave much credence to their own terminal diagnosis. Their "disease," being spiritual in nature, did not faze them in the least. But for those who do long for spiritual healing (as the words of the classic spiritual proclaim), "There is a balm in Gilead, to make the wounded whole. There is a balm in Gilead, to heal the sin-sick soul." That "balm," of course, is not some medicinal salve, but the Great Physician himself who not only can heal the body but save the soul as well. Without him our sin-sick souls are indeed incurable. With him no condition is so desperate we cannot be cured.

■ **The life-giving question is: Because my physical life is undeniably terminal, how much attention have I given to healing my sin-sick soul?**

Silence Before God

The LORD is in his holy temple; let all the earth be silent before him.

HABAKKUK 2:20

Have you ever heard the short hymn "The Lord Is in His Holy Temple," sung to quiet everybody down? The words of the hymn are basically those in today's verse, followed by: "Keep silence, keep silence before him." No wonder this song is used to dampen the decibels of a vacation Bible school filled with noisy children or to bring a congregation of adults into a meditative mode. Yet Habakkuk is not talking about the absence of noise. He is contrasting the living God with lifeless idols. The sovereign God of the universe alone was to be worshipped. While there is no reason to listen to a carved piece of wood or stone, we have every reason to listen to the God who created both wood and stone—and us! If such a God might evoke tumultuous praise from our lips, our likely first response in his glorious presence will be one of awed silence. Not just literal quietness, but a profound sense of submission.

Theologians sometimes argue about the issue of silence in Scripture. When the Scriptures do not specifically address a particular matter of religious practice, is that silence *permissive* or *prohibitive*? The answer requires us to ask whether the silence was intentional or merely coincidental. Yet when God tells us clearly what he wants, he doesn't have to explicitly rule out every possible alternative. The question is whether we are tempted to think that we have license to do what we want just because God hasn't specifically ruled it out. If that is our attitude, maybe it is time to reconsider the importance of being silent in the presence of an awesome God!

■ **The disquieting question is: Do I ever speak my mind so loudly that God's voice can't be heard?**

A Respected Family Tradition

"Will you not learn a lesson and obey my words?" declares the LORD. "Jehonadab son of Rekab ordered his descendants not to drink wine and this command has been kept. To this day they do not drink wine, because they obey their forefather's command."

JEREMIAH 35:13-14

What family do you know of today that for generations has retained the spiritual values of its godly forebears? In a fickle era of "good king, bad king, good king," it must have been rare indeed to discover that the Rekabites maintained a consistent family tradition honoring Jehonadab's moral directive. (God himself is envious! Why can't his children honor him with the same respect?) The most intriguing aspect of Jehonadab's directive is that, except for the voluntarily Nazarite vow, there was nothing in the laws of Moses requiring complete abstinence. While the decision not to drink might certainly be wise, the fact that total abstinence was merely optional highlights all the more the respect of ongoing generations for the wisdom of distant forbears.

Because God's spiritual "fatherhood" is merely analogous, care must be taken not to infer blame on God for "his children's" rebellion. That said, it's worth exploring why Jehonadab's descendants consistently honored an exceptionally high standard of conduct. There must not have been the harsh, arbitrary legalism that so often alienates children. Jehonadab apparently had a loving way of impressing on his children the wisdom behind his unusual injunction. It is probable that the deep respect Jehonadab's descendants had for the wise patriarch was engendered by their knowing a truly holy and humble man of God. And his offspring must surely have been instilled with a deep respect for God himself. Respect at the highest level breeds respect at every level. If that formula worked for Jehonadab's family, why could it not work for godly families even today?

■ **The obvious question is: What might I myself do today to foster a respect for God that will last for generations?**

Contempt for God's Word

Whenever Jehudi had read three or four columns of the scroll, the king cut them off with a scribe's knife and threw them into the firepot, until the entire scroll was burned in the fire.

JEREMIAH 36:23

The story is told of the preacher having a Bible study with a couple about a particular doctrine. Because the doctrine was contrary to what they had been taught, the preacher was not making progress. So he left a list of all the Scriptures relevant to the subject for the couple to consider before their next meeting. The following week the couple announced that those Scriptures were not in their Bible. Thinking they simply hadn't been able to locate the passages, the preacher said, "Let's turn in your Bible and take a second look." To his amazement the passages literally weren't there. The couple had cut out every one of the controversial verses! If that story is true, then we are not far removed from what took place in today's featured passage. Just imagine… Jehoiakim calmly and deliberately slicing to shreds the scroll of the Lord that had been revealed to Jeremiah! And there is also that chilling postscript: "The king and all his attendants who heard all these words showed no fear, nor did they tear their clothes." Wow!

Few would be so callous as to cut up a God-inspired scroll, as Jehoiakim did, or to literally rip out disturbing passages, as the couple above. Yet there is little difference between using scissors to excise Scriptures and purposely ignoring passages considered to be troublesome. At Judgment we are far less likely to be judged on the technical correctness of our understanding as we are on our attitude toward God's revealed Word. Culpable ignorance is no less serious a sin than willful disobedience. Indeed what could be more offensive to God than coldly carving up his divine mind!

■ **The cutting question is: Are there any verses "missing" from my Bible because I've purposely chosen to ignore them?**

The Value of Higher Learning

To these four young men God gave knowledge and understanding of all kinds of literature and learning. And Daniel could understand visions and dreams of all kinds.

DANIEL 1:17

Not long ago many Christians were highly skeptical of higher education. Their concerns had some merit because higher education was once dominated by a godless secularism having potential to turn young people into skeptics. With the advent of "Christian" education at all levels, some of this concern has waned but not entirely. After all, many of today's most notable "secular" universities were founded as "Christian" universities. Scholarship in the ivory tower is so heady that it is difficult to acknowledge there is anything higher—even God!

Today's featured passage reminds us that God delights in human learning and understanding. Because he gave us minds capable of learning and a vast universe begging to be explored, he must intend the obvious process of education. Should we be skeptical of reading books written by nonbelievers? Not necessarily. Even though many of the so-called "great books" of western civilization were written by men who didn't know God as we do, they seriously engaged all of the crucial issues of life with which we need to struggle. Their keen insight into God's moral universe stands as powerful testimony that God's fundamental values are written on the heart and capable of basic understanding by every human mind. We need only to read the extraordinary works of Shakespeare to appreciate how divine truths can emerge from brilliant literature. Whether it is art, science, music, literature, history, or economics, God himself is the founder of Universe University!

■ **The educating question is: Have I been a serious student of God's vast universe or have I disappointed God by not being more curious to learn?**

_____

_____

_____

_____

A Surprising Work of God

"A curse on anyone who is lax in doing the LORD's work! A curse on anyone who keeps their sword from bloodshed!"

JEREMIAH 48:10

No, you didn't misread that second sentence. For all the times God has condemned bloodshed, this time it is his idea! In fact wielding the sword is characterized as being "the Lord's work"! What's more, there is harsh censure for anyone unwilling to do that deadly work! Perhaps those who have fought in bloody battles as members of the military can help us make sense of this hard passage. But for those of us who have never even picked up a weapon in anger, all of this is strange indeed. As always, context is the key. Today's passage is found in the middle of Jeremiah's tirade against the people of Moab, who for years have worshiped the god Chemosh. Perhaps you recall the time when Israel's King Joram joined forces with Judah's King Jehoshaphat and the king of Edom to attack Moab, then under the leadership of King Mesha. The battle was going so badly for Mesha that, in desperation, he sacrificed his son to Chemosh! The battle actually turned in Moab's favor, intensifying all the more the Moabites' love affair with their national god.

But now the time of Moab's destruction is at hand. God is fully intent on executing punishment long promised. And for those who will be God's agents of wrath, this is no time for hesitation. The battle must be engaged! It is time for bloodshed in the name of righteousness and justice! Although God no longer asks that you and I wield literal swords drawing actual blood, there are still battles to be fought. Moral conflicts, cultural wars, and doctrinal skirmishes all beg for brave and dedicated warriors. In the important battles of our own day, "a curse on anyone who keeps their sword from bloodshed!"

■ **The disturbing question is: Can I recall *any* battle I have fiercely fought on behalf of God's righteous cause?**

No Safety for Sinners

"As surely as I live," declares the LORD, "even if you, Jehoiachin son of Jehoiakim king of Judah, were a signet ring on my right hand, I would still pull you off."

JEREMIAH 22:24

"Signed, sealed, and delivered," so goes the saying. If you've ever seen any of the ancient legal documents in England, you undoubtedly have noticed those red circles of imprinted wax just below the signatures at the bottom of the parchment. Once a document was signed by the interested parties, sealed with their official imprints, and delivered to the appropriate persons, the document was forever binding. Today we no longer use the signet (or signature) rings that made the seals official, but in ancient times the king's signet ring, especially, was of great importance. The ring not only sealed vital documents but was a sign of the king's authority. Pharaoh gave his signet ring to Joseph to signify Joseph's authority to act on Pharaoh's behalf. In the story of Esther, King Xerxes first gave his signet ring to the evil Haman. After discovering Haman's treachery, the king retrieved the ring and then gave it to the righteous Mordecai. And when Daniel was thrown into the lion's den, King Darius sealed the den with his own ring so that Daniel's situation could not be changed.

That was the idea: No document written in the king's name and sealed with his ring could be revoked. So it is a powerful statement indeed when God says that were Jehoiachin himself God's own signet ring, he would throw him away! When it comes to punishing evil, God vows to pull out all stops! In his eyes nothing is more important than doing justice. Nothing is so valuable that he wouldn't give it up to atone for sin. In fact that's exactly what God did. Jesus Christ, the empowering "signet ring" on God's right hand, was the very seal of God's irreversible promise of salvation.

■ **The ringing question is: Just how deep an impression has God's right-hand "signet ring" made on my life?**

Praying for Alien Nations Where There's Alienation

This is what the LORD Almighty, the God of Israel, says to all those I carried into exile from Jerusalem to Babylon: "…seek the peace and prosperity of the city to which I have carried you into exile. Pray to the LORD for it, because if it prospers, you too will prosper."

JEREMIAH 29:4-7

A rising tide," so it is said, "floats all boats." Whether it is affluence for some that brings a greater measure of economic security for all or perhaps the enlightenment of the few that brings insight to a whole society, the principle has much truth to it. Of course it is just another way of saying that believers can be salt and light to the wider community. It's interesting that God should tell his people in exile to become a productive part of the culture in which they have become captive. He also wants them to be prolific in offspring, no doubt looking forward to the time when they will need to repopulate the land of promise and perhaps also desiring that they win over a pagan nation by procreation as much as by proclamation. The greater the raw number of believers in a culture, the greater the percentage of faith they represent.

There is a sense in which, even in a free "Christian" nation, we are being held hostage by an alien culture. We can choose to be assimilated into that culture, withdraw in isolation, or determine to have a positive impact on the society in which we live. While God warns against spiritual assimilation, he also calls us out of self-righteous or fearful isolation. Our role as "strangers in a foreign land" is not only to be a beacon of righteous productivity and fruitful godliness but to be prayer warriors on behalf of our culture so that it might flourish spiritually. For a nation that turns to God is a nation toward whom God himself will turn.

■ **The captivating question is: What could I pray that might float the culture around me on a higher spiritual tide?**

So Callous We Don't Care

"Am I only a God nearby," declares the LORD, "and not a God far away? Who can hide in secret places so that I cannot see them?" declares the LORD. "Do not I fill heaven and earth?" declares the LORD.

JEREMIAH 23:23-24

Signs often seen in well-known tourist destinations promise that "whatever happens here stays here." The suggestion is that you can go wild in that faraway place without having to worry about a ruined reputation back home. The fact that such signs even exist confirms our tendency to think that if we can keep our sins secret enough, we're safe. Yet as our focus passage reminds us, no holiday port of call is so remote or business trip so distant that God doesn't know what we're up to. By now the myth of "secret sin" is a familiar theme. Despite the obvious implications of today's passage, the sin Jeremiah is railing against is hardly a secret sin. Jeremiah is castigating counterfeit prophets for delivering false oracles to the people. For lying, for pandering, for misleading God's people—all of which was being done openly and brashly, not in secret.

So why the reference to "secret places"? Apparently the prophets were so callous about their public sin that they were wholly indifferent to God's watchful eye. So which is worse: to sin in secret somehow hoping God doesn't see, or to sin in public and still be convinced that God doesn't see? If perhaps the former is a misguided illusion, the latter is a mad delusion! Either that or it is merely the ultimate extension of secret sin. Become sufficiently blasé about our secret sins and, before we know it, we will be so callous that sinning in open defiance of God means nothing at all. This takes us full circle back to secret sin. In which case maybe there should be signs saying: "What begins here doesn't just stay here."

The escalating question is: If I would never brazenly sin in some open way, dare I risk sinning in private, hidden ways?

Wiping the Slate Clean

"In those days, at that time," declares the LORD, "search will be made for Israel's guilt, but there will be none, and for the sins of Judah, but none will be found, for I will forgive the remnant I spare."

JEREMIAH 50:20

Ever wish you could start all over again? Whether in a job, or in a marriage, or perhaps in some strained personal relationship, it would be nice to work with a clean slate. To have a fresh start—a new beginning. Once derailed it is hard to get back on track. Sometimes it is a matter of pride, not wanting to admit where we went wrong. Sometimes there is the difficulty of overcoming relationship patterns that have become set in concrete. And sometimes the problem has simply gotten beyond our control, being in the hands of others over whom we have no control. Far more serious, of course, are our persistent sins. Can they ever be forgiven? How, possibly, can we ever wipe clean the slate of moral failure?

We, of course, have no eraser sufficient to wipe any slate clean. Only God can do that. But do we really trust that he does…or *can*? Looking at the ongoing sin in our lives, it is hard for us to truly believe God has removed our sin once and for all. Yet look at today's text. If God would have trouble removing anybody's sins, surely it would be Israel's and Judah's. But there it is in black and white—God did just that! Oh, maybe not *all* Israel and Judah were forgiven, but at least a remnant was sufficiently cured of their idolatry and graciously given a clean slate. That gives us hope as well. Within each rebellious soul is a remnant just waiting to be redeemed—or *already redeemed!* So why, with such a clean slate, should we ever want to spoil it again?

■ **The renewing question is: If God can wipe clean the slate of sin within *me*, can I not also make fresh starts in broken relationships?**

Halfhearted Repentance

Recently you repented and did what is right in my sight…But now you have turned around and profaned my name; each of you has taken back the male and female slaves you had set free to go where they wished.

JEREMIAH 34:15-16

Today's passage brings to mind one of those windup toys that keeps running into objects and changing direction. First one way then another. What a perfect picture of Israel! Along with her idolatry had come widespread contempt for the law. Yet there was just enough residue of conscience that occasionally the people would make some feeble attempt to "repent." Sadly, it never lasted long. Whether periodic occasions of national repentance or sporadic attempts at repentance by individuals, the watchword was fickleness, not faithfulness. This passage is a good case in point. Under the Mosaic law, an Israelite servant was to be given his freedom after seven years of service. So when, in a rare moment of stricken conscience, some of the people belatedly released their indentured servants, one could easily predict that their "repentance" would be short-lived. Sure enough, as soon as there were weeds to be pulled and the laundry was piled high, the released servants were quickly forced back into service!

What's so frustrating about this ancient scenario is that it sounds an awfully lot like you and me. Despite our best intentions, we too "repent," then suddenly find ourselves caught up once again in the exact same sin we thought we had abandoned. No wonder we so easily identify with Paul's lament that he kept doing the very evil he hated! But just when we think he's telling us that we're all windup toys with no control over what we run into, Paul rebukes such a notion and calls us higher. Just because we have the capacity for halfhearted repentance doesn't mean we aren't also capable of wholehearted repentance!

■ **The challenging question is: Have I given up on my sins because I've repeated them so many times, or am I all the more determined to let God help me end the maddening cycle?**

God of Velvet, God of Steel

"Very well," he said, "I will let you bake your bread over cow dung instead of human excrement."

EZEKIEL 4:15

To say the least, talk of dung and human excrement is hardly typical devotional material! Yet who can fault the enactments God directs Ezekiel to perform—from lying on his side, to baking disgusting loaves of bread, to carefully measuring out a meager quantity of food and water each day, to using dried excrement for cooking? Overall, the idea conveyed is that Judah will soon suffer such catastrophic deprivations that food and water will be extremely scarce. Baking bread over a fire of dried dung is hardly exceptional. It can be a plentiful source of fuel for cooking, but it isn't possible to go out and gather dung during a time of siege. God describes an approaching time when only human excrement will be available.

While this somewhat bizarre prophecy is fascinating in itself, far more interesting is what the startling exchange between Ezekiel and God says about God's character. Though Ezekiel adamantly protests eating anything that is defiled, it appears that Ezekiel's greater distress is having to cook with human excrement. With all the other things God imposes on him (not the least being the death of his wife), this is what Ezekiel fixated on! Even so, a most amazing thing happens. The omnipotent creator God of the universe is touched by Ezekiel's squeamishness and permits animal dung instead. If that seems insignificant and unworthy of note, why was it noted? Could it be because God wants us to know he genuinely cares how we feel? Incredible as it might seem, the tough, demanding God of heaven turns out to be Mr. Sensitive himself.

■ **The thought-provoking question is: If God cares that much about my own sensitivities, should I myself not be more sensitive to others?**

Spinning Ezekiel's Wheel

I looked, and I saw beside the cherubim four wheels, one beside each of the cherubim; the wheels sparkled like topaz. As for their appearance, the four of them looked alike; each was like a wheel intersecting a wheel.

EZEKIEL 10:9-10

Ezekiel's famous wheel might remind some of the old Negro spiritual, "Zekiel saw de wheel way up in de middle of de air." But if the song itself gives us no insight into exactly what Ezekiel saw, there are plenty of folks eager to tell us. One of the most popular interpretations assures us that the wheel was a UFO carrying extraterrestrials. Others say the wheel represents the four points of the Zodiac. For those bent on cosmology, the "wheel intersecting a wheel" is said to be a picture of the planets following the movement of the constellations. Still others believe just as strongly that the reference to wheels was inserted long after the book of Ezekiel was written, in an attempt to introduce the celestial spheres of the Greeks. Since there was no word for *spheres*, the word *wheel* was used. One can even find advocates urging a "Star Wars version," that Ezekiel's wheel was a dimensional doorway or energy portal to heaven!

One wonders if the old rabbis didn't have it just about right when they concluded that, if anyone really understood the mystical passages of Ezekiel, he would know all the secrets of creation. But that doesn't seem to stop folks from brazenly putting their own highly speculative spin on Ezekiel's wheel or from believing virtually anything they are told, no matter how ludicrous. Ever wonder why we are willing to expend enormous time and energy on the mystical parts of Scripture, yet pay such little attention to what is crystal clear?

■ **The no-spin question is: Have I let myself become obsessed with interpreting the mysterious passages in Scripture rather than focusing on what is as plain as day?**

Sins of a Nation

The word of the LORD came to me: "Son of man, if a country sins against me by being unfaithful…even if these three men—Noah, Daniel and Job—were in it, they could save only themselves by their righteousness, declares the Sovereign LORD."

EZEKIEL 14:12-14

How could we *not* be a Christian nation? Just listen to all the public pronouncements which tie us to God: "One nation under God." "In God we trust." "Endowed by their Creator." And "Nothing but the truth, so help me God." But despite all the official God-talk, is it possible that one day we might become a "godless Christian nation"? As today's passage suggests, it was certainly possible for there to be a godless nation of God! And one could make the case that other "Christian nations" are already virtually godless. So what guarantees that God will not remove his blessings from this nation or any other? Lest anyone think that a righteous remnant can forestall God's heavy hand of judgment on a nation deserving of punishment, the words of Ezekiel suggest otherwise.

The most striking part of Ezekiel's warning is the reference to Noah, Daniel, and Job—each of whom would know what it means to be spared for the sake of righteousness. There was divine deliverance for each one. But their personal deliverance did not prevent other family members from suffering, or the exile of fellow countrymen, or—especially in Noah's case—the world's entire population from being destroyed. At some point the diminishing salt and light of a shrinking remnant of the righteous can no longer delay the inevitable. We delude ourselves if we think that ours, or any nation, is permanently safe as long as there is some residue of faith in the land. Need we ask Lot how safe Sodom was because of his presence?

■ **The urgent question is: What meaningful contribution might I make to help delay the death of a nation that talks admiringly about God while increasingly turning its back on him?**

Personal Accountability for Sin

The one who sins is the one who will die. The child will not share the guilt of the parent, nor will the parent share the guilt of the child. The righteousness of the righteous will be credited to them, and the wickedness of the wicked will be charged against them.

EZEKIEL 18:20

Suppose you were walking down the street and suddenly you were arrested (and later convicted) for a crime committed by somebody else. How would you feel? Fundamental to justice is the principle of personal accountability for one's actions. As with the Israelites, one might certainly suffer *consequences* flowing from another's sin—"even to the third and fourth generation." But *guilt* for sin is always personal, not vicarious. Fortunately you cannot be held responsible for my sins, nor I for yours. Nor, as Ezekiel declares, is the sin of parents punished in their children, or vice versa. It bears repeating, "The one who sins is the one who will die," not some other person. Unfortunately the flip side of that principle is true as well. No child will ever be saved by the righteousness of his or her parents, nor parents by the righteousness of their children. We all stand or fall on our own before the Lord.

In a rather different context, the apostle Paul affirms the principle of personal accountability for sin, saying that we all die spiritually *because all have sinned*. But then he says the most remarkable thing—that "the gift is not like the trespass." Whereas the *trespass* (sin) is always personal and never vicarious, the *gift* (salvation) is always vicarious and never personal. Were it otherwise, we could claim to have personally earned our own salvation! As it is, salvation is possible only by the vicarious, atoning death of Jesus on the cross. This puts a whole new slant on Ezekiel's message—the righteousness of the *Righteous Man* will be credited to the righteous!

■ **The personal question is: Am I constantly blaming somebody else for my own faults or perhaps lamenting that I don't personally deserve to be saved?**

The Lost Art of Discrimination

Her priests do violence to my law and profane my holy things; they do not distinguish between the holy and the common; they teach that there is no difference between the unclean and the clean.

EZEKIEL 22:26

The greatest lesson of the civil rights movement was that discrimination is evil. Institutionalized discrimination, in particular, had caused inestimable damage to people of color. Along with the movement for racial equality came the call for gender equality and a ban on all other forms of discrimination. Now virtually every institution proclaims, "We do not discriminate on the basis of race, religion, gender, age, or national origin." Want to get into trouble? Try discriminating against some minority or special interest group. Despite much subtle hypocrisy, discrimination has become the nation's number-one sin. Accordingly, the media, schools, laws, and churches send out the constant message: Don't discriminate! Don't discriminate!

Unfortunately there has been a tragic, unintended repercussion. Having been told so forcefully, "Don't discriminate," we no longer *can* discriminate! Between evil discrimination and righteous discrimination. Between just and unjust causes. Between right and wrong. As with Judah under its corrupt priests, we've been taught that there's no difference between the holy and the unholy, the moral and the immoral, truth and untruth. The grand irony is that, once there is no longer any universally understood distinction between right and wrong, then the moral basis for nondiscrimination laws themselves is undermined! For the truly discriminating, there is a time to discriminate and a time not to discriminate. Unless we know the difference between black and white, we have no moral justification for telling anyone *not* to discriminate between black and white!

■ **The truly discriminating question is: Have I allowed something quite right in today's culture to blind me to something that is quite wrong?**

Longing for the Bad Old Days

So I will put a stop to the lewdness and prostitution you began in Egypt. You will not look on these things with longing or remember Egypt anymore.

EZEKIEL 23:27

The sexually explicit personification of Samaria and Jerusalem as two promiscuous sisters engaged in a lifetime of wanton prostitution is shocking to the senses. The sister representing Jerusalem comes off even worse than her "older sister" on two counts. Even though Judah looked on as Israel unabashedly prostituted herself with forbidden idolatry, Judah disdainfully spurned the obvious consequences of Israel's sin. Judah ended up being even more religiously promiscuous than Israel had ever been—so much so that God sarcastically accuses Judah of being a prostitute who eagerly *pays out* for her services rather than *being paid*! Extending the analogy back to its roots, we see that the two sisters initially became prostitutes in Egypt—a reference to the fact that the children of Israel had first been seduced by idolatry while enslaved under Pharaoh. From then on, God's people played the harlot time and again with virtually anybody who solicited them!

As highlighted in our focus verse, one of the powerful undertones throughout this rebuke is the sisters' constant replaying of their many promiscuous escapades. Memories of their earliest dalliances keep flashing through their minds—as if yearning for the good old days (which, of course, could only be the *bad* old days). Among many other reasons for the exile, apparently God intended their captivity as a way to wipe out those addictive memories that kept feeding Israel's unfaithfulness—a warning for us today of the dangers of indulging in "the bad old days." It is hard enough to be holy in the present, much less complicate matters with the wistful unholiness of our past.

■ **The lingering question is: Have I completely buried the sins of my youth, or do I keep digging up unhelpful memories?**

Mark This Day!

In the ninth year, in the tenth month on the tenth day, the word of the LORD came to me: "Son of man, record this date, this very date, because the king of Babylon has laid siege to Jerusalem this very day."

EZEKIEL 24:1-2

Yesterday, December 7, 1941—a date which will live in infamy—the United States of America was suddenly and deliberately attacked by naval and air forces of the Empire of Japan." So began the solemn radio announcement by President Franklin D. Roosevelt of the surprise attack on America's forces in the Pacific. And that date has indeed lived on in infamy—as has June 6, 1944, the day the Allies invaded Normandy. More than half a century later, terrorists attacked the World Trade Center on September 11, 2001. It is now known simply as "9/11," the day that America's invulnerable sense of security came crashing down. It is not surprising, therefore, that God would mark so precisely for Ezekiel the exact date when the king of Babylon laid siege to Jerusalem.

That day in 588 BC should also be a date we moderns remember vividly because it is a definitive marker in time connecting us with a timeless God. A God capable of instantaneously telling Ezekiel about a far distant siege speaks not only of God's omniscience and omnipresence, but confirms that the events taking place were the purposeful fulfillment of God's many predictions. The fact that God powerfully brought his will to bear on Jerusalem on a given day in history means he is a God who interacts with divine purpose. So when we are told that "*today* is the day of salvation," you can mark it on your calendar that, even this very day, God is both laying siege to evil and saving souls from destruction.

■ The timely question is: Could this seemingly ordinary day actually be a day on which, behind the scenes, God is doing something extraordinary in my life?

I Live in Hope!

And though the city will be given into the hands of the Babylonians, you, Sovereign LORD, say to me, "Buy the field with silver and have the transaction witnessed."

JEREMIAH 32:25

"When pigs fly!" comes to mind. Or, "When hell freezes over." In other words, it's impossible! Even Jeremiah had to question his own prophecy about a restoration of Israel so complete that one day there would once again be buying and selling of property in a land systematically being razed by the Babylonians. "Are you kidding me, God?" he all but asked, dumbfounded. But God was not kidding. That day would actually come. (For that matter they're still buying and selling property in Jerusalem to this very day!) In the normal course of things, it is not unusual for bombed-out cities to be rebuilt, for drought-ridden lands to be regenerated, or for deathly ill people to once again enjoy full health. But never before or since the exile and restoration of the Hebrews has there been such a clear time of destruction followed by a precisely predicted date of restoration!

However dire the circumstances in which we find ourselves, there are at least two reasons for hope. The first is that life has a funny way of turning around, sometimes when we least expect it. The fortunes of life ebb and flow naturally like the tide. Yet, for believers, there is a far more important reason, confirmed over and over again in the life of God's people. Our God delights in restoration! He loves to "make pigs fly," especially when a skeptical world insists that they can't. And how he delights in miracles! In one biblical account after another, the blind see, the lame leap, and the mute are shouting praise to God! If "the impossible" can only happen when hell freezes over, then consider it done!

■ **The hopeful question is: Have I too quickly given up all hope over some "impossible" situation that God may yet turn completely around?**

Finding Our Way Home

Set up road signs; put up guideposts. Take note of the highway, the road that you take.
Return, Virgin Israel, return to your towns.

JEREMIAH 31:21

In Grimm's famous fairy tale, Hansel and Gretel first attempt to foil their wicked father's plan to abandon them in the forest by dropping pebbles along the path, leaving a trail home. The second time around, they leave a trail of breadcrumbs, which are promptly eaten by animals in the woods. So the children become lost. More often than not, the expression, "leaving a trail of breadcrumbs," presumes breadcrumbs are the objects of choice. Maybe that works on a dry day with no hungry creatures about, but rocks would be better. Better still would be guideposts and road signs as Jeremiah suggests. If God is going to bring the Hebrews back to the land of Canaan from their captivity in exile, they need to make sure they don't lose their way. Yet it's not likely Jeremiah is literally talking about the people finding their way back home at the end of seventy years. More likely he's saying: Before you know it, you'll be coming back on the very road you left on!

Even more important is the idea that, upon their return, Israel will need to carefully follow the ancient spiritual guideposts they had so carelessly overturned. When you take a trip into unknown spiritual territory, you'd better know how to find your way back! Knowing that there are times when we have gone far astray, we would do well to establish reliable markers in our faith so that, if we ever wander from the path again, we will not be forever lost. But those markers would not be *breadcrumbs* of faith, rather *rocks* of faith. In a fairy-tale world of vanishing values, mere breadcrumbs of faith are worse than useless.

■ **The crucial question is: How can I best establish my spiritual guideposts so that I never again lose my way?**

From Checklist to Wish List

"The days are coming," declares the LORD, "when I will make a new covenant with the people of Israel and with the people of Judah…I will put my law in their minds and write it on their hearts. I will be their God, and they will be my people."

JEREMIAH 31:31,33

What is the difference between *obligation* and *desire*? Or *have to* and *want to*? It is the difference, really, between the laws of Moses and the law of Christ. Between checklist religion and wish-list faith. Under the old law it was mostly a matter of checking off each and every duty imposed upon the people of Israel. And if you managed to adhere perfectly to the law, then you could convince yourself that you were a righteous person. After all, there was the law, written in great detail in black and white, to match your life against. By contrast when Jeremiah speaks of a new covenant to come, he is talking first of all about a "law" that no longer has the look and feel of a formal legal code. Not that there isn't any law at all. In fact all the same moral laws still apply as under the laws of Moses. Yet apart from the form of the "law" itself, the primary difference is one of motivation. If law-keeping under Moses was done *in order to be* saved, law-keeping under Christ is to be done *because* we are saved. It's not what we *have* to do, but what we *wish* to do!

On one level even children know the difference between *having to do* and *wanting to do*. Whereas strict do's and don'ts are tailor-made for children, maturity brings with it an appreciation for doing things without having to be told. No wonder the law was said to be a schoolmaster preparing the way for Christ. In Christ we finally grow up!

■ **The motivating question is: Do I live my life out of duty and obligation or out of the sheer joy of serving the Lord?**

_____

_____

_____

_____

With a Vengeance

This is what the Sovereign LORD says: "Because the Philistines acted in vengeance and took revenge with malice in their hearts...I will carry out great vengeance on them and punish them in my wrath."

EZEKIEL 25:15-17

Have you ever acted out of revenge? Or *wanted* to? Of course we've all wreaked revenge when we were children. Put in its best light, revenge partly is an outworking of self-preservation. Striking back at any threatening force is a natural defense mechanism. Yet with maturity we are able to discern the distinction between true threats and mere offense. Where mere offense, we learn to make a measured response or no response at all. It's when a person never gains that maturity that the sin of revenge enters the picture. Some folks have a tit-for-tat attitude toward the world, always ready to inflict instant judgment at the drop of a hat, but that's not likely your problem or mine. Typically we grapple with revenge only when someone has done something so offensive and outrageous that it seems *right* to retaliate!

At those times, hopefully, we remember that "'It is mine to avenge; I will repay,' says the Lord." Vengeance is God's job, not ours. Yet one could be excused for asking: If revenge is a sin for man, why is vengeance a divine prerogative? Apart from maintaining order on earth by encouraging restraint, perhaps vengeance is reserved for God because only he knows all the underlying circumstances and can judge what punishment is deserved... and when. Unlike men and nations, God would never get caught up in vicious cycles of senseless revenge. For us, in the meantime, taking it on the chin is a true mark of spiritual maturity.

■ **The even more challenging question is: If I have somehow managed not to throttle people who deserve throttling, can I move to the next step of not even *wanting* to throttle them?**

The Devil, You Say!

Your heart became proud on account of your beauty, and you corrupted your wisdom because of your splendor. So I threw you to the earth; I made a spectacle of you before kings.

EZEKIEL 28:17

Most often the devil is grotesquely depicted in his notorious red suit, complete with horns and carrying a pitchfork, ready to pitch sinners into the burning cauldron of hell. Unfortunately that improbable caricature of the devil has encouraged many to completely dismiss the reality behind the devil. As we know, the devil took on the form of a serpent in Eden. And although we are not told in what form he appeared when tempting Jesus, it is not likely he was wearing a red suit! To speak of "the devil" is to speak of Satan, that great tempter and adversary whose ultimate torment in the "lake of fire" is vividly described in Revelation. Yet for all we know about Satan, there is much more we do not know. In all his "roaming through the earth," is he omnipresent like God? Does he have such power over us that anyone can legitimately say, "The devil made me do it"? And if Satan really was a rebellious "fallen angel," why would God permit him the power to do whatever he does!

As generally assumed, Ezekiel's description of the ruler of Tyre contains an oblique reference to Satan. What the ruler of Tyre had in common with Satan was the sin of pride, which in Satan's case apparently was born of beauty and splendor. But whatever his appearance, the crucial thing about Satan is that he epitomizes pride. If knowing about Satan helps us understand anything at all, it is that pride always leads to destruction. Maybe that is why God permits Satan to exist—to be a visual image reminding us of how far we too can fall if we let pride get out of control.

■ **The bedeviling question is: Do I obsessively see the devil behind every sin or perhaps foolishly never consider the effect of his evil in my life?**

Who Do You Trust?

Those women will say to you: "They misled you and overcame you—those trusted friends of yours. Your feet are sunk in the mud; your friends have deserted you."

JEREMIAH 38:22

In times of crisis it's hard to know whom to trust. Put your trust in the wrong people, and you could end up in serious trouble. Consider a civil war, for example. Who among your neighbors is a secret informant, and who is on your side? Because we can never be completely sure, it's not surprising that normally we would turn to trusted friends for advice and counsel. But what if those friends are wrong—or not as loyal as we think? The problem with pitiful King Zedekiah is that, in the panic and fear of the siege, he ended up trusting the wrong source. Why anyone would take man's word over God's is a mystery. Even if the truth is ugly, it still remains the truth! One can live in denial only so long before running headlong into the truth. Just ask Zedekiah!

Because there's no way we can be totally sure of any human advice, our safest course of action is to seek God's counsel. In times of crisis, God may be more silent than we might wish, but he will never mislead or desert us. Through thoughtful meditation on God's revealed Word and fervent personal prayer, we have the best possible assurance of getting at the truth. Of course it is always easier to ask others what they think. That way we don't have to do any of the hard work ourselves. But, as Zedekiah could tell us, asking others is risky business. If they are right, we're in good shape. If they are wrong, we're as good as dead! So when trouble is pounding at our door, maybe it's time to remember that God himself is our most trustworthy friend.

■ **The practical question is: Shouldn't I already be inquiring of God right now, before trouble is at my door and it's too late to ask?**

Safe in God's Arms

But I will rescue you on that day, declares the LORD; you will not be given into the hands of those you fear. I will save you; you will not fall by the sword but will escape with your life, because you trust in me, declares the LORD.

JEREMIAH 39:17-18

Nothing is sweeter than watching a young child's first hesitant jump into the open arms of a coaxing father. If perhaps we can no longer personally remember that palpable childhood fear, we can certainly appreciate it. Yet the unspoken message coming through tiny faces contorted by sheer terror is always a wistful, "I really want to do it!" So the father says reassuringly over and over, "Come on. I'll catch you!" As the father nudges closer to narrow the gap and bolster the child's confidence, the big moment finally comes. After hesitant false starts, all of a sudden there's take-off! The youngster takes that exhilarating leap of faith, squealing with delight. Faith is like that. Desire mixed with fear. Longing to be in the Father's arms, yet ever so hesitant.

What's wonderful about today's text is that these words of promise are being given to Ebed-Melech, the Cushite, *after the fact*. You may recall that Ebed-Melech had come to Jeremiah's rescue after Jeremiah had been lowered into a fetid, dank cistern where, without someone's intervention, he surely would have died. Despite the obvious risk involved in approaching the king on Jeremiah's behalf, Ebed-Melech did not think twice before "jumping." And why? Because, says the text, he trusted in the Lord. Apparently Ebed-Melech had jumped in faith so many times before that fear had given way permanently to trust. Whenever we come to a point in our own lives requiring a similar leap of faith, it is reassuring to know that we've jumped successfully before. Practice may not make perfect, but it does make permanent.

■ **The question of trust is: Why am I still so hesitant to trust God after all the times he's already coaxed me and caught me?**

_____

_____

_____

_____

In the Depths of Despair

See, LORD, how distressed I am! I am in torment within, and in my heart I am disturbed, for I have been most rebellious. Outside, the sword bereaves; inside, there is only death.

LAMENTATIONS 1:20

When was the last time you were in the depths of genuine despair? What moment was so spiritually harrowing that you felt all was lost? Maybe you've never experienced the unique despair associated with sin, but for those who have, nothing comes close by comparison. Unlike even the devastation associated with death or disease, the utter terror born of moral failure is haunting. Only that kind of torment can make one appreciate the agonizing depth of lament recorded in Lamentations. With war, famine, and disease rapidly overtaking the people of Jerusalem, the question "Why?" must have plagued the minds of all who struggled to survive. And the obvious, painful answer was even more haunting: *Because of sin*! Sin that easily could have been avoided. Sin that seemed harmless at the time. Sin that everybody else was doing and thus appeared acceptable. Sin that is so easily committed, yet so impossible to undo. Sin that *always* has consequences.

When sin, and sin alone, is the root cause of grief, how great is that grief! Yet, in some respects, despair over sin and its consequences is to be welcomed. It's a wake-up call! If our sin was not already so obviously wrong that it couldn't get our attention, then what except pain and despair would do the trick? This poses an interesting question for those who have never experienced spiritual devastation. Is it because of a lack of sin or because the sins you've committed have not moved you to despair? Pity the sinner whose sins have no devastating consequences! Without a wake-up call, what reason is there to wake up?

■ **The alarming question is: If ever again I find myself in horrendous spiritual despair, will I hit "snooze" and turn over or open my eyes?**

Faithful as the Rising Sun

Because of the LORD's great love we are not consumed, for his compassions never fail. They are new every morning; great is your faithfulness.

LAMENTATIONS 3:22-23

And there was evening, and there was morning—the first day." And the next. And the next. Praise God for mornings! If creative types ever see a sunrise, it is only because they've worked all through the night! But for everyone else, the rising sun brings the exciting promise of a new day. The troubles of the previous day, if perhaps persistent, are not specifically to be repeated. Sufficient, indeed, is the evil of each day! Once ended, that day is forever past. Hope is always in tomorrow because—until the Lord returns—there will always be a tomorrow. And new beginnings. And God's unending faithfulness. How can we know that? Because the sun keeps coming up every day! The sun and the moon and the earth all remain faithful in their assigned courses, reminding us day by day that the One who made them all is himself faithful. As sure as there is night and day, God's love is constant. His compassion never fails.

In a modern world of unrivaled, unsettling change, the one thing we most desire is constancy. No hymn articulates that desire better than Henry Francis Lyte's classic prayer "Abide with Me," ironically written long before the catastrophic changes of our time. "Change and decay in all around I see," Lyte bemoans. He then petitions on behalf of us all, "O thou who changest not, abide with me!" Even when we must pass through the dark night of death, God's faithfulness will not fail. As life on earth becomes an eternal yesterday, our prayer is God's promise: "Heaven's morning breaks, and earth's vain shadows flee; in life and death, O Lord, abide with me."

■ **The reassuring question is: When the sun comes up tomorrow, might it just remind me of the hope renewed each day by God's constancy?**

_____

_____

_____

_____

Sincerely Seeking Direction

Be sure of this: I warn you today that you made a fatal mistake when you sent me to the Lord your God and said, "Pray to the LORD our God for us; tell us everything he says and we will do it."

JEREMIAH 42:19-20

When Br'er Rabbit got stuck on Tar Baby and fell victim to Br'er Fox, he "prayed" repeatedly that Br'er Fox wouldn't throw him into the briar patch. But that "prayer" was a ruse because the briar patch was exactly where Br'er Rabbit wanted to go! Is it possible that our own prayers can be just as self-serving? Conscientious believers are always in prayer that God will lead them. That is particularly true when crucial, life-changing decisions must be made: What job? What marriage? Which school? Which church? Where should we live? What house? There could hardly have been a more vital need for God's direction than in the aftermath of Jerusalem's destruction. It is not surprising that the ragtag remnant would seek out Jeremiah to learn God's will in the matter. "Pray that the LORD your God will tell us where we should go and what we should do," they implored. Yet quite unbelievably when Jeremiah conveyed God's message that they were not to go down into Egypt, they called Jeremiah a liar and went anyway!

As it subsequently appears, the only reason these folks went to Jeremiah in the first place was in hopes of getting God's blessing for what they had already decided to do. If that sounds crass, or arrogant, or stupid, have we ourselves ever been guilty of doing the same thing? When we pray for God's direction, do our own plans ever become the answer we are really after? If so, we deserve whatever true briar patch we get thrown into, and it won't be the comfortable briar patch we were hoping for!

■ **The prayerful question is: When I ask God to lead me, are his options only my options, or am I truly willing to be flung into whatever circumstance he chooses?**

Entertained, Not Pained

Indeed, to them you are nothing more than one who sings love songs with a beautiful voice and plays an instrument well, for they hear your words but do not put them into practice.

EZEKIEL 33:32

What is the difference between a Christian concert and a sermon? Maybe nothing, maybe everything. It is possible for a concert to be a sermon and also possible for a sermon to be a concert. In the latter case, the fact that a sermon turns into a concert might be the fault of the one preaching the sermon. (More and more pulpits have been turned into stages.) Or maybe it is the fault of those who regard the sermon as a concert. Here Ezekiel unquestionably brings a sobering message from the Lord, but the people receive it as little more than light entertainment. They probably even told Ezekiel on the way out how eloquent he was. Or perhaps how much his sermon (aimed directly at them) was needed by others. Where people's minds are during the most thoughtful and provocative of sermons is a mystery, though none of us is immune.

For example have you ever sat through a sermon calling you to higher purity and dallied with impure thoughts? Or listened to an impassioned plea to become less materialistic while envying the expensive car you saw on the way in? Or tolerated the preacher droning on about the need for fasting while trying to decide where to have lunch after church? We're downright pitiful, aren't we? Something deep inside tells us we ought to assemble and listen as God speaks to us, but when he does, it is as if we are a thousand miles away. Maybe it's time for a reality check. Heard any good sermons lately? Then again what do we mean by "good"? Good for what we *want* to hear, or good for what we *need* to hear?

■ **The confronting question is: How many sermons speaking directly to me have I managed to conveniently ignore?**

When Dead Bones Come to Life!

Then he said to me, "Prophesy to these bones and say to them, 'Dry bones, hear the word of the LORD! This is what the Sovereign LORD says to these bones: I will make breath enter you, and you will come to life.' "

EZEKIEL 37:4-5

Ezekiel's vision of dry bones coming to life has inspired one of the greatest spirituals of all time. What a macabre, hilarious picture comes to mind as the skeleton is gradually assembled, piece by piece from toe to head. As in, "Toe bone connected to de foot bone; de foot bone connected to de ankle bone," and so forth! Most amazing of all is the fantastic prophecy: "Dem bones, dem bones gonna walk aroun', I hear the Word of the Lord!" Whether or not we could hear the Word of the Lord, odds are if we saw a bunch of bones walking around in a cemetery, we'd be outta there! Skeletons are made for graves, not for rattling around all over the place. God's sense of humor is topped only by his sense of the miraculous. When it comes to dry bones coming to life, God is dead serious. Not only for Israel but for us.

In Israel's case this is a prophecy about a dead nation being restored to life following the Exile. Who would ever think it? In our case it's about spiritually dead people being brought to new life in Christ. Dead, buried, and suddenly dancing! Not only in this life, but in the life to come. Dead, buried, and one day resurrected. Who would ever think it? Well, no one actually, except for two things. The first is that God made good on his promise to restore Israel. The second is that God went a giant step further in Jesus' resurrection from the tomb. Dead, buried, and then marvelously alive! If that doesn't set your toes to dancing, what will?

■ **The rattling question is: If God can bring even dry bones to life, is there anything about my spiritual deadness he cannot wholly transform?**

Taking False Security in Righteousness

If I tell a righteous person that they will surely live, but then they trust in their righteousness and do evil, none of the righteous things that person has done will be remembered; they will die for the evil they have done.

EZEKIEL 33:13

Are you sure you are going to heaven? Before any of us answers that question, perhaps we would do well to take a deep breath and approach the question more thoughtfully than we normally do. For believers in Christ, the usual immediate answer is, "Yes, absolutely! I've been saved." But if you were to ask "Are you righteous?" you'd likely hear a far more hesitant response acknowledging the obvious, that none of us is wholly righteous. Although it is certainly true that our "righteousness" is imputed from Christ's, there must also be something equally true about today's text. Importantly, if our eternal security is dependent on God's own faithfulness, here God says that he has already assured this righteous person that they will *surely* live. Yet despite God's promise, it is obvious that this person can also *surely* die! The alarming message is that even a long life of righteousness could end up counting for nothing. Where one lapses irreversibly into a life of evil, a previous life of righteousness is no guarantee of spiritual security.

How, then, can we be sure of our salvation? As our text suggests, the answer lies in where we put our trust. If we're trusting in our own righteousness, we are only as safe as each day's righteousness. Yet as strange as it might seem, it only gets worse if we are trusting in our salvation itself to save us! As Paul reminds us when he asks, "Shall we go on sinning so that grace may increase?" (Romans 6:1), there is a fine line between *trusting in* our salvation and *trading on* our salvation. In the end, certainty about heaven is all about trusting God, not ourselves.

■ **The compelling question is: Have I ever seriously considered the subtle distinction between *saved* and *safe*?**

Regardless of the Consequences

"If we are thrown into the blazing furnace, the God we serve is able to deliver us from it, and he will deliver us from Your Majesty's hand. But even if he does not, we want you to know, Your Majesty, that we will not serve your gods or worship the image of gold you have set up."

DANIEL 3:17-18

What young children most remember about the bedtime Bible story of Shadrach, Meshach, and Abednego is that they were miraculously saved from the fiery furnace. And that exciting story is well worth remembering, even for us. A stop-action, slow-motion look at the biblical account reveals an extraordinary God with extraordinary power working in extraordinary ways. If God could save three men under these dramatic circumstances, then there is absolutely nothing God cannot do in my life or yours! Yet perhaps the more thrilling story is what leads up to the fiery furnace. When King Nebuchadnezzar threatened to throw these three Hebrews into the fiery furnace for refusing to bow down to his golden idol, they gave the determined reply highlighted in today's passage. That too is worth a second look.

If there was anything that Shadrach, Meshach, and Abednego were sure of, it was that God not only had the *power* to rescue them, but *would* rescue them! Though most would agree that God has that same power to rescue us even today, few of us indeed would confidently expect God to actually invoke that power in a similar life-and-death circumstance. Yet their remarkable confidence in God's saving power is not even the real story here. Rather, it is their determination to remain faithful to God whether or not he rescued them. Have we become jaded, knowing the happy ending? Countless martyrs have died *without* rescue! As might we some day—even if the only thing at stake for us is our job, our families, or our virtue.

■ **The provocative question is: What would I be willing to give up for the Lord, even if there was no hope of rescue?**

Catching a Greater Vision

Son of man, describe the temple to the people of Israel, that they may be ashamed of their sins. Let them consider its perfection, and if they are ashamed of all they have done, make known to them the design of the temple—its arrangement, its exits and entrances—its whole design and all its regulations and laws.

EZEKIEL 43:10-11

Why should anyone be moved to repentance by looking at a set of architectural drawings? (Good question for any church contemplating a building program!) But this is no ordinary set of plans. It wasn't even the blueprints for the temple that was to be reconstructed in Jerusalem. It was just a vision. But, oh, what a vision! Languishing in captivity with plenty of time to reflect on why they were in that predicament, the Jews were being forced to contrast their low estate with the former glory of the kingdom before they had turned to idolatry. At that time Israel's holiness was bound up in her laws, her priesthood, her sacrifices, and—most symbolically of all—her marvelous temple, which now lay in ruins. So to be given a grand vision of a new and glorious temple was to be reminded of how truly far they had fallen. More than that it was a call to return to a life consistent with that grand vision. To *catch* the vision. To *respond* to the vision. To *live worthy* of the vision.

But if it was only a vision, why all the intricate details? Why all the emphasis on entrances and exits? Perhaps to whet their appetites for the ins and outs of a radically different kind of kingdom and the time when that mysterious "Prince" would appear. One cannot help but think of another, similar vision, which we ourselves have been given in John's Revelation. Yet to focus on the mysterious details, as we typically do, is to miss the incredible power of such a grand vision to humble us, rebuke us, encourage us, and inspire us.

■ **The captivating question is: Is my vision of heaven truly grand enough to call me higher?**

The Name Says It All

And the name of the city from that time on will be: THE LORD IS THERE.

EZEKIEL 48:35

Can you identify the cities that match these nicknames: The City of Brotherly Love, The Big Apple, Big D, Music City USA, Sin City, Beantown, Tinseltown, and Motown? Typically nicknames for cities have some connection with either the actual name itself (Philadelphia or Dallas) or with something for which the city is known (Nashville's music industry or Boston's baked beans). Even biblically, Nibshan was known as the "City of Salt," Jericho as the "City of Palms," and, of course, Jerusalem as the "City of David." So when Ezekiel is given the vision of the new temple and the lands surrounding it, what could be more appropriate than a new name? More than just the often used "City of God" or "City of the Lord," the name of this visionary city will be: THE LORD IS THERE. Given God's omnipresence, perhaps that nickname should be unremarkable—unless, of course, there is to be something radically different about this coming city.

If John's Revelation is anything to go by, the "Holy City" yet to come will feel God's presence in a way never before experienced. In fact by contrast with Ezekiel's vision, in John's vision there isn't even a temple in the Holy City because "the Lord God Almighty and the Lamb are its temple." Nor will there be any need for the sun or the moon because "the glory of God gives it light." If the Lord's presence is already with us (even in Sin City!), how much more intimately we will know him in the Holy City to come! Where every eye will see him, and no one will ever again ask, "Where is God?" In that great eternal city on the other side, *THE LORD IS THERE*!

■ **The vital question is: Have I truly named the name of the One in whose holy presence I want to live forever?**

Out of Touch with Reality

Immediately what had been said about Nebuchadnezzar was fulfilled. He was driven away from people and ate grass like the ox. His body was drenched with the dew of heaven until his hair grew like the feathers of an eagle and his nails like the claws of a bird.

DANIEL 4:33

The bizarre account of mad King Nebuchadnezzar reminds one of mad King George III of England (1738–1820). When King George's health deteriorated, he began to act in strange, often embarrassing ways. Once he pressed his affections on Elizabeth Spencer, claiming that she was his queen and that Charlotte (his wife) was an impostor. George gave orders to people who were long since dead, imagined that London was flooded, and on Christmas Day called his pillow Prince Octavius! Evidence now suggests that King George suffered from porphyria, perhaps aggravated by arsenic in the medicine given to cure his seeming insanity. Like Nebuchadnezzar, King George eventually came back to his senses as if nothing had happened. What the two kings shared in common was temporarily being out of touch with reality.

In one sense that's true of all of us. When we speak of "this life" and "the life to come," we are talking about two radically different realities. Even within "this life," there are two competing realities as different as night and day. On Pentecost when the apostles were filled with the Holy Spirit and everyone heard them in their own language, many thought the apostles were drunk. They had no clue about the level of reality on which the Holy Spirit operates or the sublime level of spiritual reality being proclaimed. The message that day was about the need to move from one level of reality (this world) to a far higher level of reality (the kingdom of Christ). For those unwilling to acknowledge the critical difference, it can only be said that—not unlike Kings George and Nebuchadnezzar—they are temporarily indulging in the "insane"!

■ **The maddening question is: In which of the two competing realities do I mostly live?**

The Good, the Bad, and the Ugly

He replied, "You are talking like a foolish woman. Shall we accept good from God, and not trouble?"

JOB 2:10

Listen to virtually any newscast reporting some calamity, and you are likely to hear some survivor say, "I just thank God that I was spared!" Maybe God truly did save that person from injury or death—it wouldn't be the first time. But what are we to think about all the other people in that plane or building who didn't make it out alive? Are we to blame God for their deaths? As Job begins to sort out the perplexing conundrum of suffering, he is certainly right to acknowledge the obvious, that not everything that happens—whether good or bad—can be laid directly at God's feet. Yet even supposing that it could, Job is teaching us an even more important lesson: We should praise God in any event, whether it be blessings or curses. After all, we go out with exactly what we bring in—nothing!

To speak this philosophically and glibly of suffering does not mean that we don't have many hard questions to put before God, as did Job himself. It only means that we are able to put our suffering into a larger context. It also means that we are more hesitant to attribute to God whatever pain we experience. Perhaps we might think that if God sends us good, he is just as likely to send us trouble. On the other hand, it makes just as much sense to say that *because* God sends us good, it is not likely he would turn and send us trouble! In the ebb and flow of life, sometimes things are good and sometimes they are bad. What's important throughout it all is that we acknowledge God's overarching sovereignty and praise him for an eventual escape from whatever suffering we might encounter.

■ **The painful question is: Have I learned yet to praise God as much when I am truly hurting as when I am wildly ecstatic?**

Logical, but Wrong!

If God places no trust in his servants, if he charges his angels with error, how much more those who live in houses of clay, whose foundations are in the dust, who are crushed more readily than a moth!

JOB 4:18-19

Suppose that police radar indicates a car is going 80 mph. At that speed the car would travel 80 miles during a period of an hour. Right? Is it then logical to say that an hour prior to being stopped by the police the speeding car had been 80 miles away? It's certainly not illogical and might even be right, but it might also be wrong. The odds are that the driver came onto the highway only a few miles down the road and accelerated up to 80 mph. Just as that which is true is not always logical, that which is logical is not always true. In today's featured passage, Job's friend Eliphaz is quite sure that Job is suffering because Job has sinned. Doesn't one logically follow the other, he reasons. If God punished even his rebellious angels, why not mere mortals on earth? Seems logical, doesn't it? And certainly Eliphaz is right, that God punishes both men and angels for their sin. But does that logical hypothesis explain Job's suffering…or ours?

When Eliphaz goes further to argue that those who sow trouble reap trouble, he is still thinking logically. Almost always sin has adverse consequences. Yet Eliphaz exposes the vulnerability of his logic when he asks, "Who, being innocent, has ever perished?" Let's see…babies in the womb and Christian martyrs? What about our Lord himself? It's the same cause-and-effect bugaboo we've seen many times before. If the innocent often suffer through no fault of their own, then suffering is not necessarily caused by sin. The only thing we can say, which is both logical and true, is that human logic alone is not always the final answer.

■ **The logical question is: Do I rely too strongly on my own reasoning to understand a God who doesn't always follow my logic?**

Spitting into the Wind

How then can I dispute with him? How can I find words to argue with him? Though I were innocent, I could not answer him; I could only plead with my Judge for mercy.

JOB 9:14-15

To paraphrase Jim Croce's popular lyrics, you don't tug on Superman's cape, you don't spit into the wind, you don't pull the mask off that old Lone Ranger, and—most certainly—you don't mess around with God! Not that God relishes playing a tough guy. It's just the sheer distance between God and man that makes any desire for a genuine conversation rather fanciful. For all that Job would like to say to God (and hear *from* God), he is frustratingly aware of the cosmic gap between himself and God. Have you ever picked up a tiny ant and held it in your hand? Imagine suddenly hearing that minuscule creature calling your name and trying to have a conversation! If we put ourselves in the place of that lowly ant and envisioned ourselves in the hand of God, we would begin to get some idea of how Job felt.

So is it just spitting into the wind to talk to God? Are we off limits for wanting merely to *touch* God's cape or to catch a glimpse of what is behind the mask he often wears? If at times it seems God is stiff-arming us, at other times he practically opens his arms and hugs us! One of the ironies of the book of Job is that it is a personal gift to us from this "unapproachable" God. It is his way of telling us more about himself. Of being intimate with us. Of letting us know that he cares about how we feel when we are hurting. If God didn't care, why bother with revealing himself in the first place? And so we pray in desperation, comforted by the assurance that the Spirit himself supplies the very words we can never find.

■ **The daunting question is: How trusting am I that God's silence doesn't mean he's turned a deaf ear?**

A God Who Longs for Us

If someone dies, will they live again? All the days of my hard service I will wait for my renewal to come. You will call and I will answer you; you will long for the creature your hands have made.

JOB 14:14-15

On this date in history, horrendous death flashed before the eyes of a world watching aghast in total disbelief. Few who witnessed the shocking scenes unfolding at the World Trade Center that day can ever forget the chilling images, especially of "the jumpers" instinctively attempting to escape the conflagration. Death took on a whole new meaning that fateful day. Then again many of us have also known death far more personally, perhaps as we held the hands of loved ones as their souls winged their way into the life to come. Or is that last part just wishful thinking? *Is there really life after death?* Will those unknown desperate "jumpers" or the loved ones we knew so well really rise to live again?

Although for the Jews in exile the concept of resurrection was vague, it is clear from passages such as today's text that the idea of life after death was firmly entrenched in hearts of faith. Indeed even pagans took the afterlife seriously, as best evidenced by the Egyptian tombs. But if there is almost universal acceptance of life after death, rarely do we spend much thought on that profound reality. To get a better handle on the dynamics of *why* we will live again, we would do well to put Job's words into God's own mouth. After all, it is God who is speaking to us through this literary masterpiece. So it's as if God himself were saying to each one of us personally: "I will call, and you will answer. For I desperately yearn for you." Can there possibly be a more astounding thought than God eagerly awaiting my death, longing to hold me close!

■ **The perplexing question is: Why do I fear death so much when God is yearning to welcome me home?**

Our Advocate and Friend

Even now my witness is in heaven; my advocate is on high. My intercessor is my friend as my eyes pour out tears to God; on behalf of a man he pleads with God as one pleads for a friend.

JOB 16:19-21

Courtroom drama has been televised out of proportion to what actually takes place in the halls of justice. Yet we are familiar with the roles played by the various actors in a trial. The judge presides over the proceedings, the lawyers argue their clients' causes, and the witnesses, hopefully, tell us the truth. Sitting in the gallery are friends and family interested in the outcome of the case. Naturally we expect each of the participants to play their own unique role. The judge isn't going to testify as a witness, the lawyers aren't going to assume the bench, and—as much as they might want to—the friends and family in the courtroom are not going to suddenly jump up and argue the case. All of which makes today's passage so interesting.

Alluding to the Christ to come (of whom Job could have had no clue), Job speaks of a unique process of justice in which the Son of God in heaven is not only his lawyer advocating his cause before the Great Judge, but is also his chief witness testifying to the truth about his life. More intriguing is Job's confidence that this advocate doesn't just argue his case as a lawyer, but actually intercedes as a distraught companion begging mercy on behalf of his friend. Unaware of the messianic events still to unfold, Job speaks only wishfully. Yet in doing so, ironically, he becomes our own intercessor to the Father, pleading our need for all of the above—a respected advocate, a truthful witness, and a caring friend. With Christ's coming, the verdict is now in. Job has won his case!

■ **The question on trial is: Even with Christ as my advocate, witness, and friend, am I living my life in such a way that I make my case easier or more difficult?**

Vanishing in the Mist

Those who have seen him will say, "Where is he?" Like a dream he flies away, no more to be found, banished like a vision of the night. The eye that saw him will not see him again; his place will look on him no more.

JOB 20:7-9

Do you have any old family photos in black and white or maybe sepia that show your ancestors with those mandatory solemn faces and wearing old-timey frocks? Or do you perhaps watch those classic old black and white films featuring an earlier generation of actors? If so, do you ever stop to think that those people are now long gone? If that seems obvious to us, it would not have seemed so obvious to them when they were in their heyday. Oh sure, they all knew they would eventually die, but no time soon. Now consider your own high school or college yearbook. Odds are that a number of your contemporaries have already died. And the day will come when those who follow after us will look at *our* pictures and simply take it for granted that we have been dead and gone for a long time.

Although in today's passage Zophar is speaking specifically of the wicked, the fact is that—when it comes to the brevity of life—we are all in the same boat. We are here for the briefest of time, then quickly gone like a passing dream or vision in the night. If that is cause for depression, it is also reason to celebrate each day that we are given and make it as productive as possible. If a chain is no stronger than its weakest link, what strength will we give to generations unknown that follow after us? Amazing though it may be, how we live our lives cannot help but have an impact on someone down the road who knows us only through some cracked or faded photo.

■ **The long-range question is: If my time on earth will influence future generations of unknown souls, what legacy am I leaving?**

What Does God Get Out of It?

Can a man be of benefit to God? Can even a wise person benefit him? What pleasure would it give the Almighty if you were righteous? What would he gain if your ways were blameless?

JOB 22:2-3

Job's friend Eliphaz could hardly be more cynical in asking these questions. Because he doesn't believe Job is as righteous as he claims, Eliphaz is taunting Job with the thought that God couldn't care less if Job were completely and totally righteous. This raises a few good questions: What's in it for God? Why did he make man in the first place? And what pleasure, if any, does God get when we are righteous? We can only speculate, of course, but surely there must be something to the idea that we were created in God's image and are called God's "children." Why do parents have children, knowing in advance how much trouble they can be? Despite recognizing the great risk of disappointment associated with bringing children into the world, even new parents intuitively sense the special fulfillment that comes in having offspring. Naturally it is hard to think that God, being God, would need that kind of fulfillment. It's not as if God is somehow incomplete or lacking anything…is he?

By his nature God is the very picture of completeness. But that is not to say God likes being alone any more than we do. Because we are like him and he like us, God must also relish the joy of fellowship. Yet for a holy God, there is obviously a limitation on his ability to fellowship with that which is unholy…which would be *us*! Why then would God *not* take pleasure in our righteousness? This means that God can have even closer fellowship with those who are righteous. Because all parents find pleasure in children who are well-behaved and respectful, should our heavenly Father feel any different about us?

■ **The flip-sided question is: If God takes pleasure in my righteousness, how must he feel when I am *not* righteous?**

Can Man Be Righteous?

How then can a mortal be righteous before God? How can one born of woman be pure? If even the moon is not bright and the stars are not pure in his eyes, how much less a mortal, who is but a maggot—a human being, who is only a worm!

JOB 25:4-6

What kind of genius does it take to call attention to the obvious? Bildad must be awfully proud of himself to ask such profound questions! Compared with God, who indeed can be righteous? But having stated the obvious, is there nothing more to consider? For example, what are we to do with the many Scriptures that call us to righteousness? Or those that promise abundant blessings for *being* righteous? Sure sounds like God himself thinks we should be righteous and *can be!* Indeed, will he not judge us for *not* being righteous? So although it's true that we could never be as righteous as God, it doesn't mean that we can't be righteous to the extent that God expects us to be righteous. Isn't that equally obvious? What's fascinating about the obvious is that typically there is something equally obvious hidden just beneath the surface that makes the obvious not so obvious!

In this passage, for instance, there are some less-than-obvious points shouting for attention. The first is that Bildad's second question ("How can one born of woman be pure?") has an answer as important as it is surprising. While normally such a thing would be highly improbable, the fact is that Jesus of Nazareth, though born of a woman, was unquestionably pure. "But he was *God*," someone quickly insists. True, but he was also the Son of Man, and for good reason—to demonstrate that the "sons of man" can be righteous! Far from being "maggots" and "worms" incapable of righteousness, you and I *can* be pure. And *must* be.

■ **The obvious question is: Do I ever use God's matchless purity as a feeble excuse for telling myself that I'm just too human and helpless to be pure?**

Learning to Discern

For the ear tests words as the tongue tastes food. Let us discern for ourselves what is right;
let us learn together what is good.

JOB 34:3-4

All of us can instantly taste the difference between *sweet* and *sour*. The same goes for salty and unsalty, spicy and bland, frothy and smooth. We certainly know what chicken tastes like, even if snake and other suspect foods are proverbially said to "taste like chicken"! And who couldn't recognize a burger with their eyes closed! But just how fine-tuned is your palate? If a gourmet chef were eating a dish prepared by somebody else, that chef probably would be able to recognize most of the secret ingredients. Any cook familiar with spices and flavorings will usually be able to identify tastes the rest of us wouldn't have a clue about. Most of us just dig in and enjoy the overall result, wholly undiscerning. Pretty much like we typically listen.

When it comes to listening, normally we can distinguish between loud and soft, near and distant, human and nonhuman. Most can recognize differences in pitch and tone. Usually we can even distinguish between serious talk and jesting. Yet how many "listening gourmets" are there? How many of us can discern what we *hear* as proficiently as what we *taste*? Even fine listeners may have no discernment whatsoever when it comes to distinguishing between different kinds of talk—say, talk that is truthful and talk that is subtly deceptive. Or talk that is logical and talk that never connects all the dots. How many people, for instance, can recognize when an argument fails to carefully distinguish between Issue A and Issue B? Learning to "taste" words with discretion is a godly art. What's at stake is the crucial discernment of ideas, teachings, doctrines, and ultimately truth. Not all words have the same flavor. Some are deliciously right while others are disgustingly wrong.

■ **The discerning question is: How good am I at listening critically and carefully analyzing what I hear?**

Seeing Is Believing

You said, "Listen now, and I will speak; I will question you, and you shall answer me." My ears had heard of you but now my eyes have seen you. Therefore I despise myself and repent in dust and ashes.

JOB 42:4-6

Have you visited modern Israel? If so, you will know how illuminating that experience is to your understanding of the Scriptures. Perhaps all your life you've read about Jerusalem and had some vague idea in your mind about how it might have looked during biblical times. Despite obvious changes over the centuries, you would be surprised how much remains of the old city of Jerusalem since Jesus and the apostles walked on some of those very stones. And if you have ever wondered how a pilgrim traveling *south* to Jerusalem could be "going up" to Jerusalem, as numerous passages indicate, to be in Israel is to understand the topography of the land. Jerusalem is higher in elevation than some cities to the north. And don't forget to walk through Hezekiah's tunnel or to visit the ruins of Jericho and the Sea of Galilee. Merely to *hear* about Israel is nothing like *seeing* it for yourself.

Yet Israel is merely the setting for the greatest story ever told—the story of sin and salvation, of disobedience and punishment, of obedience and blessing. It is the story of covenant, and sacrifice, and redemption, and—above all—God himself. Maybe you've heard that marvelous story a thousand times. Maybe you are hearing it for the first time. Either way it's one thing to *hear*, but another to *see*! It's one thing to *know*, and another to *understand*. Indeed, it's one thing to *understand* and another to *act upon* that understanding. Not until we have personally experienced the difference between being lost and being saved can we say that we truly "see" the God of our salvation.

■ **The important question is: Do I know a lot about God but still have a long way to go before truly "seeing" him?**

_____

_____

_____

_____

The Cry of the Faithful

If we had forgotten the name of our God or spread out our hands to a foreign god, would not God have discovered it, since he knows the secrets of the heart? Yet for your sake we face death all day long; we are considered as sheep to be slaughtered.

PSALM 44:20-22

In a variety of different ways, the classic question we keep asking over and over is: Why do bad things happen to good people? Never has that question been more sharply focused than for the faithful remnant who, along with their idolatrous neighbors, were victims of the brutality experienced during the exile. Though they had not bowed their knees to idols, they were being punished along with all the others who had. So how could that punishment be just? It's a timeless question asked by generations of the faithful who have faced undeserved suffering. An easy answer, of course, would be that it wasn't punishment at all, only a matter of chance circumstances in which all of us get caught up from time to time. Yet that only begs the question of why God would allow his faithful people to suffer at the hands of sheer fate.

More intriguing is another possibility typically overlooked in the conversation—that the faithful remnant may not be completely without responsibility for what is happening to them. Just because they didn't personally bow down to idols isn't the end of the story. What had they done to stop their neighbors from worshipping idols? What words of rebuke had they passed along to the priests who they knew were either winking at the people's sin or actually joining in sin with them? What had they done to warn their children against forsaking God? When bad things happen to good people, the definition of *good* is always worth a second look.

■ **The probing question is: If I feel like I don't deserve the bad things happening to me, is it possible I've overlooked what I might have done to prevent some of them from happening?**

Singing the Blues

There on the poplars we hung our harps, for there our captors asked us for songs, our tormentors demanded songs of joy; they said, "Sing us one of the songs of Zion!" How can we sing the songs of the LORD while in a foreign land?

PSALM 137:2-4

As popularized in song, this poignant passage begins with the familiar words: "By the rivers of Babylon, we sat and wept when we remembered Zion." Perhaps no words better capture the heaviness of heart that followed in the wake of the deportations to Babylon. Exiled far from home, discouraged, and hopeless, the Hebrews couldn't think about the former glory of Jerusalem without weeping. How far indeed they had fallen! And to make matters worse, the locals taunted the Hebrews to sing some of their national songs. Undoubtedly the Babylonians knew how important Israel's psalms were to the fabric of Hebrew society, so—seizing on their captives' despondency—the Babylonians hatefully tried to "rub it in." And did a good job of it! How could the Hebrews sing while feeling so sad? Yet the irony is that their lament about not being able to sing is captured in a *song*—which they must have *sung*!

Wouldn't you love to know *how* they sang this song? If our own genre of songs is anything to go by, odds are they were singing the blues. "Blues" songs are almost always mournful laments emerging from deep wells of hurt and pain. They speak of broken hearts, broken backs, and broken lives. Ever known that kind of pain? Do you know what it's like to have such a heavy heart you don't feel like singing? If so, the best way out of the doldrums, oddly enough, is to sing your way out! Sing the blues if you must, but *sing*! Whenever the heart is heavy, music is just what the doctor ordered.

■ **The energizing question is: Have I ever considered the power of music to stir my soul when I am down in the dumps—especially music that articulates the depths of my despair?**

A Different Kind of Kingdom

He was given authority, glory and sovereign power; all nations and peoples of every language worshiped him. His dominion is an everlasting dominion that will not pass away, and his kingdom is one that will never be destroyed.

DANIEL 7:14

The rise and fall of nations and empires has been widely chronicled over the centuries. We may be more familiar with Egypt, Babylon, Persia, Greece, and Rome, but other great cultures have also come and gone, including the Mayans, the Incas, and the Ottomans. At the height of each of those empires and cultures there weren't likely any residents who anticipated that culture's demise. Yet eventually all of them fell, as will the seemingly invincible world powers of our own time. The underlying causes behind this cycle of nations have also been well documented, from ascendancy, to decline, to extinction. National arrogance and pride have led to internal moral decay, ushering in a vulnerability to external forces previously considered unthinkable. Far from insuring a great culture's longevity, its power, prosperity, and prestige inevitably bring about its own undoing.

What Daniel sees in his marvelous vision is a being that looks ever so human, but who is ushered into the presence of the Ancient of Days and made ruler over a kingdom that never ends. What may have been a mystery to Daniel is no mystery to us. That flesh-and-blood Son of Man was Jesus Christ the Son of God, who—having been raised triumphantly from the dead—ascended through the clouds into heaven in a scene strikingly reminiscent of Daniel's vision. In that wondrous ascension, Christ transcended every human notion of authority, rule, and reign. Unlike any human kingdom, his spiritual kingdom will last forever. No decline and no fall. No corruption and no decay. So who wouldn't want to be part of a kingdom like that?

■ **The timely question is: Why should I fear the current decline and fall of culture if my true citizenship is in an eternal kingdom?**

The Frustrating Matter of Prayer

As soon as you began to pray, a word went out, which I have come to tell you, for you are highly esteemed.

DANIEL 9:23

Wouldn't it be great if every time we prayed (or even occasionally) Gabriel would show up to tell us God's response? But he doesn't, does he? Maybe this frustration explains why many people never pray or pray only perfunctory prayers as if never expecting any answer. But how are we to account for all the millions of people who *do* pray and pray fervently as if they really believe God answers their prayers? Just knowing that Gabriel apparently didn't show up every time Daniel prayed should be of some encouragement, as is the fact that the Bible records hundreds of prayers that seemingly received no response whatsoever from God. What's more, if today's verse tells us anything at all, it is that God is listening to us from the moment we begin to pray! If that doesn't set the mind racing, what does? The God of the universe listening to *me*?

If we get frustrated not hearing clear answers to our prayers, imagine how frustrated God must be when he doesn't hear particularly meaningful prayers from us! Think back on all your prayers. Were any worthy of a divine conversation? Were they serious prayers? Specific prayers? Passionate prayers? Humble prayers? In particular, how many of your prayers have been deeply confessional prayers like Daniel's? Most of us would have to confess that we rarely pray such agonizing confessional prayers. Most of our prayers are "wish-list prayers." To sit in anguish and pour out our sins before a holy God might be a new experience for many of us, but well worth doing. Yet it's hard not to think that, for such a prayer, God is too touched to speak.

■ **The prayerful question is: When was the last time any prayer of mine might possibly have moved God to tears?**

Dirt or Derision?

Finally these men said, "We will never find any basis for charges against this man Daniel unless it has something to do with the law of his God."

DANIEL 6:5

If someone wanted to dig up dirt on you, how difficult would it be? To his eternal credit, Daniel was squeaky clean. No matter how hard they tried, Daniel's enemies could turn up nothing whatsoever to impugn his character. No dirt or scandal. Not even rumors of whiffs of traces! In fact the only reputation he had was for being wholeheartedly loyal to his God and resolutely obedient to the exacting laws of the Jews. So if Daniel had any Achilles' heel, his enemies concluded, it was his unflinching faith. And it was there that they laid their trap. Because they knew Daniel would not obey any law that ran afoul of God's law, all they needed was the king's decree punishing anyone praying to any god or other man. No sooner had Daniel courageously prayed in defiance of the king's decree than he found himself in that legendary lions' den.

That Daniel's enemies had to resort to exploiting his faith tells us about more than Daniel's personal integrity. If total dedication to God's law produces such an impeccable character, what must that say about the law itself, if not that it is uniquely and perfectly designed to be character-forming? And if that is the case, then the opposite must be equally true. Whenever a person's moral character can easily be impugned, you can rest assured that in some serious way God's law has been ignored. This brings us full circle to the opening question. If it wouldn't be all that difficult for someone to dig up dirt on you and me, maybe it is time we think again about just how committed we are to God's law.

■ **The arresting question is: What would I find more troublesome about my life, the dirt someone could turn up or having a faith commitment so weak that no enemy would think to exploit it?**

The Pedigree of Faith

The following came up from the towns of Tel Melah, Tel Harsha, Kerub, Addon and Immer, but they could not show that their families were descended from Israel.

EZRA 2:59

Genealogies are all the rage. For some, tracing one's ancestry is fascinating and fun. For others it is serious business. While it can have some risks, tracing one's family tree and learning of one's forebears is a great way of bridging generations. Indeed, one's pedigree can be vitally important to one's personal identity. One can only guess how disconsolate the people referred to in our text must have been over not being able to prove their Jewish bloodline at a time of national patriotic fervor. For Jews, more than for most, lineage was crucial. Nothing could be more important than proving they were the offspring of Abraham because it was with the children of Abraham alone that God had covenanted his promised blessings. No wonder the Scriptures are filled with genealogical records. To be a "son of Abraham" was to have a unique relationship with the God of heaven.

With Christ's appearance came a whole new way of proving one's spiritual identity. Although Jesus himself had the most extensive genealogy of anybody (all the way back to Adam…and God!), he forever changed the genealogical rules. No longer is one a "son of Abraham" by ancestry or lineage, but by faith. All who are children of God by faith in Christ Jesus are "sons of Abraham" and heirs to the spiritual promises made to Abraham. Whether Jew or Gentile, Christ's disciples have all "descended from Israel." We *are* the spiritual Israel! So if you want to trace your bloodline of faith, it's always only one generation back, to the blood shed on the cross. To be a child of God is to have the most easily provable lineage ever!

■ **The identifying question is: Is my pedigree of faith determined mostly by my family tree or by my own personal, loving response to Jesus Christ?**

Rest and Rise!

As for you, go your way till the end. You will rest, and then at the end of the days you will rise to receive your allotted inheritance.

DANIEL 12:13

For those in the military hardly anything is more welcome than "R & R." Particularly during times of hostility, rest and relaxation is just what the weary soldier needs to regroup physically, mentally, and emotionally. Cruelly, of course, the much-anticipated break from the horrors of war is but a temporary respite before the soldier must return to the front line. While today's text presents us with an intriguing parallel, we are introduced to a rather different "R & R" experienced, certainly, by every soldier who is killed in battle and eventually by each of us. Here at the end of his life, Daniel is told that he will *rest* for a time and then *rise* on the great Day of Resurrection when the multitudes who now "sleep" will awake—some to eternal life and others to eternal condemnation. As with Daniel, *rest* and *rise* is the destined "R & R" for each living soul who dies. Far from being just a temporary respite, however, it is the final respite from the fearful struggles of this embattled world.

If one lives long enough, advancing age has a way of becoming a battle for survival. Body parts just don't work like they used to. The mind itself begins to play tricks. And gone is the energy and strength of youth! If you don't yet know what it means to feel worn out all over, that day is likely to come. In the end we all need a good long rest. And that is God's promise. But resting forever would find us "asleep" forever, and that simply won't do. If there is a *resting*, there is also a *rising*! As soldiers of the cross, what could be more welcome than that glorious R & R!

■ **The challenging question is: If I look forward to the day of my rising, do I look forward with equal excitement to my destined period of rest?**

Under God's Protective Eye

But the eye of their God was watching over the elders of the Jews, and they were not stopped until a report could go to Darius and his written reply be received.

EZRA 5:5

On the side of a dollar bill opposite from the bust of George Washington is a seal featuring an unfinished pyramid having thirteen steps representing the original thirteen states and the country's future expansion. Atop the pyramid is the "Eye of Providence," and above it in Latin are the words *Annuit Cœptis*, meaning "He is favorable to our undertakings." The idea is that God is watching over the United States to bring prosperity and security. Whereas we have previously considered the all-seeing eye of God as sternly monitoring our earthly actions, the "Eye of Providence" is a visionary eye. A protective eye. In today's text the eye of God was not just *watching*, but *watching over* Israel's elders to ensure that nothing got in the way of their making progress on the temple. If we feel uncomfortable with God watching our every thought and deed, perhaps we take comfort in knowing that, moment by moment, God is watching over us!

By some happy coincidence, immediately to the right of the words *Annuit Cœptis* are the words *In God We Trust*. Why *shouldn't* we trust God, knowing that his protective eye is looking after us in every adverse circumstance? If God could break into history to intervene in the political dynamics surrounding the restoration of the Jews, he can certainly break into history at any other time on behalf of his people. Why then do we place such heavy reliance on the dollar bill itself (or stacks of them!) rather than the profound assurance of God's protective providence so graphically depicted even on our money?

■ **The comforting question is: If I am facing some difficult challenge in my life, how can I not be wonderfully encouraged by knowing that God is truly watching over me?**

Toward a Great Glory

"Who of you is left who saw this house in its former glory? How does it look to you now? Does it not seem to you like nothing?…The glory of this present house will be greater than the glory of the former house," says the LORD Almighty.

HAGGAI 2:3,9

Did you ever go back to a house you once lived in as a child, only to be disappointed at how small it was? Now that we are grownups, houses that once seemed huge seem more like doll houses. So we can understand the disappointment of elderly Jews contemplating the rather less grand temple planned on the site of the old. Yet Haggai insists that the glory of the new would far exceed the old. One wonders if Haggai isn't pointing to a more profound glory yet to be associated with the temple that one day would evolve from the one under construction. For when Herod later refurbishes this same temple, it will be honored with an earthly visitation of the incarnate God. During his life and ministry, Jesus would literally walk on stones being laid during this very restoration. As both a twelve-year-old youngster and later an outraged Messiah cleansing the temple of its abuse, the Lord of heaven would bring a special glory to the temple by his personal presence!

Because we ourselves are said to be the "temples" in which God now dwells, we might at first question just how glorious our "temples" could ever be, especially given the sin that has so corrupted them since an age of pristine innocence. While we can never go back and recapture our former innocence, the quite wonderful promise for God's children is that, with Christ's personal presence in our lives, "the glory of this present house will be greater than the glory of the former house."

■ **The edifying question is: If ever I long for the former days of childlike innocence, am I not buoyed by the thought that, in Christ, I now experience the far greater glory of his forgiving presence?**

Where the Real Power Resides

So he said to me, "This is the word of the LORD to Zerubbabel: 'Not by might nor by power, but by my Spirit,' says the LORD Almighty."

ZECHARIAH 4:6

Ever feel absolutely hopeless for the task ahead? Faced with determined enemies from without and beset by fellow immigrants more interested in building their own houses than erecting the temple of the Lord, Zechariah must have wondered what strength he could possibly muster to complete the task to which he had been called. Neither a powerful king nor an influential priest, Zechariah was just a lowly prophet of God, spurring the people to action…at a snail's pace! It is human nature, of course, to think that all we need to accomplish the task is simply a matter of mustering more punch and power. Maybe that explains why we bang on faulty appliances, as if a demonstration of brute force will convince the dratted thing to work! Whatever the situation, God reminds both Zechariah and us that doing the seemingly impossible is within his power alone, not ours.

For those of us who believe, the question is not what God *can* do but what he *will* do, or perhaps *does* do. Could the answer to that question lie in the particular task at hand? Whereas God might leave us to our own devices to accomplish goals of our own making, of one thing we can be sure: If the task ahead is God's own plan, there is no way that we can fail! Does God's temple need to be rebuilt? It will happen! As will any other daunting task to which God might call us. To think that we've got to dream up powerful schemes to further God's kingdom is to forget that all God needs is one or two "who are anointed to serve the Lord of all the earth"!

■ **The daunting question is: Might I myself be one of those "one or two" through whom God's Spirit might even now be moving mightily to accomplish some seemingly impossible task?**

Why Do We Worship?

Ask all the people of the land and the priests, "When you fasted and mourned in the fifth and seventh months for the past seventy years, was it really for me that you fasted?"

ZECHARIAH 7:5

Perhaps you have gone to church all your life, week in and week out. Some of us were "gospel greedy," going twice on Sunday and yet another night during the week. For others there were special religious seasons and celebrations to be observed. Maybe even times of fasting or feasting. If you are blessed to be past seventy, perhaps you can especially appreciate the question in today's featured passage. Paraphrasing only slightly: When you attended all those religious services over the past seventy years, was it really for God that you did it? At any age that may seem like a particularly odd question. *Why else* would we devote all that time to church activities if not for God!

Here's a reality check. Think back on last Sunday. Assuming you went to church, can you recall having any conscious thought about getting up and getting dressed in eager anticipation of meeting with God? Was there any question in your mind about whether you would go to church, or did you just take that for granted because it was Sunday morning? Did you go simply out of habit? And if you didn't particularly want to go to church but did anyway, why was that? Was it out of obligation? When you actually got to church, what did you enjoy most? Was it the music, the Lord's Supper or Eucharist, the sermon—or perhaps the socializing? And how did you feel as you left the church building? Had you truly communed with God? Serious soul-searching just might reveal that we may "worship" regularly for numerous reasons other than strictly to please God. But do we really think that pleases God?

■ **The thorny question is: If it's not really and truly for God that I "go to worship," is it still worth going through the motions?**

Skipping the Traces

They would not be like their ancestors—a stubborn and rebellious generation, whose hearts were not loyal to God, whose spirits were not faithful to him.

PSALM 78:8

After reading over half the Bible, does it occur to you that there's an awful lot of seemingly endless repetition? Why do we hear over and over about Israel's unfaithfulness and rebellion? Why does God keep repeating that after he has punished Israel he will restore them…and that the Jews will finally shed their penchant for idolatry and honor him as the one true God? Why so much emphasis on Israel and the Jews when there were many more nations on the face of the earth? Could it be God knows that, like the Jews, we too are "a stubborn and rebellious generation" and that repetition is sometimes necessary to get through to stubborn folks? As believers in Christ, we too are God's "chosen" people. Any lessons appropriate for a rebellious "chosen" people are appropriate for us as well.

The timing of this particular psalm—coming after the exile—suggests the importance not only of Israel's past rebellion but of their emerging reformation as a nation. What all this repetition emphasizes most is that there's no spiritual rebellion that cannot ultimately be turned around into faithfulness. No departure from God so extreme that there's no way back. No persistent sin that can't be overcome. No bad habit that can't be broken. And we're not talking about nations as *nations,* but nations as *individuals*—like you and me! Israel's long, sad—yet now exhilarating—history is a powerful parable worth repeating. Maybe, as with Israel, it might take a traumatic personal exile to get our attention, but just imagine the dramatic and lasting transformation when we finally come home!

■ **The potentially transforming question is: Is there any persistent sin in my life that God will discipline me to overcome?**

The Day of Salvation

The stone the builders rejected has become the cornerstone; the LORD has done this, and it is marvelous in our eyes. The LORD has done it this very day; let us rejoice today and be glad.

PSALM 118:22-24

On a particularly beautiful day, it is not unusual to hear someone exclaim, "This is the day the Lord has made!" (quoting a more traditional translation of this verse). Praise God for beautiful days and rainy days as well, for every day is "the day the Lord has made." But this familiar line is contained within a psalm of salvation from sin, especially pertinent to the Jews who were being reconciled to God after their notorious descent into idolatry. For all of us who have ever experienced our own descent into sin, there is little wonder why there should be rejoicing at the thought of being forgiven and restored. Yet there is also an allusion here as to how that salvation would come about. The hope of salvation for mankind would come on a day like any other day except for one pivotal event, never before experienced and never to be repeated. On that day the "stone" widely rejected by first-century Jews would become the very capstone of God's plan to save sinners.

We are talking, of course, about Jesus Christ, who died on the cross for your sins and mine. On that day of unfathomable divine sacrifice, the spiritual destiny of the world forever changed. So in a broader sense, there's not just *one*, but *three* days of salvation that the Lord has made. First is that day in history when Jesus bore our sins on Calvary. Second is that life-changing day when we submitted our lives to Christ in full obedience. And still to come is that glorious day when Christ will return to claim his own. When it comes to any of these three marvelous days, not even the most beautiful day can compare!

■ **The comforting question is: When days are particularly dreary, can I not still truly exult in "the day the Lord has made"—the day of my salvation?**

Sowing Tears of Joy

Those who sow with tears will reap with songs of joy. Those who go out weeping, carrying seed to sow, will return with songs of joy, carrying sheaves with them.

PSALM 126:5-6

No pain, no gain" is as true as it is trite. Each of us has more than proved this obvious truth simply by emerging into the world at the cost of great pain to our mothers who—despite the pain—were filled with joy. Today's featured passage is all about pain and gain. About exile and restoration. Resignation and exhilaration. Hopelessness and hope. Seventy years of scorn, rebuke, and humiliation certainly ought to get one's attention! It could just as easily have backfired, generating bitterness and resentment against God. Indeed many of the Jews died during the exile, having never witnessed the promised restoration. Not all tears reap joy. It is only after we finally emerge from the pain that we can fully appreciate what we have gone through to get there. In the midst of the ordeal, there is mostly pain—not gain.

So what about those who, throughout an entire lifetime, *never* experience the joy? In a hurting, seldom-seen "third world" are millions whose tragically brief lives are filled only with tears, whether shed or unshed. They're the truly hungry. The perpetually diseased. The oppressed and brutalized who dread the approaching shadows of each night and fear the knock on the door…if they even have a door. For those of us fortunate enough never to experience such abject horror and despair, what greater joy we might feel if somehow, someway we could actually increase our lesser pain in order to lessen their greater pain. For all of us, of course, the ultimate joy can never be known in this life—only in the life to come when we will look back on whatever degree of pain we have known as if it never existed!

■ **The hope-filled question is: What "seeds of pain" am I sowing now that soon will bloom into sheer joy?**

_____

_____

_____

_____

Inviting Bells

On that day HOLY TO THE LORD will be inscribed on the bells of the horses, and the cooking pots in the LORD's house will be like the sacred bowls in front of the altar.

ZECHARIAH 14:20

Would it surprise you to know that bells are mentioned in Scripture in only two contexts? The first is in connection with Aaron the high priest, whose robe was designed by God to have a hem of pomegranates alternating with tiny gold bells. Why the bells? Quite incredibly, "The sound of the bells will be heard when he enters the Holy Place before the LORD and when he comes out, so that he will not die" (Exodus 28:35). Apparently the purpose of the bells was to announce Aaron's coming into the presence of the Holy One, as if mortal man dare not approach God casually or unannounced. In a sense the bells acted as a "doorbell," seeking an invitation into God's very presence. Who would deign to simply barge in without ringing the bell? Yet mysterious as today's featured verse is, it seems to send an entirely opposite signal. As Zechariah anticipates the coming of the Messiah, he speaks of a day when "holy bells" will not be on priestly garments, but on horses!

With the coming of Christ, the eternal High Priest, we have now entered into a radically new era in the relationship between God and man. No longer does God hold us at arm's length. No longer must we stand on formalities. As his children we don't have to ring the doorbell to gain an entrance into our Father's presence. Day or night, in good times and bad, he is always freely accessible. In the person of Jesus, praise God, the distance between the secular and the sacred, the mortal and the immortal, has been forever narrowed to the width of a cross!

■ **The ringing question is: How often do I take advantage of this new freedom to come into God's holy presence?**

A Twofold Tale of Courage

But when the attendants delivered the king's command, Queen Vashti refused to come.
Then the king became furious and burned with anger.

ESTHER 1:12

The wonderful story of Esther's legendary courage quite rightly bears her name. As Mordecai predicted, Esther had indeed come into a royal position for just such a crucial time. While God was obviously at work behind the scenes, it was Esther's courage in risking her life that saved a generation of Jews from what could have been the first holocaust. Yet Esther was not the only character in this inspiring story of courage. We mustn't overlook Queen Vashti and the pivotal role she also played in this historic episode. Without her extraordinary courage in refusing the king's command, the rest of the story never would have happened. Some might ask by what right Vashti refused the king's command. Whether Vashti was a "believer" is unclear. Yet sensing that the king wanted to display her physical beauty before his court in a drunkenly perverse and prideful way, Vashti rightly refused to lower herself to such a degrading display.

Vashti's resolute moral courage was rewarded by being made an example to all other wives. Wouldn't do for the other women to follow her defiant, insubordinate lead, now would it! All the king and his officials could think about was making sure that men were the unchallenged "rulers" in their homes. The high moral ground prompting Vashti's "insubordination" would have been completely lost on them, as it so often is with those who are devoid of spiritual values. And not just them, but also with those of us who openly espouse spiritual values but—at points of critical testing—lack the moral resolve of these two courageous women.

■ **The moment-of-truth question is: Am I sufficiently courageous to do the right thing even when the consequences are potentially disastrous?**

Hurting Only Ourselves

So they impaled Haman on the pole he had set up for Mordecai. Then the king's fury subsided.

ESTHER 7:10

The expression "Hoist on his own petard," was immortalized by Shakespeare in *Hamlet*. Historically, a "petard" was a primitive explosive device used in medieval warfare to make a breach in a fortification by blowing up a gate or a wall. Should the devise fail to operate properly, it was easy for the "bomber" himself to be hoisted into the air and killed. In such a case, the intended plan to harm others ironically backfired. Hence Shakespeare's use of the phrase as Hamlet alters the death warrant intended for himself to be death warrants for Claudius' two messengers, Rosencrantz and Guildenstern. They were thus "hoist on their own petards," as was the evil Haman, who was impaled on a pole he himself had set up. The scene is almost comical—like those cartoons in which the evil character is scorched when the bomb intended for his nemesis explodes in his own face.

If only self-inflicted bombs were comic relief. Unfortunately, being hoisted on one's own petard happens too often simply to dismiss it with a laugh. At some point most of us have personally felt the very blast we intended for others. Even what might seem like doing justice to others sometimes has a way of boomeranging to our own peril. Whatever the context, he who fights fire with fire is liable to be burned. That's why the Bible is as sensible as it is theological. The many admonitions to self-control, tolerance, and forgiveness are not just arbitrary rules to be obeyed but sound, practical advice.

■ **The sensible question is: Next time I'm tempted to strike out at someone who deserves it, might the visual image of being hoisted on a petard be a helpful thought?**

Sniffing at the Lord's Table

"But you profane it by saying, 'The Lord's table is defiled,' and, 'Its food is contemptible.' And you say, 'What a burden!' and you sniff at it contemptuously," says the LORD Almighty.

MALACHI 1:12-13

"Actions speak louder than words," so it is said. And sometimes actions speak volumes when no words are spoken. Such is the case here, where the people's deplorable temple sacrifices virtually shouted out what they would never dare say. Without actually *saying*, "the Lord's table is contemptible," they had made the Lord's table an object of contempt by offering blemished sacrifices. It is hard not to be struck by the obvious parallel with the Lord's Supper, a ritual which we often describe as "meeting around the Lord's table." Is it possible that there is some way in which we might unknowingly "sniff contemptuously" at the Lord's Supper?

Consider the frequency—or lack of it—with which we even come around the Lord's table. When Jesus instituted the Supper (around a table), he said that as often as we partake of it, we proclaim his death until he comes again. Some of us are doing precious little proclaiming! Then there is the matter of participating in a worthy manner. Not that we are *worthy* to partake, but certainly we must not take it in a manner unbefitting the profound significance of the occasion. In fact the more regularly we gather around the Lord's table, the more contemptuous we can be. Familiarity can indeed breed contempt. Of course today's passage would suggest that it's what we are bringing in sacrifice to the Lord that counts most. To participate in the Lord's Supper without giving over our lives to Christ merely mocks the ritual. To observe Christ's sacrifice without wholehearted personal sacrifice is to sniff contemptuously at the sacred emblems.

■ **The humbling question is: When I gather around the Lord's table, do I truly do honor to that sublimely meaningful moment?**

Not Just Talking the Talk

I was ashamed to ask the king for soldiers and horsemen to protect us from enemies on the road, because we had told the king, "The gracious hand of our God is on everyone who looks to him, but his great anger is against all who forsake him."

EZRA 8:22

Doesn't the adage wisely warn us not to put all our eggs in one basket? Better to hedge our bets and put some of our eggs in another basket…just in case. Doesn't it simply make sense to have a backup plan? So when it comes to trusting in God, is there any reason not to exercise prudence? Surely God does not want us to be silly about our faith. To throw all caution to the wind. To let go of the steering wheel believing that God will guide us safely down the highway around every curve and bend! We can understand, then, that Ezra's first thought was to ask for soldiers to accompany his band of people who were about to embark on a journey rife with danger from deadly enemies. Given the obvious threat, it would have been a wise precaution. Yet Ezra also knew that, after all his talk about God's protective hand, asking for such protection would send the wrong signal to skeptical nonbelievers. If Ezra's God was able to protect him, why would he need soldiers?

One simply has to believe that Ezra's subsequent prayer for God's protection was uttered in sheer terror. With the courage that only profound faith can muster, Ezra was putting all his eggs in one basket! When was the last time you and I put everything on the line because of our faith? When did we refuse to hedge our bets, trusting God completely with our very lives? It's one thing to talk big about God's protection and provision, but another thing altogether to make that risk-it-all leap of faith.

■ The embarrassing question is: How often do I pray for God's protection, then put my reliance for protection in any and everything *but* God?

_____

_____

_____

_____

Less Than We Deserve

What has happened to us is a result of our evil deeds and our great guilt, and yet, our God, you have punished us less than our sins deserved and have given us a remnant like this.

EZRA 9:13

Open the morning newspaper on almost any given day and it's likely you will see an article reporting some ludicrously lenient sentence handed down by a liberal, wet-noodle judge. The beast who raped a vulnerable ten-year-old girl is let off with the time served awaiting trial. Or maybe it is the drunk driver who killed a whole family, yet gets not so much as a day's time in jail. With good cause the community is outraged. "Why don't criminals get what they deserve?" we demand! But that is how we speak when we are talking about *criminals*. When it comes to our own sins, few of us would wish to be punished according to what we deserve. The problem is that the line between sinners who violate man's law and sinners who violate God's law is more blurred than we would like. Much of man's law was God's law all along—especially any law having moral implications. So in God's sight, you and I are also criminals, law-breakers, culprits, and outlaws. Do we not, then, deserve more punishment than we receive?

Ezra thought so. Not that he desired greater punishment. His point was how gracious God is despite our great sin. Yet far from being a liberal, wet-noodle judge who places such blame on society that the offender is simply let off the hook, God is merciful specifically in order to instill in each of us a greater desire to mend our sinful ways. Too often we take advantage of his mercy and continue sinning. But it needn't be that way. If ever we could see the vastness of God's mercy in relationship to the seriousness of our sin, we'd renounce sin forever!

■ **The ever-disturbing question is: How am I most moved by God's mercy—to greater purity or to greater sin?**

When Body Language Speaks

I had not been sad in his presence before, so the king asked me, "Why does your face look so sad when you are not ill? This can be nothing but sadness of heart."

NEHEMIAH 2:1-2

Do you remember Casper the friendly ghost? Depicted as a bouncing baby, Casper was too cute to be ghostly. When you and I think of ghosts, we tend to think of disembodied spirits, just as the apostles did when the risen Jesus suddenly appeared to them through a bolted door. But, like Jesus, Casper had form and body and substance. When Casper was happy, he was dancing. When he was sad, he was drooping. Not a word had to be said for us to know how he was feeling. As with humans, Casper exhibited a universal body language. If we think of our own bodies as packages in which our spirits dwell (something like Casper), we shouldn't be surprised that our "packages" are affected by whatever mood our spirit is in. No wonder our "packages" expand to their complete height when our team wins the game or droop and slouch when our team loses.

Has anyone asked lately why you are looking so "down"? If more than one friend dares to ask, maybe we are more "down" than even we ourselves know. Of course we can all put on a good face, even when we are crying inside. But listen closely and even strangers might be telling us that something is visibly wrong. When this happens, generally it is a spirit problem—indeed, often a *spiritual* problem. If perhaps we can't always control "spirit problems" (as with the death of a loved one), we have complete control over "spiritual problems." So when folks start talking about our being "down," maybe it's time to check whether our inner "Casper" has been misbehaving.

■ **The intriguing question is: Do I appreciate how what I do in my body affects my inner spirit, which in turn gives shape and expression to my body language?**

_____

_____

_____

_____

Workers Prepared for Battle

Those who carried materials did their work with one hand and held a weapon in the other, and each of the builders wore his sword at his side as he worked.

NEHEMIAH 4:17-18

A whole generation brought up on multitasking thinks nothing of organizing their minds around any number of competing screens, modes, or functions. Then again, from time immemorial mothers have been adroit multitaskers, managing the disparate demands of their households. When Nehemiah encountered opposition to his rebuilding of the walls of Jerusalem, he raised multitasking to a new level for his time. To fend off attacks from the enemy, Nehemiah conceived of a brilliant strategy using "citizen-soldiers." Hammer, saw, or trowel in one hand was balanced by shield, spear, or sword in the other. While the work progressed at breakneck speed, lookouts along the wall kept watch for any assault. When the trumpet sounded, all the workers quickly left their assigned positions to join in repelling the attack, and then it was immediately back to work—weapon in hand.

This marvelous Old Testament story is the perfect picture of how we should live our lives: productive in our daily work, but with the sword of the Spirit by our side, ready to fend off any threats from a disbelieving world. Having often segregated our profession of faith from our daily professions, we can find ourselves vulnerable to Satan's surprise attacks. If we are to build a home, church, or society of lasting quality, it will take not only the usual tools of parenting and leadership but the written Word embedded into the soul. If at first it is awkward doing our jobs while firmly holding a weapon, the surprise is how much easier any task becomes when we are always prepared to do battle with a threatening world.

■ **The soul-searching question is: Am I good at multitasking in every area of my life except my faith life?**

Leadership with Integrity

I put in charge of Jerusalem my brother Hanani, along with Hananiah the commander of the citadel, because he was a man of integrity and feared God more than most people do.

NEHEMIAH 7:2

Some might call it nepotism. In fact one wonders if Nehemiah isn't being somewhat defensive even to explain why he put his brother in charge. Did he perhaps feel a need to justify his decision to his critics? Man of integrity that he was, Nehemiah surely can't be faulted for giving his brother too glowing a recommendation. So why not place the best man in the job, even if he happens to be your brother? In light of current experience, Nehemiah's emphasis on integrity as a quality of leadership is refreshing. Even in Christian circles, leadership with integrity can be hard to find. Not surprisingly, people of integrity often prefer being in the background while people without it seek the limelight. For those who are bent on self-promotion, integrity can stand in the way. To get ahead it's tempting to live in the shadowlands of truth. To embellish one's portfolio where others are too humble to tout their (often greater) achievements.

Integrity, of course, is not just about telling the truth. It is a character trait that reflects a far deeper set of values pervasive in a person's life. Note the connection which Nehemiah makes between integrity and fearing God. Despite the lip service one might make to faith and religion, show us a leader who lacks integrity and you can be sure that what he lacks most is a genuine fear of God. One's lack of integrity begins with one's lack of relationship with God. *Lying* only happens because of what is *underlying*. So praise God for Nehemiah's brother, and shame on all Christian leaders who fall below his high standard.

■ **The question for even non-leaders is: Am I a person of such integrity that God himself could feel comfortable putting me in charge of some special task, however lowly?**

The Joy of Grief

Nehemiah said, "Go and enjoy choice food and sweet drinks, and send some to those who have nothing prepared. This day is holy to our Lord. Do not grieve, for the joy of the LORD is your strength."

NEHEMIAH 8:10

You'd think fasting would be more appropriate than feasting, wouldn't you? Upon hearing the law of Moses being read, the Jews must surely have been struck by how far they had strayed from its commands. Yet they were told not to grieve, but rather to celebrate! Did God not want them to grieve over their sin? Are you and I not to grieve over our own? Maybe the answer lies in the genuineness of their anguish. Had they *not* grieved at the hearing of the law, surely they would not have been told to celebrate. But because they *did* sincerely weep and mourn, the surprising message was to wipe away their tears and celebrate the day of the Lord! What they needed at that point was not more self-flagellation, but experiencing the joy of God's forgiveness and grace.

By comparison how do you and I react to sin? Are we *anguished* by our sins, or are we perhaps far too cavalier about them? Do we celebrate God's grace and forgiveness all too quickly, without first genuinely grieving over our many transgressions? Being obsessively morbid about our sins can't be spiritually healthy, but when was the last time we even wept about them? Sure, we sometimes weep at the *consequences* of our sin, but rarely do we bathe the sins themselves in penitent tears. Could this possibly explain why we often do not feel the sense of joy we otherwise might when we assemble to celebrate the day of the Lord? The irony of spiritual celebration is that the highest joy can only follow the deepest anguish.

■ **The disturbing question is: If my worship experience is less than ecstatic, could it be that I have robbed myself of joy by failing to grasp the seriousness of the sin from which I have been saved?**

How Shall We Be Remembered?

Remember me for this also, my God, and show mercy to me according to your great love.

NEHEMIAH 13:22

If you could write your own eulogy, what favorable things would you say about yourself? What do you think others might say? Today most eulogies focus on one's secular achievements. For Nehemiah the greater concern was not how his contemporaries might remember him, but how God would assess his time on earth. Of all the great things Nehemiah had accomplished, it was not the rebuilding of Jerusalem's walls that was uppermost in his mind. Rather, it was his moral reforms for which Nehemiah prayed to be remembered. Had he not—like the Messiah to come—cleansed the temple of its corruption? Had he not upbraided the Jews for violating the Sabbath and intermarrying with heathens? Building a wall in the face of fierce opposition was nothing compared with the moral fortitude he had shown as the spiritual leader of the Jews during the tumultuous period of restoration. To his eternal credit, spiritual loyalty was the epitaph and legacy Nehemiah most coveted.

In eulogies, it is rare to mention the spiritual loyalty exhibited by the deceased, more rare to mention their character flaws, and especially rare to mention his or her secret sins. That Nehemiah wanted God to remember the good that he had done underscores how acutely aware Nehemiah was of the flaws in his life that needed God's mercy. Our eternal destiny will not be decided on the basis of some cosmic balance sheet comparing assets and liabilities. Yet knowing how sinful we are, it is understandable that we would want to make sure that God didn't overlook whatever good there is in us.

■ **The question of legacy is: If God should ask me what spiritual accomplishments I would wish for him to remember, what would be my reply?**

_____

_____

_____

_____

The Allure of Health and Wealth

Jabez cried out to the God of Israel, "Oh, that you would bless me and enlarge my territory! Let your hand be with me, and keep me from harm so that I will be free from pain." And God granted his request.

1 CHRONICLES 4:10

No wonder this is such a popular passage! Who wouldn't want to be pain free and blessed with material abundance? In recent times the prayer of Jabez has been rescued from obscurity in Israel's ancient chronicles to become a standard fixture in contemporary Christian thought. Didn't God grant Jabez' request? And, if Jabez', why not yours or mine? As God's children, apparently all we have to do is name it and claim it—well, as long as we are not in some third world country where Christians regularly live in hunger and poverty despite all their prayers. And then there are those intriguing beatitudes that speak of the poor in spirit being happy…though nonetheless poor. Did Jesus himself promise health and wealth for his disciples? One does well to proceed cautiously when praying the prayer of Jabez.

So what are we to make of the fact that Jabez' prayer was granted? Perhaps there is a clue in Jabez' name (sounding like the Hebrew word for *pain*), which suggests God knew something special about his particular needs. Yet if God gives us only what is good for us, how often is wealth really to our benefit? And if life without pain is to be desired, why did our Lord himself experience such excruciating pain? In light of all the passages which call us to suffer as Christians and to sacrifice our abundance for the needs of others, any selfish prayers would seem wholly out of order for believers. Then again if Jesus himself could pray that he be spared the cup of pain, so can we…as long as we remember he was *not* spared!

■ **The painful question is: If ever I'm tempted to pray for health or wealth, are my motives worthy of such a prayer?**

From Birthright to a New Birth

Reuben…was the firstborn, but when he defiled his father's marriage bed, his rights as firstborn were given to the sons of Joseph son of Israel; so he could not be listed in the genealogical record in accordance with his birthright.

1 CHRONICLES 5:1

As we bring the Old Testament to a close in this chronological arrangement of the Scriptures, what might seem to be a throwaway parenthetical thought is the perfect summary of the relationship between ancient Israel and God and a wonderful bridge to the wider family of God soon to emerge. As Jacob's firstborn son, Reuben stood to inherit the lion's share of Israel's estate. Yet because Reuben had acted wickedly toward his father, his inheritance was given to the two sons of Joseph. The obvious analogy is striking. Like Reuben himself, the nation of Israel had played the harlot with God, defiling the "marriage" covenant by which they should have fully inherited the blessings God had intended for them. Their exclusive inheritance would now be shared with the spiritual offspring of another "Joseph" soon to come. Just as Reuben was not completely deprived of his inheritance in the land of promise, so too the Jews would not be wholly robbed of their spiritual inheritance in Christ. Yet their loss of an exclusive relationship with God would be the whole world's gain, to be shared alike with God's firstborn nation.

Are we children of God through Christ Jesus? If so, the glorious inheritance from the Father is ours for the taking. He who has promised is faithful! But will we be "listed in the genealogical record in accordance with [our] birthright," or will we act so wickedly in breach of our marriage vows that we forfeit our inheritance? Whatever our particular understanding of eternal security, Reuben represents a clarion call to purity and faithfulness among the children of God.

■ **The sobering question is: Am I living worthily of the glorious inheritance I have been promised?**

A Four-Hundred-Year Silence

They will say, "Where is this 'coming' he promised? Ever since our ancestors died, everything goes on as it has since the beginning of creation."

2 PETER 3:4

The question posed in today's passage comes four hundred years after the end of the Old Testament record. Yet it must surely have been the very question on the minds of all those who, in the meantime, eagerly looked forward to the coming of the promised Messiah. When would he appear? How long must they wait for the mighty kingdom he would establish? Why was God so silent? We ourselves can identify with many of the same questions. Now that Christ has come and promised to return, when will he come again? How long must *we* wait? Having revealed himself to us in the person of Jesus and in the inspired Scripture of the New Testament, why is God still so silent? The problem is only exacerbated when *their* four hundred years has now turned into *our* two millennia. Although many in succeeding generations have been convinced that Christ would come in their lifetime, so far those believers have lived and died only in expectation, not fulfillment. Christ will indeed come in some generation's lifetime, but it may not be our own.

So how do we deal with such delay? Become cynical and give up our faith? Become obsessed with signs of an imminent coming, even if they prove to be wrong yet again? Of one thing we can be sure: No matter how long it takes, Christ *is* coming again! How do we know? Because, despite the long delay between the two Testaments, Christ did indeed appear, precisely as promised. Just as surely, we too can count on his glorious reappearing. It may not be in our lifetime, but it certainly *could* be.

■ **The only question is: If Christ should suddenly appear even today, would I be ready?**

The Importance of Scripture

All Scripture is God-breathed and is useful for teaching, rebuking, correcting and training in righteousness, so that the servant of God may be thoroughly equipped for every good work.

2 TIMOTHY 3:16-17

Considering the profound implications, the historical debate over inclusion of the so-called Apocrypha in the canon of Scripture is no small concern. If that which is gifted to us from God's mind to ours is the exclusive guide to our eternal destiny, then it is vital not to confuse his divine Word with anything that is *not* God-breathed. How God could inspire human thought and pen unerringly to convey his sublime truths is a mystery far beyond our comprehension. Whether in the genre of law, history, prophecy, poetry, or epistle, God's inspired Word is nothing short of lifesaving and life-shaping. The writings of the Apocrypha reflect many of the same truths found in the 66 books of the Bible. So the crucial question is: What can we rely on with complete certainty as being the pure, unadulterated, revealed mind of God?

Were we left solely with human discernment to answer that question, we should never be satisfied. One simply has to trust that God's hand has been guiding the process all along. Why should God reveal his mind to man only to allow man to frustrate divine revelation? For that matter, why should God reveal his mind to *you* and *me* only for us to ignore what he has revealed? How many countless people have contentiously debated the issues surrounding the canon of Scripture while leading lives that would be an affront to virtually any book that might be nominated for inclusion in Scripture? Even complete skeptics would know better than that!

■ **So the most important question of all is: How do I measure up to the obvious truths that are all around me, especially those that are in my Bible?**

The Influence of Secular Thinking

See to it that no one takes you captive through hollow and deceptive philosophy, which depends on human tradition and the elemental spiritual forces of this world rather than on Christ.

COLOSSIANS 2:8

In the years leading up to the coming of Christ, confusion reigns supreme—politically, socially, and religiously. A far more complex world has emerged since the nation of Israel was intact and under the theocratic rule of God. With the domination of each foreign power, the Jews have become increasingly immersed in secular values. Their penchant for idolatry has given way to a more philosophical and intellectual approach to religion. Even within Judaism, priests have taken second place to rabbis whose seat of power is not the temple, but synagogues. As what will become known as the first century AD fast approaches, observance of the law has become a system of strict legalism, and competing doctrinal camps pit Jew against Jew in sectarian strife, principally between Pharisees and Sadducees.

Which is worse, pagan idolatry or intellectual secularism? For all their ignorance of the one true God, at least pagan idolaters recognized a spiritual dimension interfacing with every aspect of life. There were gods and goddesses for virtually every activity known to man, and worship was a way of life. By contrast, intellectual secularism elevated human thinking as the sole object of respectability, if not adulation. Quite incredibly, secular humanists were asking, "Is there a God?" Even today we find ourselves far more at risk from intellectual secularism than classic idolatry—except for the irony that, thanks to culture's elevation of humanism, we now have a new form of "I"-dolatry! Just when real progress was made possible through Christ, have we now come full circle?

■ **The compelling question is: Despite my deep faith, how much of my thinking is unwittingly both secular and idolatrous?**

God Wrapped in Flesh!

The Word became flesh and made his dwelling among us. We have seen his glory, the glory of the one and only Son who came from the Father, full of grace and truth.

JOHN 1:14

If ever an idea were beyond our grasp, surely it must be the thought that the Creator God of the universe could take on a human nature. How, possibly, does an eternal being fit within the temporal limitations of mortal man? How can an ethereal spirit be wrapped in human flesh? Is not the concept of "incarnate God" the ultimate oxymoron, something in the nature of a square circle? To believe John's Gospel is to believe in "squircles," or at least one in particular. Yet John's consummate prologue is unequivocal: To believe in Jesus is to believe he was the one and only "God-man," as much human as divine and as fully God as fully man. Creator and creature all in one! To say Jesus was the "Son of God" is not to suggest that he himself wasn't God, but only some divinely procreated offspring of God. Though conceptually a "son" in relation to his "Father," the incarnate Jesus was one in essence with the Father, not unlike a man who simultaneously is the son of his father and the father of his son.

The mystery of incarnation is not limited to Jesus of Nazareth. Although we are hardly divine spirits, the truth remains that we are also spirit beings wrapped in flesh. In our human essence, we too are "squircles," being mortal, yet capable of immortality. Were it otherwise, at death we would no longer exist in any form whatsoever. So to believe in Jesus' incarnation is to believe in our own earthly incarnation and in our eternal incarnation in resurrection bodies yet to come!

■ **The challenging question is: If in some ineffable way my incarnate spirit is not unlike God's incarnate spirit, how—even today—can I be more like a true "son of God"?**

_____

_____

_____

_____

Knowing One's True Father

Now Jesus himself was about thirty years old when he began his ministry. He was the son, so it was thought, of Joseph, the son of Heli.

LUKE 3:23

Who is your father? Unless perhaps we were adopted or raised under circumstances of parental obscurity, all of us know who our fathers are. Why, then, would today's text contain that enigmatic line, "so it was thought"? Was Joseph *not* Jesus' biological father? In point of fact, of course he *wasn't*. Even before we get to the detailed accounts of Jesus' birth, we are presented here with the astounding fact that Jesus was born of a woman, but not of a man. Although Jesus' lineage is traced in separate genealogies through both Joseph and Mary, in biological terms Joseph did not provide the seed for Jesus' birth. Jesus' virgin birth was nothing short of a divine miracle—which is not to say that Jesus was any less human. Why else record his human lineage all the way back to Adam if not to drive home Jesus' humanity with an unassailable genealogical record? But equally important is Jesus' spiritual lineage, which because of his virgin birth, is necessarily traced to his heavenly Father.

Everyone has a different view of their father. Some despise their fathers while others adore theirs. For those whose fathers have been a blessing, it is God they can thank for providing such good examples of fatherhood. For those whose fathers have been a curse, Jesus' birth provides a wonderful way of looking at fatherhood in a whole new light. As is the case with of all God's children by faith, our biological fathers may have brought us into the world, but it is our spiritual Father who has given us true life.

■ **The question of spiritual lineage is: Who has been the greater influence in my life, my biological father or my heavenly Father?**

_____

_____

_____

_____

Resting in Peace

Simeon took him in his arms and praised God, saying: "Sovereign Lord, as you have promised, you may now dismiss your servant in peace. For my eyes have seen your salvation."

LUKE 2:28-30

The initials R.I.P. are found on so many tombstones that they now appear on virtually all cartoon depictions of marble headstones in spooky graveyards. By those initials the final farewell to the dead is: Rest In Peace. The idea, of course, is that death is a peaceful repose from the tumultuous cares of life. Imagining the souls of the dead actually lying there in the grave—as if having a prolonged snooze in a comfortable bed on a rainy morning—hardly speaks to the reality of the situation. Yet it is also true that the euphemism for death most often used in Scripture is "sleep," or perhaps "resting with his fathers." So R.I.P. may not be as far off the mark as one might think, especially when considering the story of Simeon holding the baby Jesus in his arms.

What a tribute to this man of faith—that God would have promised him a personal view of the Messiah within his lifetime! And what a thrill it must have been for him to literally hold the Savior of the world and see his tender smile. If ever there were an appropriate time for someone to say, "I can die happy now," this was it. In effect, that's what Simeon said in his *Nunc Dimittis* (now dismiss me), celebrated in both music and art, notably by Rembrandt. Why was Simeon happy to die at that point? Because he had seen God's salvation brought into the world. So what would make *us* rest in peace? Having found the cure for cancer? Seeing children happily married? Maybe we're all thinking far too carnally. What possibly could make us ready to meet our Maker more than being assured of our own salvation?

■ **The crucial question is: Am I sure I have personally held the Savior of the world in my own believing arms?**

That Wondrous Moment of Knowing

"Why were you searching for me?" he asked. "Didn't you know I had to be in my Father's house?"

LUKE 2:49

Ouch! Did the precocious twelve-year-old Jesus really answer his mother so impudently? After all, he *had* stayed behind in Jerusalem without so much as a hint about what he was up to. Unless we assume that Jesus fully comprehended his unique personhood from the moment he was born, there must have been some definable moment when he came to understand his divine nature. At what point did the young Jesus realize he was the eternal God in human flesh? Had Mary ever told him the incredible story of his birth? Or that he was destined to be Israel's Messiah? One wonders if the dialogue Jesus had with the rabbis didn't mark the moment when Jesus came to a full realization that he was indeed the Christ of prophecy. Hadn't he been born in Bethlehem precisely as Micah had prophesied? Had he not been called out of Egypt just as Hosea had said?

If this was the moment when Jesus finally put it all together, his response to Mary takes on a whole new tone. As if seeking her confirmation, did Jesus pointedly ask Mary: Didn't *you*, of all people, know what I have finally come to realize? Why else is this temple scene the only specific event recorded in the first thirty years of Jesus' life? This raises the pivotal question for all of us: At what moment did we fully accept our spiritual identity? If we knew and loved Jesus at a very early age, when did we have sufficient maturity to make a lifelong commitment and seal it with a specific act of humble obedience? At what moment did we intentionally walk into our Father's house and feel extraordinarily comfortable being there?

■ **The grateful question is: Who do I have to personally thank for gradually preparing my heart for such a profound epiphany?**

No More Lame Excuses!

The tempter came to him and said, "If you are the Son of God, tell these stones to become bread."

MATTHEW 4:3

When reflecting on Jesus' wilderness confrontation with the devil, it is tempting to think that this account is given to demonstrate how Jesus successfully withstood all of the same temptations you and I face. While Jesus did in fact triumph over every temptation, have we possibly overlooked something important? First, have you ever been tempted to turn a rock into bread? Or to jump off a tall building expecting angels to swoop down and rescue you? Nor I! These temptations are not aimed at Jesus *the man*, but Jesus *the Son of God*. This leads to a second clue: the devil's sarcastic lead-in, "*If* you are the Son of God…" The devil knows full well that Jesus is the Son of God! He is taunting Jesus, testing his commitment to being truly human. But Jesus doesn't take the bait. Certainly Jesus could have turned the stones into bread as surely as he would soon turn water into wine. Yet Jesus adamantly refuses to use his divinity to selfish advantage.

If Jesus could master temptation only because of his divine nature, the Scripture's assurance that he was tempted in every way like ourselves, but without sin, would be a complete sham. And if that were the case, why should we lesser mortals even try? Apart from shedding his blood for our sins, Jesus came into the world as a fellow human being in order to rid us of any excuse for sin—especially that overused line, "But I'm only human!" In the desert Jesus refused to use his *divinity* as a crutch, robbing us of any foolish notion that we can use our *humanity* as a crutch.

■ **The tempting question is: Have I lamely used my humanity as an excuse for what I could well resist?**

Saving the Best Till Last

Then he called the bridegroom aside and said, "Everyone brings out the choice wine first and then the cheaper wine after the guests have had too much to drink; but you have saved the best till now."

JOHN 2:9-10

That Jesus should take time out of his busy ministry to attend a wedding celebration speaks wonderfully about how highly he regarded the institution of marriage. Even if it was likely a family affair, Jesus' presence certainly brought great honor to the wedding couple. Their celebration was also a fitting backdrop to Jesus' first miracle, although without his mother's urging it might not have happened. As miracles go, turning water into wine was fairly unremarkable. But, as the master of the banquet quickly recognized, this was no ordinary wine. Contrary to common practice, this finest of wines had been served last, not first as would have been expected. Why fine wine, and why was it served last? Apart from verifying that Jesus' miracle was no cheap imitation or watered-down fluke, perhaps there are valuable lessons to be learned by all who have ever taken the vows of marriage.

The excitement of a wedding gets marriages started off on the right foot. Through the honeymoon stage, it's all love and kisses. But not even the best of marriages can maintain that high note. There are peaks and valleys, good times and hard times, the highest of highs and difficult, daunting challenges far greater than ever imagined. What to do, then, when the wine of love runs out? Perhaps the best advice comes from what Mary said to the servants: "Do whatever he [Jesus] tells you." How could any couple possibly do better than that? And the reward? As virtually all married couples can attest, through good times and bad the Master of miracles saves the very best till last!

■ **The question to celebrate is: How many times in my own marriage has the wine seemingly run out, only to be replenished with even finer wine than before?**

Fishing with Patience

Going on from there, he saw two other brothers, James son of Zebedee and his brother John. They were in a boat with their father Zebedee, preparing their nets. Jesus called them, and immediately they left the boat and their father and followed him.

MATTHEW 4:21-22

Just like that? You mean to say that Jesus simply calls out for complete strangers to follow him, and quick as a flash they drop whatever they're doing—livelihoods and all—and sign up for a mission they know virtually nothing about? Well, not exactly. Clearly there is far more to the story than we are told. One has to do a bit of sleuthing (in various accounts recording events witnessed by Jesus' mother and her sister), but it is highly probable that Mary's sister was actually the mother of the "sons of Zebedee." In which case, James and John would not have been strangers at all, but rather Jesus' first cousins. And they were fishing partners of Simon Peter and his brother Andrew, who were also called. Not only that, but these four were the ones who had only recently witnessed that miraculous, boat-bulging catch of fish! And they would have been familiar with Jesus' teachings because they undoubtedly were listening as Jesus preached the gospel to the lakeside crowd from Simon's boat. So there we have it—the other side of the story!

All of which suggests a practical lesson for those of us who would take up the call to evangelize others. As with ordinary fishermen, lesson number one for those who would be fishers of men is patience. Souls can't be won for Christ overnight. It often takes time to build trusting relationships that will allow the gospel message to come through unimpeded. Would we even want conversions so fast that there was little time for deep reflection and genuine commitment? Patience is not just a virtue. With evangelism—it's vital!

■ **The question that calls is: Have I been in such an eager rush to evangelize that I've shaken lost souls off the hook?**

When Mercy Means More

But go and learn what this means: "I desire mercy, not sacrifice." For I have not come to call the righteous, but sinners.

MATTHEW 9:13

Our featured text makes one wonder if we've rushed past a fabulous lesson by not taking into account the importance of a name. Today's verse is Jesus' response to criticism about attending a banquet that Matthew held for Jesus with a crowd of tax collectors and others whom the Pharisees called "sinners." Why tax collectors? Because Matthew was a tax collector—one of those traitorous fellow Jews who worked for the hated Romans and notoriously pocketed part of what they collected. Interestingly, only Matthew, not Mark or Luke, gives us the reference to Hosea's line, "I desire mercy, not sacrifice." And even more intriguing, Mark and Luke both refer to Matthew by his other name, Levi.

You can almost imagine the first meeting between Levi and Jesus—perhaps Levi was trying to collect taxes on the great catch of fish Jesus miraculously produced. Jesus, tongue-in-cheek, might have protested that the haul was a gift from God, then gotten Levi's attention by asking, "Have you paid your own gift tax, Levi…or is it *Matthew*?" "Do we know each other?" asks a stunned Levi. "What I know," says Jesus, "is that your other name, *Matthew,* means 'gift from God,' and that you owe God far more than this legalized thievery you're engaged in!" Whatever the conversation, it led to one of the greatest conversions and transformations ever! Appreciating God's mercy as few others, Levi insisted on being called Matthew and couldn't wait to share with all his fellow "sinners" the man Jesus, whose own name means "the Lord saves"!

■ **The identifying question is: If I proudly wear the name *Christian*, have I forgotten that it is a word signifying God's great gift of mercy to me, the sinner?**

No Worries!

Therefore do not worry about tomorrow, for tomorrow will worry about itself. Each day has enough trouble of its own.

MATTHEW 6:34

Wouldn't it be interesting to know how many doctor visits could be eliminated if only we didn't worry? How many millions of nights of lost sleep could be recovered? How many countless hours would be freed up for positive thoughts and maybe even solutions to the problems folks worry about? In Jesus' Sermon on the Mount, the worry he is most concerned about is not whether aging parents are properly being taken care of, or whether children are safe while away from home, or whether the cancer will do its deadly work before a daughter's wedding. The target of Jesus' teaching is our fretting about things that don't really matter in the big picture, such as daily food, drink, and clothing. There are those for whom having the next meal is truly a worry, but that probably doesn't apply to you and me. Yet consider how much time we waste on where we will eat, what we will eat, and what we will wear when we go out to eat! For a more modern audience, Jesus might well have included worry about stock market fluctuations, or rising or falling house prices, or whether we'll be laid off in the next corporate takeover. Maybe too—terrorist attacks, or global warming, or wars over which we have no control.

The problem with worry is not just that it is unhealthy and a waste of time, but that it often represents a lack of trust in God's providence. Or fails to grasp the bigger, more important picture. Or wrongly prioritizes physical needs over our greater spiritual needs. In short, worry is usually symptomatic of far more significant underlying causes. And if there is anything we should really worry about, that would be it!

■ **The worrying question is: Which of my many unnecessary worries are a worry to God?**

Asking All the Hard Questions

When the men came to Jesus, they said, "John the Baptist sent us to you to ask, 'Are you the one who is to come, or should we expect someone else?' "

LUKE 7:20

Of all people, John shouldn't have the slightest doubt about Jesus being the Messiah! He personally immersed Jesus in the Jordan and witnessed the Spirit descending upon him as the booming voice from heaven declared him to be God's own Son. In fact, when John said that he would not have known Jesus except for being divinely instructed that the descending Spirit would be a sign of the Messiah, John couldn't have been speaking literally. After all, his mother and Jesus' mother were relatives so the two boys must've been cousins growing up in fairly close proximity. And at the Jordan, remember that John hesitated to immerse Jesus, knowing him to be supremely righteous. Surely they had discussed their mutual ministries before or after their Jordan meeting. Why, then, John's question?

Who knows what tricks the mind can play for even the most confident of prisoners in a rotting jail? Maybe John truly did have doubts. But a more plausible explanation is that, sensing impending death, John is burdened with convincing his own disciples to switch their loyalty to Jesus. Maybe John's disciples were arguing that Jesus had done nothing to stir the political waters or to raise the army against Rome like most Jews expected of the coming Messiah. So perhaps John wants his disciples to "hear it from the horse's mouth," so to speak. Whatever prompts the question, it is a good one and one each of us must ask for ourselves. What does Jesus mean to you and me personally? What kind of Christ do we want him to be? Is it possible we have missed the real person of Jesus?

■ **The difficult question is: Have I myself asked all the hard questions of Jesus I really ought to ask?**

An Uncomfortable Calling

Sell your possessions and give to the poor. Provide purses for yourselves that will not wear out, a treasure in heaven that will never fail, where no thief comes near and no moth destroys. For where your treasure is, there your heart will be also.

LUKE 12:33-34

There's no end to how we can rationalize away this passage. Surely Jesus wasn't speaking literally, otherwise we would be too poor to share! (That logic didn't deter those first-century Christians who, immediately after Pentecost, literally sold their possessions.) Or surely it's sufficient if we have hearts that would be *willing* to sell everything if some drastic need ever arose (please, God, don't let that happen!). For most of us, it would be remarkable enough simply to reduce our level of materialism by half, or a third, or even a tenth! How glibly we speak of "disposable income," the money we have left over after rent or mortgages, utilities, groceries, and other "necessary" items. What part of that "disposable income" goes to meet the needs of the poor, instead of expensive vacations, big-boy toys, and fashion items?

We sometimes say "He wears his heart on his sleeve" about someone who lets his emotions show for all the world to see. On a deeper spiritual level, we also wear our hearts on our *designer* sleeves, and expensive cars, and upmarket homes. Through whatever possessions are our personal "treasures," even those of us with moderate incomes are declaring our excessive materialism loudly and clearly to a watching world. As Jesus said, "Where your treasure is, there your heart will be also"…fully on display. But it is when we reverse the order of Jesus' words that the real indictment hits home: For where your heart is, there your treasure will be also. Want to know how spiritually healthy our hearts are? Just look at our checkbooks and credit card statements.

■ **The disturbing question is: What does my incessant addiction to materialism say about my heart?**

Teaching with Kingdom Insight

He said to them, "Therefore every teacher of the law who has become a disciple in the kingdom of heaven is like the owner of a house who brings out of his storeroom new treasures as well as old."

MATTHEW 13:52

Did you attend a Christian college or university? If so, what made it distinctively "Christian"? A faculty and student body composed mostly of believers? Required chapel programs and Bible courses? Prayers or Scripture readings in class? Were you ever asked to think "Christianly" about English, math, science, history, art, or music? Did your teachers relate biblical principles to each subject, or did you learn only what a business or engineering major at the secular university across town would've learned? In today's text it's not likely that Jesus was directly addressing today's Christian schools. He was alluding to the highly respected rabbis who taught the law of Moses with great flourish, but whose teaching was uninformed by the profound kingdom principles that, even then, Christ was explaining through the simplest of parables. In the closest parallel today, how many respected theologians teach religion with great brilliance, yet undermine their students' faith by teaching a marvelously inspired text robbed of kingdom power?

Turning to other "teachers of the law," how many capable Christian law professors teach torts, tax, contracts, or property with little or no mention of man-discovered law and its relation to man-made law? Without applying profound kingdom truths to whatever course is under instruction, even the best teachers have little to offer an inquiring world. By contrast, even those who are not teachers by profession can convey the greatest insights ever shared, simply by looking at a humble flower and using its design and beauty to tell some lost soul about God's kingdom.

■ **The never-too-late question is: What profound treasures is my education lacking that greater kingdom insight might yet provide?**

Touching, or Being Touched?

At once Jesus realized that power had gone out from him. He turned around in the crowd and asked, "Who touched my clothes?"

MARK 5:30

Healed by merely touching Jesus' cloak? Oh, to be able to do that ourselves! Have cancer? Touch Jesus' cloak! Suffering from arthritis? Reach for his cloak! In so brief a space, we can only begin to touch on all the dynamics involved in this incident. For instance, what power-surge did Jesus feel coursing through his body when the woman's hand touched him? And how but *divinely* did his body discern that hers was different from all the other hands reaching out to touch the popular prophet? Yet, if *divinely,* why did Jesus have to ask who touched him? The great mystery of God-in-flesh remains! But the most intriguing question is: Was this humble woman healed by touching Jesus or by being touched? Jesus' answer was, "Daughter, your faith has healed you." Had she never been touched *by* Jesus, the woman herself never would have reached out in faith to touch him.

Not all of Jesus' healings involved touching, but many did. He touched the eyes of the blind, the ears of the deaf, and the cold hands of the dead—as if to underscore the source of the miracle. But it is when Jesus touches the heart that his power is most transforming. Through faith in Christ, the spiritually blind can see, the spiritually deaf can hear, and the spiritually dead are raised to new life. Few believers in history have personally touched either Jesus or his clothes, but all believers have been touched by Jesus in a way none of us ever could've expected. And, as with Jesus that day, it is in our souls that the power of God's Holy Spirit courses freely to transform, renew, and even heal.

■ **The groping question is: Have I wistfully hoped for God's transforming power in my life, yet never allowed him close enough to truly touch my soul?**

Prince of...Division!

Do not suppose that I have come to bring peace to the earth. I did not come to bring peace, but a sword.

MATTHEW 10:34

Were the angels wrong when they heralded Jesus' birth with joyful songs of "peace on earth, good will to men"? Was Jesus contradicting himself when he rebuked Peter, warning that "all who draw the sword will die by the sword"? Suddenly we hear Jesus saying he didn't come to bring peace, but a sword! That he has come to put parents and children at odds with one another, and sibling against sibling! Just when we think we know the character of Jesus—and *like* it—we are surprised. Despite how sharply Jesus puts it, it is obvious that he is simply acknowledging the inevitable consequences of his mission to bring peace and reconciliation between God and man. Because that peace comes solely through Jesus' lordship, any denial of his lordship sets the believer and the unbeliever in opposite camps. What harmony can there be between light and darkness, good and evil, faith and disbelief? What harmony can there be between father and son, mother and daughter, or brother and sister when one submits to Jesus' lordship and the other rejects it? It doesn't mean they must literally hate each other, but what core values do they have in common?

Jesus' observation about bringing division is a warning about what we may be called to give up for our faith, including our relationships with family members. Countless parents know the pain of alienation from their children, and vice versa. Untold numbers of siblings can never know the joy of genuine Christian fellowship with those who share precious childhood memories. For all the peace there is in Christ, faith is not for the fainthearted!

■ **The daunting question is: Have I allowed *any* earthly relationship to become more important than my commitment to Christ?**

When There's Reason to Doubt

Immediately Jesus reached out his hand and caught him. "You of little faith," he said, "why did you doubt?"

MATTHEW 14:31

Some ask, "Why did Peter doubt?" Yet the amazing thing is that Peter ever climbed out of that tossing boat and *tried* to walk on water! Maybe we've been too critical of Peter. Wouldn't it be interesting to have heard the Lord's tone when he was chastising Peter? It's hard to believe Jesus was giving him too rough a time. In point of fact, there are any number of circumstances in which there is good reason to doubt. When you think about it, faith makes no earthly sense. If it did, then it wouldn't be faith! Faith is a leap of logic—a bizarre thought that the mind does not easily accommodate. Consider miracles themselves. Miracles are miracles because they are not natural. What, for example, could be more mind-stretching than the incarnation of God? And certainly the resurrection of Jesus defies all human understanding. If a reasonable person does not have some legitimate doubts along the road to faith, one rightly wonders about the depth of his or her faith.

So, believer that you are, what do you have doubts about? Ever wonder how God could allow evil to exist? Or why God lets Satan have what power he has? Or why God doesn't answer all our prayers for the sick and dying among our family and friends? Or if it is *really* true that we will live on beyond the grave? If you have ever had serious doubts about any of these, join the crowd. It is one thing to step out in faith when the seas around us are glassy calm; another thing altogether to put one foot in front of the other in the face of life's storms.

■ **The question of faith is: If sometimes I have genuine doubts about God, do I stop to consider the sea of doubts I would drown in if God weren't in the picture at all?**

When Ignorance Is Anything but Bliss

Do you still not see or understand? Are your hearts hardened? Do you have eyes but fail to see, and ears but fail to hear?

MARK 8:17-18

Just how challenged are you by the thought that you know what you know (because you know it), but you don't know what you don't know (because you don't know it)? In other words—we can never comfortably assume we know everything we need to know. The student who is sure that she knows enough to get an A may be sadly disappointed to get a C instead, all because the teacher is testing not only what she knows, but what she doesn't know. You know? So imagine how disconcerting it must've been for Jesus to have his closest disciples so blind to what he'd been trying to teach them through parables, miracles, and innumerable direct discourses. How many times would it take, do you suppose, for Jesus' disciples to appreciate that he often spoke of spiritual realities in material terms? Yet when Jesus starts talking about "the yeast of the Pharisees," the disciples assume he is talking about their not having any bread to eat. Were that his concern, Jesus reminds them he could produce bread miraculously, as he had done twice when feeding the multitudes. Only by further explanation did they realize he was speaking of the corrupting (yeast-like) power of Pharisaical legalism.

From our Scripture-informed vantage point, the disciples look pretty pitiful and undiscerning. *You and I would never have been so stupid!* But if Jesus' own disciples, who spoke with him face-to-face, were blind to higher spiritual realities, why should we assume that we ourselves are not so mired in worldly thinking that we too fail to grasp huge spiritual truths that are staring us in the face?

■ **The alarming question is: For all that I think I know about the kingdom of God, what profound truths am I still missing?**

Toward a Greater Faith

Immediately the boy's father exclaimed, "I do believe; help me overcome my unbelief!"

MARK 9:24

Do you believe that Jesus is the Christ, the Son of the living God? (YES/NO) Do you believe in the virgin birth? (YES/NO) Do you believe in the resurrection of the dead? (YES/NO) Do you believe that the Bible is the inspired Word of God? (YES/NO) Do you believe that, with enough faith, you could literally move a mountain from one location to another? (YES/NO) Many of us could easily answer "yes" to the first four questions, but we're probably more hesitant about that last one. Some might indulge in the possibility suggested by Jesus that, if we truly did have enough faith, we could actually move Mt. Everest to the Sahara! Others would dismiss the notion saying that Jesus didn't intend for his words to be taken literally. But the moving of mountains is not the daily test of our beliefs. It's relationships, and illnesses, and temptations, and a host of other real-world challenges to faith.

In today's passage, the test for the boy's father was whether he truly believed Jesus could heal the lad. Why else bring him to Jesus? And yet there was that subtle qualifier: "If you can…" But when Jesus seized on that hesitation, out came that wondrous confessional prayer that has been an inspiration to so many strugglers: Yes I believe, Lord! Only help me to move the mountain of unbelief that remains. Believing the affirmations of Christian faith is light-years away from having the depth of faith that makes those affirmations fully empowering. Most of us are staunch believers and fearful unbelievers all at the same time. Were there not so great a gap of faith in all of us, Everest itself would have reason to tremble!

◼ **The gaping question is: As a person of faith, do I pray that God will further strengthen my faith?**

Judging with Humility

But Jesus bent down and started to write on the ground with his finger. When they kept on questioning him, he straightened up and said to them, "Let any one of you who is without sin be the first to throw a stone at her."

JOHN 8:6-7

Wouldn't you give almost anything to know what Jesus was writing in the dust that day? There's been much speculation, but whatever he actually wrote had an immediate effect on the men who were accusing the woman caught in adultery. Was Jesus writing the names of each of the men and perhaps the sins they themselves had committed? No wonder they fled! Not only would it have vindicated Jesus' divinity (the issue being tested by dragging the woman before Jesus), but it would also have exposed these accusers' deplorable hypocrisy. Certainly they were already suspect for not equally condemning the *man* caught in adultery, but making that objection would have shifted the focus away from their own sinfulness. What they needed to see was that, while they were pointing one finger at the woman, three fingers were pointing back at themselves! Who better deserved being told off by Jesus?

Unfortunately, an unintended perversity has evolved from today's passage. How many times have we heard someone say, "Let him who is without sin cast the first stone"? It usually happens when people are rebuking moral judgment against a target they feel is undeserving—often themselves! This verse has become a favorite proof text for a nonjudgmental culture, despite Jesus' judgmental warning to the woman that she should stop sinning. Far from being a general prohibition against judging immorality in others, the point of the story is to temper our moral judgments with the recognition that we too are sinners. If others need our moral censure (and they do), none need it more than ourselves.

■ **The question of judgment is: Am I privately as outraged at my own moral failure as I am publicly outraged at the sins of others?**

Blind Slaves All

He replied, "Whether he is a sinner or not, I don't know. One thing I do know. I was blind but now I see!"

JOHN 9:25

No hymn is more well-known than "Amazing Grace," that joyous anthem of God's mercy to sinners written by John Newton, former master of a slave ship who knew profoundly what it meant to be a sinner transformed by grace. Drawing from today's text, Newton spiritualized the words of the blind man whose sight was miraculously restored. "I once was lost, but now am found," rings Newton's immortal words, "was blind, but now I see." Jesus ruled out any connection between *physical* blindness and sin. But there's a direct connection between *spiritual* blindness and sin. Most spiritual blindness is a myopic disorder manifesting itself in nearsightedness. When Jesus told the Pharisees that they were from below (this world) while he was from above (not of this world), they could only see the up-close world of which they were a part, not the spiritual realm from which Jesus had come. Proudly religious though they were, their thinking was carnal and their insight limited. Though fully sighted, they were blind.

It's ironic that Newton's great sin was participating in the ghastly eighteenth-century slave trade—for in Jesus' words, "Everyone who sins is a slave to sin" (John 8:34). That includes you and me—all of us blinded to our enslavement by a world happy to barter us for mere trinkets. We're in bondage to this world's paltry values, and we can't even see it! Or refuse to see it! Though fully sighted, we too are blind. That we catch even a glimpse of God's mercy as we sing "Amazing Grace" is a wonder. But what a marvelous, merciful wonder it is!

■ **The amazing question is: If I once was blind but now I see, why do I allow my vision to be blurred by a world eager to enslave me all over again?**

The Imperfect Hostess

"Martha, Martha," the Lord answered, "you are worried and upset about many things, but few things are needed—or indeed only one. Mary has chosen what is better, and it will not be taken away from her."

LUKE 10:41-42

Sounds a bit harsh, doesn't it? It's all well and good that Mary should want to sit at Jesus' feet and drink in his wisdom, but if there was to be any food and drink later on, somebody had to organize it. That somebody was Martha, desperately trying to set a table worthy of the Messiah. Maybe the problem Jesus detected was all the worry associated with Martha's efforts. Did every detail have to be fussed over? Was Martha too caught up with presentation or perhaps how the guests would rate the dinner? Was the meal more about *her* than about Jesus? Or might the root problem have been something else? Jumping ahead to when Jesus is talking to Martha about the death of Lazarus, her brother, he says to Martha, "Whoever lives by believing in me will never die. Do you believe this?" Martha's nonresponsive response is ever so telling. "Yes, Lord…I believe that you are the Messiah, the Son of God, who is to come into the world," she said. Notice how her answer doesn't quite match up with Jesus' question?

If the events in today's passage are any indication, by contrast Mary might well have responded, "Yes, I believe that those who put their faith in you will have eternal life." Did one sister think *religiously* while the other sister thought *spiritually*? If there is anything at all to this speculative musing, a tie between Martha's stiffly formalized religious belief system and her overattention to the formalities surrounding a dinner would not be surprising. Bless her heart, even as Jesus calls for the gravestone to be rolled away, Martha can only think about the odor! One likes to think that, as Lazarus emerged alive from the tomb, Martha forgot all about what they would have for lunch!

■ **The worrying question is: In what subtle ways does my view of religion affect my view of everyday activities?**

Money in an Hourglass

No one can serve two masters. Either you will hate the one and love the other, or you will be devoted to the one and despise the other. You cannot serve both God and money.

LUKE 16:13

This familiar passage could certainly stand on its own, if necessary, for who can miss its compelling message? Yet there is much to be gained from the larger context of Luke's account. From the beginning to the end of today's reading are two intertwining themes. The first theme is about the need for timely repentance. There is a point of no return, Jesus insists, when the opportunity to be kingdom people passes away forever. It is that heart-stopping moment when the owner of the house has closed the door and it is too late to gain entry. And it is that great banquet so many will miss out on because they have offered one feeble excuse after another. More famously still, it is that proverbial rich man in Hadean anguish being told that it's too late to send a warning to his brothers. At some point in each instance, it's simply too late!

The more obvious theme is the danger of being mastered by the love of money. There's the parable of the dishonest manager, prompting Jesus' warning that friends are more important eternally than financial shrewdness. There's that line about being trustworthy in handling worldly wealth so that we can be entrusted with true (spiritual) riches. And finally there's the story of that *rich man* ignoring Lazarus, the poor beggar he practically trips over at his gate every morning. Perhaps surprisingly, the target audience of Jesus' teaching about God and money were those proudly pious Pharisees, "who loved money," says the text. At that point the two themes merge into a single message aimed even at us. Before it is too late, we've got to decide by whom or by what will *we* be mastered?

■ **The urgent question is: How much time do I have left to get my convoluted priorities straight?**

_____

_____

_____

_____

A God Who Lets Us Die

But some of them said, "Could not he who opened the eyes of the blind man have kept this man from dying?"

JOHN 11:37

We have prayed to God with every fiber of our being that he spare the life of our loved one or friend. If he could raise the dead, surely he can *keep them from dying*! But when death steals away the object of our prayers, who could blame us for asking, "Why didn't you do something, God?" There is more than a hint of anger in the question being asked by Lazarus' grieving friends as Jesus belatedly arrives on the scene. When both Martha and Mary mention that Lazarus would not have died if Jesus had been present, the tone seems not of anger, but affirmation—and perhaps even slight hope for some miracle after the fact. Yet what good is it to affirm God's power to save from death if, in the end, he doesn't use that power? Why does God let our loved ones die? Indeed, why does he let *us* die?

Given the ultimate necessity of man's mortality in order to experience immortality, could it be that we are asking the wrong question? Maybe we should be asking why God lets any of us *live*. Practically speaking, it is amazing that any of us have survived the ever-present dangers of childhood. Had we been born in primitive times, many of us would not have lived as long as we have. Some of us, indeed, have been at death's door without its ever opening. Why didn't we die then? Did we survive simply because we had good doctors and the right medicine, or—with prayers ascending on our behalf—might God have reached down in mercy to spare us? Who says God doesn't save from death! But surely God can't answer every prayer for continued life, else what is heaven for?

■ **The intriguing question is: If perhaps God has let my loved one die, have I seriously considered why he has let me live?**

Eunuchs for the Kingdom

For there are eunuchs who were born that way, and there are eunuchs who have been made eunuchs by others—and there are those who choose to live like eunuchs for the sake of the kingdom of heaven. The one who can accept this should accept it.

MATTHEW 19:12

It's no secret that Jesus took a hard line on divorce and remarriage. Sternly rebuffing those rabbis who taught that a man could divorce his wife for virtually any reason, Jesus reaffirmed the creation principle: "Till death us do part." Had you asked those rabbis if adultery was a sin, they'd quickly say yes. Imagine their shock, then, when Jesus insisted that divorcing one's wife and marrying another woman was tantamount to adultery! Even Jesus' own disciples thought that was a bit harsh! In the midst of this conversation about divorce, suddenly Jesus begins talking about eunuchs! Eunuchs who were born impotent, eunuchs who had been involuntarily castrated, and those who had made themselves eunuchs. (Avoiding connotations of self-mutilation, the most literal translation reads, "have kept themselves eunuchs.") And why have these *acted* as if they were eunuchs? For the sake of the kingdom!

Jesus is not suggesting either a general policy of celibacy or celibacy for special classes of Christians. In the immediate context, he is reinforcing strictures against remarriage following any divorce outside divine guidelines. If that was a hard teaching for his disciples—and for us today—Jesus insists that there are hard choices to be made *for the sake of the kingdom.* Maybe it has to do with not remarrying in the wake of an unauthorized divorce. Maybe it has to do with not entering into forbidden sexual relationships despite urges to do so, or turning down that lucrative job requiring a compromise of integrity. Whatever great personal price one has to pay to maintain kingdom values, God never promised us a spiritual rose garden.

■ **The hard question is: What difficult choices am I willing to make *for the sake of the kingdom*?**

Which Jesus Do We Want to See?

Now there were some Greeks among those who went up to worship at the festival. They came to Philip, who was from Bethsaida in Galilee, with a request. "Sir," they said, "we would like to see Jesus."

JOHN 12:20-21

Celebrities invariably draw crowds. From adoring fans, to curiosity seekers, to lunatics and assassins, celebrities must endure everything that comes with fame. So it's not surprising when these Greeks approach Philip, hoping for an up-close look at the miracle worker everybody was buzzing about. It's possible that the men genuinely wanted to become disciples, but there is no mention of it. In fact when Jesus is told of their request, his odd response suggests otherwise. Saying neither yes or no, Jesus starts talking about how the person who loves this present world will lose everything while the one who forfeits the good life will receive eternal life. Did Jesus miss the question, or was it the Greeks who missed the point? If all they wanted was to *see* Jesus, he had no intention of becoming a freak show. He wasn't calling for *curiosity seekers,* but *spiritual seekers.* Seekers who were willing to pay far more than peep show prices. Seekers willing to lay down their earthly lives for a heavenly cause.

After all these centuries, folks still want to see Jesus, and the clamoring crowd continues to be a mixture of adoring disciples and mere curiosity seekers. Given that mix, you and I need to do some serious soul-searching about our relationship with Jesus. What do we really hope to gain by knowing him? Just to make sure that we end up in heaven rather than hell? Or to feel good about ourselves, wearing a name associated with the Righteous One? Is it still the miracle worker we're after? Wanting to see Jesus for all the wrong reasons is to miss the man altogether.

■ **The question for seekers is: If the tables were turned, what reason have I given Jesus to desire a closer look at me?**

The Challenge of Forgiving

And when you stand praying, if you hold anything against anyone, forgive them, so that your Father in heaven may forgive you your sins.

MARK 11:25

F orgive us our trespasses as we forgive those who trespass against us," goes the line from Jesus' model prayer—the one we call "The Lord's Prayer" and repeat so perfunctorily. Thankfully, the word is *trespasses,* not *sins!* Compared to sins, *trespasses* appear benign. It seems less of a big deal if we merely *trespass* against God. But if we consider the trespasses committed against us, suddenly it's a big deal! On the receiving end, trespasses are outrageous, mean, spiteful, and *downright unforgivable*! Who do these people think they are? If they haven't asked for forgiveness, they don't deserve forgiveness! All of which makes perfect sense…until we consider our crucified Lord saying, "Father, forgive them, for they do not know what they are doing."

At the heart of the gospel is the problem of sin and the need for forgiveness. The story line of the Bible is that sin has separated us from God and that faith in Christ is the means whereby God forgives us. But there is more involved than this legal satisfaction of "debt" in aid of obtaining eternal life. We need to be forgiven because without forgiveness we cannot live with the burden of sin. The uncomfortable truth is that neither can our worst enemies—whether they realize it or not. Yes, we should hold them accountable for their actions, but we also must forgive them. If we can't forgive *those sinners,* how can we expect God to forgive *us sinners*? Indeed, how can we expect *those sinners* ever to seek God's eternal forgiveness? Forgiving and being forgiven just might be the hardest revolving door we will ever walk through!

■ **The unforgiving question is: Who, today, do I need to really and truly forgive?**

Jesus in Our Midst

The King will reply, "Truly I tell you, whatever you did for one of the least of these brothers and sisters of mine, you did for me."

MATTHEW 25:40

Pictures of Jesus are often painted to match our particular expectations. Consider for example, William Dyce's portrayal of Jesus in *The Man of Sorrows* (1860). Meant to depict Jesus' temptation in the wilderness, we see a Leonardo-like Christ in the midst of a barren Scottish Highlands landscape! And then there is Jean Beraud's *Christ in the House of the Pharisee* (1891), a bizarre attempt to transplant Jesus into nineteenth-century bourgeois Paris! We all want Jesus to fit into our own time, culture, and context. Invariably we end up re-creating Jesus in *our* own image. Yet the intriguing question remains: What *did* Jesus look like? Few people are aware that Jesus painted a masterful self-portrait that, even now, hangs in Matthew's gallery.

At first glance you see Jesus wearing a crown of gold and flowing regal robes. But the longer you stare, the more you notice other forms emerging from the thick brushstrokes. For example, there's a woman suffering from some debilitating illness; and also a man with a gaunt, twisted face looking out anxiously from behind prison bars. Toward the bottom of the painting you see a young child with a hideously bloated stomach, obviously starving. And near the top is a weathered old man facing into a bitter wind, wearing the most threadbare of clothing. Clearly, that is how Jesus wants us to see him—as hungry, imprisoned, diseased, and threadbare. Though painted in words, this picture is a vivid reminder that we see Jesus every hour of every day in the faces of all the strugglers whom Jesus himself came to serve—and calls us to serve.

■ **The question Jesus poses is: Am I staring right at him but still missing the picture?**

Faithless Faith

Yet at the same time many even among the leaders believed in him. But because of the Pharisees they would not openly acknowledge their faith for fear they would be put out of the synagogue; for they loved human praise more than praise from God.

JOHN 12:42-43

Something is seriously wrong with this passage. How can anybody have "faith" in Jesus the Son of God, yet not be willing to confess that faith—especially for fear of the consequences? Isn't faith in Christ, by definition, a belief in all that Jesus taught and practiced? If Jesus commanded his disciples to follow him no matter the cost, what remains of faith if we are not willing to do just that? If Jesus calls us to choose between honoring God or honoring man, how can honoring man over God exhibit even a patina of true faith? Surely these religious leaders did not believe in the Jesus you and I know! And yet John's Gospel clearly says they did. John even contrasts them with others who, despite Jesus' miracles, did *not* believe. So here we have it: Respected Jewish leaders who intellectually affirmed that Jesus was the One sent from God, but weren't willing to stand up for that conviction for fear that they would lose their vaunted positions and be kicked out of their local synagogues. Incredible!

What does this travesty of faith tell us except that mere intellectual acknowledgment of Christ is meaningless. To sign up to a belief system without being bold enough to confess that belief is a sham and a farce. It lacks fundamental integrity. Then again, just how far removed are these unbelieving believers from you and me? How many times have *we* silenced our faith for fear of losing favor with someone? How many times have *we* kept quiet about crucial doctrinal issues lest we get dumped from leadership positions or get snubbed by the congregation? And we call ourselves *believers*?

■ **The question of faith is: In what ways have I denounced my faith by refusing to openly acknowledge what I truly believe?**

Washing Even the Dirtiest Feet

Now that I, your Lord and Teacher, have washed your feet, you also should wash one another's feet.

JOHN 13:14

When Peter protests Jesus' kneeling down to wash his feet, Jesus insists that he's teaching the disciples an invaluable lesson about the need to serve others, no matter how "important" one might be. If the Lord could get down on his knees and wash filthy feet—typically a job for servants—then there was no reason why his disciples shouldn't do the same. The need to wash feet as an act of hospitality has little modern application. To elevate footwashing to the status of religious ritual might serve as a reminder of Jesus' lesson on servanthood but risks missing the whole point. Certainly Jesus was not talking about washing feet that are already clean, merely as an act of ceremonial humility. He is using the customary courtesy of washing first-century, sandaled feet to make a statement that, in the kingdom of Christ, no one should think he is above getting his hands dirty serving others.

Though we normally focus on Jesus washing Peter's feet, we mustn't overlook a far more important point. It was not just Peter's feet Jesus washed, but also the feet of the man who only minutes later would leave the upper room to betray him. Was Judas worthy of being served that way? Apparently Jesus thought so because he did not distinguish between Judas and the other disciples. Without doubt, Judas' betrayal was a grave sin. But by his repeated denials of even knowing Jesus, Peter too would soon betray Jesus—as would the other disciples, all of whom fled in Jesus' greatest hour of need. If we refuse to wash the feet of the worst of us, it hardly matters that we might wash the feet of the best of us.

■ **The cleansing question is: If I'm pretty good at serving others, does that include even those who might have the "dirtiest feet"?**

Known by Our Love

They may be brought to complete unity. Then the world will know that you sent me and have loved them even as you have loved me.

JOHN 17:23

A line from the popular hymn reads: "They will know we are Christians by our love." *They,* of course, being an unbelieving world. And make no mistake—they *are watching*! First, they witness Christ-honoring believers in scores of disparate denominations and fellowships. Then, there are those denominational subgroups who don't see eye to eye. Even the casual observer can see all the acrimonious infighting among people singing from the same hymnbook. If "they" are to know us as Christians by our love, what message are we sending with our division and strife? We must be careful, of course, not to overstate the case. A skeptical world is never going to understand the crucial importance of contending earnestly for the truth, even when that results in the kind of division of which Jesus himself warned. Sincere doctrinal differences affirm a commitment to truth.

If conscientious conflicts were the only problem, even cynics might be more understanding. However, because even worthy, necessary, and honorable battles are rarely fought in a spirit of humility and Christian love, the high ground we might otherwise claim quickly erodes. And what possibly can justify all the petty conflicts over personalities, power struggles, finances, and church politics? What must Christ himself be thinking? Surely it is time we all took sober inventory of just how loving we show ourselves to be. Our neighbors aren't simply watching the lack of unity among denominations and fellowships generally. They are watching *you and me*!

■ **The sobering question is: If the world based its judgment about Christ solely upon how I love fellow believers, would they move nearer to Christ or farther away?**

Overcoming Temptation

Watch and pray so that you will not fall into temptation. The spirit is willing, but the flesh is weak.

MATTHEW 26:41

Every instinct in Jesus' body wanted to cut and run. Why else pray, "If possible, Father, take this cup from me"? No less than you or I, Jesus did not want to die an agonizing death. In that deceptively peaceful garden on an ominously dark night, the divine Son of God was first and foremost the earthly Son of Man, complete with the instinct to survive. Yet not even Jesus' closest disciples stayed awake to bolster his resolve. So to Peter, especially, Jesus issues the caution in today's featured verse. It would not be long before Peter would deny knowing Jesus, despite protesting so vehemently that he would never betray the Lord. But here's the intriguing question: Was Jesus' warning meant for Peter and the others or *for himself*? At that particular moment, who but Jesus was in the throes of temptation? Who was having an internal battle between what he knew he *must* do and what he *wanted* to do? If even the incarnate Lord of heaven experienced the excruciating conflict between flesh and spirit, there is a lesson to be learned by all of us.

To have a willing spirit is not enough. As we know, the body sometimes seems to have a mind of its own. Yet neither spirit nor body acts apart from the other. Because human cravings are ultimately subject to an inner will shaped by the spirit, the challenge is to keep that crucial link connected through watchfulness and prayer. No wonder Jesus prayed so fervently in the garden that the Father's will would be his own, so as to conquer the human instincts he was battling. The lesson, then, for today? Without prayer we don't have a prayer!

■ **The obvious question is: If my highest spiritual aspirations are not enough to keep my body in check, isn't it time my spirit got down on its knees?**

Getting What We Need Instead

[Pilate asked], "Do you want me to release 'the king of the Jews'?" They shouted back, "No, not him! Give us Barabbas!"

JOHN 18:39-40

Calling Jesus "king of the Jews" heightened the frenzy of the chief priests. In a last-ditch effort to have Jesus crucified, they had spread out among the crowd and begun to shout, "Away with this man! Release Barabbas to us!" Barabbas was a popular bandit who had been arrested after an insurrection in which a Roman soldier had been killed. Pilate gave them a second chance and asked whom between the two should he release: the Galilean or Barabbas. Incited once again, the crowd roared back, "Barabbas!" Despite the inconceivable depravity of the mob, a grand scheme was unfolding that neither they nor Pilate ever could've imagined. In calling for the release of Barabbas, the people were going to get, not the *man they wanted*, but the *Son of Man they needed*. Lost on them was the significance of the name they were shouting. That strikingly odd name *Bar-Abbas*, meaning "son of his father," was even then pointing to the incarnate Son of God whose death would make possible their very redemption—for *they* were the prisoners who needed release. And who would free them from their enslavement to sin? By divine irony, not the criminal Barabbas whom the mob wanted released, but instead, the innocent *Bar-Abbas* they wanted to crucify.

In all the discussions about how God answers prayers, it is not likely that the name Barabbas ever surfaces, but it should. How often, like the mob, might we get something far more beneficial than that for which we are praying? If "we must be careful what we pray for," as the saying goes, we should also not be surprised that a loving God takes even unworthy pleas and turns them into unimagined blessings!

■ **The ironic question is: Have I sometimes prayed for the wrong things, only to be given exactly what I need?**

The Perfect Passover Lamb

But when they came to Jesus and found that he was already dead, they did not break his legs.

JOHN 19:33

Was it merely fortuity that Jesus' legs were not broken? Breaking the legs was done to hasten death by making it impossible to lift one's self up to breathe. But Jesus was already dead…precisely at the same hour that all the pascal lambs were being slain in preparation for the Passover meal. It is a complex premise, but the traditional understanding that the "Last Supper" was a Passover meal is fraught with difficulties exposed primarily by John's Gospel. What seems obvious (the disciples preparing the upper room for the Passover, and Jesus saying he desired to eat the Passover with them) turns out to be not so obvious when other passages are considered. For example, during the "Last Supper," the eleven speculated that Judas had been sent to get supplies for the feast, which would've been unlikely had the feast already begun. And the next morning, Gentile-wary Jews refused to enter Pilate's palace, wanting "to be able to eat the Passover."

The possibility that the "Last Supper" was not actually a Passover meal is rich with potential meaning. Assuming Jesus did not *eat* a Passover lamb but *was* the Passover Lamb, the same ceremonial rules would have applied to him as to any other pascal lamb, including the injunction that no bone was to be broken. (It's unhelpful that the King James Version has Jesus saying, "This is my body, which is *broken* for you," particularly in light of Paul's play on words urging that Christ's spiritual body—the church—should not be broken!) By contrast with the perfect Lamb of God, only you and I are spiritually broken and in need of healing.

■ **The disturbing question is: Just how truly broken up am I about the brokenness in me that caused Jesus to suffer?**

_____

_____

_____

_____

_____

Proof Beyond Doubt

Then Simon Peter…saw the strips of linen lying there, as well as the cloth that had been wrapped around Jesus' head. The cloth was still lying in its place, separate from the linen.

JOHN 20:6-7

In the latest version of the NIV, the burial cloth is neither "folded" nor "rolled," as is common in most translations. Pity, since the detail is a priceless clue worthy of the finest, most mysterious whodunits. Surely we are not simply to believe that Jesus was a neat freak. But neither is any grave robber. Who, hurriedly stealing away Jesus' body, would have taken the time to fold the burial cloth? Remember all the controversy (to this day) over whether Jesus was really and truly raised from the dead or whether Jesus' disciples had surreptitiously removed his body from the tomb? The wide-ranging implications are crucial, not the least of which is our own hope of being resurrected. When doubting Thomas insisted on seeing the nail wounds in Jesus' hands, he was not alone in wanting solid evidence. Who of us doesn't? After all, we are staking our very faith on it! And you and I are twenty centuries removed from the event! No wonder Jesus said to Thomas, "Blessed are those who have not seen [my wounds as you have] and yet have believed."

Do you ever wonder why we believe what we do? Is it because we simply *want* to believe it, like Santa Claus or a fascinating fairy tale? Indeed, what makes people believe in *non-Christian* faiths? Are we all following blindly along, taking the word of our families or teachers that our particular belief system is superior to all others? For true seekers, belief will always be a leap of faith—but faith without fact is only wishful thinking. No surprise, then, that John tells us he recorded Jesus' miracles so that you and I might believe in Jesus, through whom alone we can have eternal life.

■ **The urgent question is: If I don't yet have faith in Jesus, have I simply ignored the overwhelming evidence?**

Gifted with the Holy Spirit

Peter replied, "Repent and be baptized, every one of you, in the name of Jesus Christ for the forgiveness of your sins. And you will receive the gift of the Holy Spirit."

ACTS 2:38

Do you not know that your bodies are temples of the Holy Spirit, who is in you?" Paul will later write in 1 Corinthians 6:19. Is this just a picture, or does Paul mean that literally? If what Peter says in today's text is to be taken at face value, Paul had something quite specific in mind. It *is* a picture—but one framed in reality. Neither "gifts of the Spirit" nor "fruit of the Spirit" quite captures the sense. The former speaks of extraordinary, Spirit-given abilities such as prophecy, speaking in tongues, or interpretation. The latter signifies virtues flowing from the Spirit-led life, such as love, joy, and peace. Distinguished from either of these is an active indwelling of the Holy Spirit in every true disciple of Christ. What Peter promises is a soul-penetrating, inner gifting of God's divine presence, enabling our prayers, illuminating our understanding of the written Word, and producing in us those fruits of the Spirit.

It is this indwelling presence that invites Paul's analogy of our bodies as living temples in which the Holy Spirit abides. Inescapably conjured is the image of Jesus cleansing the temple and gracing it with his presence. Ridding the temple in Jerusalem of its corruption and vice, Jesus symbolically restored his Father's house to its pristine condition—the idea, precisely, behind the repentance for which Peter called. Repentance brings an openness to renewal, restoration, and refurbishment. It is our personal invitation to God to scrub our "temples" clean and make us holy through the purifying waters of baptism. So if, in fact, Paul's Spirit-filled temple analogy is "a picture," surely it is a picture worth a thousand words!

■ **The purifying question is: If I truly wish to have the presence of God in my life, have I allowed my temple to be washed and filled?**

Discipled in a Different School

When they saw the courage of Peter and John and realized that they were unschooled, ordinary men, they were astonished and they took note that these men had been with Jesus.

ACTS 4:13

Jerusalem's brightest scholars and esteemed chief priests had never seen anything like it. Here were ordinary, uneducated men who were extraordinarily insightful and articulate, yet without either degree or pedigree. They were not learned rabbis or teachers of the law, yet their wisdom, sacrificial devotion, and Spirit-transformed character was remarkable. Who *were* these guys? They were disciples of Jesus—and everyone noticed. Interestingly, they were not initially called "Christians." They were referred to as Jesus' *disciples.* All who followed Jesus in those early years were known as his *disciples,* not the least being Jesus' specially chosen apostles. The twelve had given up everything to sit at the feet of the Master Teacher for three years of intensive, on-the-job training. Who needs books about The Book when you are in the presence of the one who *wrote* The Book!

Have we possibly missed something terribly important about the "Great Commission"? Oh, we've responded to Jesus' call to evangelism, sending missionaries out to convert and baptize people of every nation. But have we truly made them *disciples* of Jesus, "teaching them to obey everything I have commanded you"? *Converting* is one thing; *discipling* is another. What is the ratio of nominal "Christians" to dedicated "disciples"? Could this crucial difference explain the biblical illiteracy and spiritual shallowness plaguing the church today? To be a disciple of Jesus demands more than being a church-going, Bible-believing "Christian." It means making a conscious, concerted effort, not just to know and love Jesus, but to become *like* him.

■ **The compelling question is: Isn't it time I moved beyond merely being a Christian to being a serious disciple of Jesus?**

The Purpose of Prayer

While they were stoning him, Stephen prayed, "Lord Jesus, receive my spirit." Then he fell on his knees and cried out, "Lord, do not hold this sin against them."

ACTS 7:59-60

Reading today's text, do you get a sense of déjà vu? While hanging in agony on the cross, Jesus himself had said, "Father, into your hands I commit my spirit" (Luke 23:46), and "Father, forgive them, for they do not know what they are doing" (verse 34). For one's dying thoughts to be focused on the forgiveness of one's enemies must surely be the ultimate tribute. Yet how are we to understand the nature of the prayers uttered by both Jesus and Stephen? Are we to believe that God actually answered their prayers by instantly forgiving their tormentors? We know for a certainty that God did not instantly forgive the crowds baying for Jesus' blood. Many of them were the same blood-stained people to whom Peter and the other apostles preached their Pentecost sermon, calling for them to repent and be baptized for the forgiveness of their sins. So had God not answered the prayer even of his own Son?

More pertinent is the question of how, when, and under what circumstances God answers *our* prayers. Who among us hasn't prayed fervently that God would heal someone with a terminal illness, only to watch them die? Is prayer an exercise in futility, or do we simply accept that it is for us to pray and for God to heal…or not to heal? Surely the same principle applies to God forgiving our enemies, or else God would be compelled to forgive everyone on whose behalf we fervently prayed! Because that obviously cannot be the case, the question remains: Why pray for our enemies? Could it be that prayers for others are more for *our* soul's good than for *theirs*?

■ **The question dying to be asked is: Have I considered that I am spiritually shaped by the prayers that I pray (or don't pray) on behalf of others?**

Radical Transformation

As he neared Damascus on his journey, suddenly a light from heaven flashed around him.
He fell to the ground and heard a voice say to him, "Saul, Saul, why do you persecute me?"

ACTS 9:3-4

Even the secular press will sometimes refer to a politician or other public figure as having had a "Damascus road experience"—a sudden turnabout of conviction or policy. In Saul's case there was a radical transformation without equal. A feared persecutor of Jesus' disciples, Saul was a prime target for God's attention, but not for punishment. God had determined a special mission for Saul before he was ever born—but timing was everything. Saul was more useful to God as a *protector* of God's people after having been a *persecutor* of God's people. Who, but a zealous enemy, could be so zealous for the right cause? Who, but one who had inflicted so much pain, could endure so much pain for his Lord? Who, but one so narrow-mindedly Jewish, could best appreciate the need for outreach to a non-Jewish world? Every convert is a transformed soul, but few have known such an extraordinary metamorphosis.

But for those of us who have never experienced a Saul-like radical transformation, maybe we've taken our "conversion experience" for granted. If it was more of a natural progression than a sudden break with a sinful past, how revved up can we be about such a conversion? What incredible story do we have to tell? Indeed, some may consider themselves to be Christians without anything that remotely could be described as a conversion experience. Maybe we don't have to be blinded by light along a highway, but if we've never had a "Damascus road experience" of *some* kind, just how useful will Jesus find us?

■ **The probing question is: If I've never experienced a radical transformation of my outward faith life, have I been truly transformed from within?**

Joy Beyond Belief

When she recognized Peter's voice, she was so overjoyed she ran back without opening it and exclaimed, "Peter is at the door!" "You're out of your mind," they told her. When she kept insisting that it was so, they said, "It must be his angel."

ACTS 12:14-15

So what were they praying for, those who had rushed to the house of Mary and John Mark when news spread of Peter's imprisonment? That God would deliver Peter safely? That God's providential hand of protection would keep him from harm? Yet when Peter shows up at the house, having been miraculously released from prison by an angel, these prayerful people were incredulous! The servant girl was either crazy or had seen Peter's angel! Yet if Peter did have an angel, what are angels for? More to the point, if nothing extraordinary is going to happen, then what are *prayers* for? Do we not pray to invoke God's divine power when we ourselves have reached the end of human capability? Need a miracle? Pray to God! So if we get precisely what we have been praying for, why should we ever be shocked?

The answer, of course, is that our prayers are rarely answered in such a dramatic fashion. How wonderful it would be, for instance, if we prayed that all who are currently imprisoned around the world as martyrs for Christ would be released tonight without harm…and suddenly they all showed up at our door! Certainly, God could snap his fingers and make that happen, but *will* he? And if he did, would we be any less astounded than the people praying for Peter? So what are we to make of the popular expression, "Expect a miracle"? If perhaps we have little reason to *expect* a miracle each and every time, who would want it said of us that we didn't believe it even when it happened?

■ **The prayerful question is: Do I pray with such confidence in God's power that I would never be surprised if he answered even the most challenging of prayers?**

It's a Rough Road to the Kingdom

"We must go through many hardships to enter the kingdom of God," they said.

ACTS 14:22

When and how did you first enter the kingdom of God? Was it associated with a penitent prayer, or a commitment in your heart, or perhaps your baptism? If so, you likely can identify with Jesus telling Nicodemus that "no one can enter the kingdom of God unless he is born of water and the Spirit" (John 3:5). Sounds like a definable moment in time, doesn't it? Yet all the other "kingdom passages" seem not to describe a single act of conversion. Indeed, today's featured verse is addressed to baptized believers! To people who, if you asked them, would have said they were "in the kingdom." So how can people who are already *in* the kingdom still have to "go through many hardships *to enter* the kingdom of God"? Is there a difference between being "in the church" and "in the kingdom"? Just about the moment we are ready to say, "No, they're one and the same," suddenly there is cause to wonder…

Even before the church was established, Jesus was teaching about entering the kingdom. "You cannot enter the kingdom," he said, loosely translated, "unless your righteousness surpasses that of the Pharisees. It may even mean plucking out your eye if it is causing you to sin. And if you are not willing to sell everything you have to give to the poor, then you can never enter the kingdom of heaven. For the rich, the kingdom is hard to enter! What's more, if you want to enter the kingdom, you will have to become as trusting as a little child." If we have never gone through real hardships because of our faith, we may be in the church but still quite distant from "the kingdom."

■ **The tough question is: In light of Jesus' teaching, how far do I yet have to go to enter the kingdom of God?**

Dead Men Walking

I have been crucified with Christ and I no longer live, but Christ lives in me.

GALATIANS 2:20

Prisoners awaiting execution on death row are said to be "dead men walking." They might possibly have their lives spared by reversed convictions or pardons, but in the meantime, they are as good as dead. Ironic, isn't it, that disciples of Jesus are also "dead men walking," though in a different sense altogether. We are not *awaiting* death, but are *already* dead. To identify with Christ in name is to identify with Christ in his death, burial, and resurrection, as pictured most vividly in Christian baptism. Having died to self, we are buried in the watery grave and are raised to walk a new life! But metaphors without an underlying reality are merely nice pictures. How many of us can honestly say that we have been "crucified with Christ"? (Nail prints, anyone?) How many of us have gone down into the watery grave without ever fully dying to self? We would think it unimaginably cruel to be buried alive, but countless believers have "been dunked" without experiencing the death that such a burial assumes. So what is that but being buried alive? How spiritually suffocating it must be!

One way or the other, everybody has to die twice. Unless the Lord returns in our lifetime, everyone is going to die physically. But there is that "second death" to think about, the destruction of the soul that Jesus spoke of and that John mentions in his Revelation. The "second death" in the eternal realm is for those who have not already died to Christ in this life. So the choice is ours. How do we want to experience our "second death," *crucified* with Christ or *condemned* by Christ?

■ **The excruciating question is: Am I a dead person walking with Christ, or a pretend Christian who has yet to truly die?**

A Holy Hunger for Truth

Now the Bereans were of more noble character than those in Thessalonica, for they received the message with great eagerness and examined the Scriptures every day to see if what Paul said was true.

ACTS 17:11

Remember that conversation between Jesus and Pilate when Jesus said, "I came into the world to testify to the truth; everyone on the side of truth listens to me"? Famously, Pilate responded, "What is truth?" The definite article here is conspicuous by its omission. Pilate didn't ask "What is *the* truth?" (which assumes the existence of truth itself), but "What is *truth*?" (as if asking whether there is such a thing as ultimate truth). If Pilate had his doubts about some higher truth, he nevertheless had a keen sense of judicial truth that led him to believe that Jesus was innocent. Unfortunately, he was also aware of another competing truth: that he risked Caesar's disfavor if Jesus—who claimed to be "a king"—were let go. That baser truth won out over a much more profound truth. One can only wonder what might have resulted had Pilate been more convinced about higher truth itself.

In an increasingly relativistic world, the dogged pursuit of truth is fast becoming a rare commodity. If there is no ultimate truth, why should we invest our hearts and minds in searching for *the* truth among competing truth claims? For the Bereans to be divinely applauded for their passionate pursuit of the truth must mean, first and foremost, that they valued truth above all else. The Bereans had a holy hunger for divine truth, which they knew intuitively could be found in the Scriptures alone, not in any mere mortal. And so the words of every man were carefully, prayerfully, and stringently measured against God's divinely revealed truth. If anyone was ever "on the side of truth," the Bereans were!

■ **The searching question is: Do I have such a consuming passion for truth that I scrupulously test everything I hear against that standard?**

Raising Our Ambitions Lower

Make it your ambition to lead a quiet life: You should mind your own business and work with your hands, just as we told you, so that your daily life may win the respect of outsiders and so that you will not be dependent on anybody.

1 THESSALONIANS 4:11-12

He's an ambitious young man, isn't he?" we often say with admiration. Or, "Her ambition is to be a doctor, isn't that wonderful?" By way of disapproval, we might even say, "Too bad he doesn't have more ambition!" For most parents, instilling a sense of ambition in their children seems fundamental. Who would want them growing up without having the best jobs, homes, and status they can acquire? Some professions can hardly be attained without heaps of ambition. Ever known a politician who wasn't ambitious? Or a wealthy business tycoon? A driving ambition is the motivation behind virtually every human success story. At the very least, it is ambition that gets most of us through school and all those dreaded studies thrown our way.

How striking it is, then, to hear Paul speaking of a radically different kind of ambition, and even to put it in terms of "studying," as some translations render it. Paul, a man himself of great ambition, urges us to study to lead a quiet life. In an increasingly clamorous and frantic world, living a spiritually reflective life will require all the more concerted effort. How do you lead a quiet, godly life while frenetically climbing the ladder? Maybe you can't. And if not, which is more important? For all the ambition that parents might wish to instill in their children, perhaps the most important lesson of all is teaching children how to live reflective, godly, and righteous lives. Then again, how is that crucial lesson going to be received if parents themselves are too busy achieving their own career-oriented ambitions?

■ **The question for reflection is: Now that I've spent a good part of my life being ambitious, is it not time to study about living a more meditative and godly life?**

Lord Willing!

But as he left, he promised, "I will come back if it is God's will." Then he set sail from Ephesus.

ACTS 18:21

Time was when you heard the phrase, "Lord willing" sprinkled throughout daily conversation. That the phrase "Lord willing" has mostly gone out of fashion is probably not a great fashion statement. Seems that now it's all about us, not God. Whatever background role God might have had is relegated to celestial matters. Many are not even sure God is still actively at work in his world. Certainly, few of us could tell exciting stories of God's direct intervention to thwart our future plans as Paul could. Do you recall when Paul's plans were divinely altered on his second missionary journey? As Luke records it, "When they came to the border of Mysia, they tried to enter Bithynia, but the Spirit of Jesus would not allow them to." (Wouldn't you like to know exactly how that happened?) It was shortly thereafter that Paul received his "Macedonian call" in a nighttime vision. So Paul was not lightly uttering trite words when he invoked "God's will" regarding his hoped-for return to Ephesus. As it happens, the Lord must have been willing because Paul would indeed spend more time in Ephesus.

It would be reassuring if people today would grace their speech with "God willing." (Imagine the impact if the president and members of Congress regularly used it with reference to national intentions!) Of course we would never want to use the term strictly from habit without a firm belief that, in truth and in fact, God *might* or *might not* be willing. How wonderfully transformed all of us would be if we took seriously the proverb, "In his heart a man plans his course, but the LORD determines his steps" (Proverbs 16:9).

■ **The interesting question is: Do I ever consciously factor God's will into my future plans?**

Carnal Christianity

Brothers and sisters, I could not address you as people who live by the Spirit but as people who are still worldly—mere infants in Christ.

1 CORINTHIANS 3:1

Division was wrecking the church in Corinth. Quite unbelievably, various ones were claiming allegiance to Peter, or Paul, or Apollos! Even those who maintained allegiance only to Christ had become a cliquish fellowship to themselves. So much for Jesus' prayer for unity! When you consider the mix of Jews and Gentiles in Corinth, you can begin to make sense of this. By their culture, Jewish Christians would have been more attracted to the excitement of miraculous signs; while the Gentile Christians, being more intellectually-minded, preferred a focus on reason and heady doctrine. Paul's response was blunt and incisive. Despite the unity that their common baptism into Christ ought to have produced, he argued, they had all missed the central message of the cross. For Jews with a long history of miracles, had any exciting miracle saved Jesus from the cross? For Gentiles enamored with human wisdom and philosophy, did the cross make any earthly sense? Put simply, the cross of Christ defied all worldly yearnings and expectations. The road to unity (and beyond) was through being *spiritually mature*, not *carnally immature*.

Just how much has changed since Paul wrote his scathing letter? Are we not still carnally minded and worldly? How would you describe our various worship experiences—truly God-focused or self-satisfying? Our view of the end times—transcendent spiritual triumph or cataclysmic earthly upheaval? Or our understanding of the nature of heaven and our resurrected bodies: otherworldly or still very much this-worldly? "When I was a child, I talked like a child, I thought like a child, I reasoned like a child." Carnal Christianity is not simply a mark of spiritual immaturity, but a quintessential oxymoron.

■ **The cross-focused question is: If I were crucified alongside Jesus, would I be looking down at the earth or lifting my human eyes spiritually higher?**

With Freedom, Responsibility

"I have the right to do anything," you say—but not everything is beneficial. "I have the right to do anything"—but not everything is constructive. No one should seek their own good, but the good of others.

1 CORINTHIANS 10:23-24

There is a saying in law that "your right to swing your fist ends at my nose." This legal truism helps explain today's intriguing text. For Jews, having suffocated for generations under the strictures of the law, freedom in Christ was heady stuff. Even for Gentiles, Christian liberation without pagan license had great appeal. But freedom and liberation can easily erode into self-indulgence and irresponsibility, especially with regard to others. So here we find Paul issuing a caution to those Corinthians flaunting their new-found freedom in the presence of weaker Christians, not thinking how their high-flying liberation might lead others astray. Paul does not dispute the basic premise that, in Christ, the prohibitions of strict legalism have given way to the grace of permission. Yet this new "permission" assumes the same process of maturation that gradually weans a child from the black and white rules necessary for the very young. With increased freedom always comes increased responsibility.

In a rights-obsessed society, it's difficult for any of us to exercise forbearance. Yet that is precisely what those in Christ are expected to do. Would any of us cross the street simply because we have a right to do so, if it could not be done safely by the child following in our footsteps? Or thoughtlessly open a bottle of wine in the presence of a struggling alcoholic? Without question, there's nothing wrong in seeking our own good—but never at the expense of the vulnerable. Even if the answer to the question "Do I have a right to do it?" is *yes*, that is never the final question.

■ **The question for the mature is: Who might be watching what I myself do in complete innocence and yet be influenced to their detriment?**

The Greatest Is Love

If I speak in the tongues of men or of angels, but do not have love, I am only a resounding gong or a clanging cymbal.

1 CORINTHIANS 13:1

When the Beatles sang that famous song "All You Need Is Love," odds are they were overlooking faith, obedience, purity, and a host of other spiritual requisites. Yet they weren't far from kingdom teaching. Simply comparing faith, hope, and love, Paul tells us that "the greatest of these is love" (1 Corinthians 13:13). Not silly love. Not "in love" love. Even though Paul's teaching about love is certainly applicable for marriage, this famous thirteenth chapter was not written merely to be a wedding backdrop. This "love chapter" is sandwiched between two other chapters dealing with the use of such spiritual gifts as prophesying and tongues. Quite incredibly, many of the Corinthians were turning their charismatic gifts into an occasion for envy, jealously, and pride—hardly *love*! Paul calls them on the carpet, warning that, without love, having a spiritual gift is useless.

If not romantic love, or loving one's enemies, or showing love to strangers, what kind of love is Paul talking about? Have you ever noticed that some of the most unloving people in the world are those who are the most religious? Or that certain major world religions are notoriously devoid of love? If love of "the higher good" is not the most basic motivating force behind one's religion or personal faith, nothing but an unloving perversion can result. One can assert the most fervent faith in God, and even the hope of eternal life, but have neither if one lacks love. The difference between "good" (such as having spiritual gifts) and "the greater good" (making humble use of them) is what mature Christian love is all about. Anyone can love the "good." Few know what it means to love "the greater good."

■ **The question of truly loving is: If perhaps appreciating "the good" comes easy for me, how motivated am I by "the greater good"?**

Brand-New or Recycled?

And just as we have borne the image of the earthly man, so shall we bear the image of the heavenly man.

1 CORINTHIANS 15:49

Everybody seems to have a different idea about what our resurrected bodies will be like. Some imagine them to be angel-like, complete with wings. Others wonder if they'll be more like disembodied spirits. Most think that we'll have virtually the same bodies as here on earth—just "new and improved." None of us can be sure, but Paul goes to great lengths to explain that our resurrection bodies will be completely different from what we see in the mirror. He speaks of seeds not being the same as that which is harvested. (Think watermelon seeds and watermelons!) Indeed, having the same recognizable bodies would present an immediate problem, considering the range in earthly bodies from aborted fetuses to stillborn infants to disfigured adults and "old wrinklies." And will there be racial or gender distinctions on the other side? Even the details of the Resurrection are mind-boggling. If our decaying bodies are truly "dust to dust," will it be a matter of vacuuming and reassembling? And what of the belief that we go immediately to heaven when we die…even before the Resurrection? What bodies do we have in the meantime? Or the belief that we are raptured into heaven and then brought back down to some kind of earthly reign? How does that work, body-wise?

When Jesus rebuked the Resurrection-skeptical Sadducees by saying that in heaven there is no marriage, he was signaling that in the eternal realm life is nothing remotely like what we experience today. Given that unpredictability, Paul's discussion takes on added meaning. Just as we bear Adam's likeness in this life, in the life to come we will bear the likeness of Christ—but only, ironically, if we *already* bear his likeness!

■ **The predictable question is: In all honesty, how closely do I bear the likeness of Jesus while in my *present* body?**

Tough Love

For I wrote you out of great distress and anguish of heart and with many tears, not to grieve you but to let you know the depth of my love for you.

2 CORINTHIANS 2:4

We have all experienced that classic line from our parents: "This hurts me more than it does you." Naturally, few of us on the receiving end ever really believed it, but with time and maturity we grew to appreciate the truth behind the sentiment. Today's featured passage follows in the same vein. Master of finesse that he was, Paul was not reticent in calling the Corinthians on the carpet. The letter we know as 1 Corinthians is a stinger! No wonder we find 2 Corinthians more conciliatory. Paul wants the Corinthians to know that he has rebuked them solely out of love and concern for their souls—not out of anger or as revenge against those who have questioned his apostleship. Just as the doctor sometimes has to hurt us to heal us, Paul knew he had no real option but to lance the boil.

So what do we do when we find ourselves having to forcefully confront someone we love for their own good? Whether we call it rebuke, intervention, or admonition, it is never without pain to ourselves as well as to the target of our loving arrows. Maybe this partially explains why we exercise what has been termed "tough love" less often than we probably should. It is enough that we are hesitant to sit in judgment of another, knowing our own faults. But we also know that calling someone to task is rarely appreciated, even by those who ought to know that love is our only motivation. So are we simply to stand by and watch someone we love self-destruct, or must we not take action against all instinct? Sometimes hurting the one we love is truly the greatest love.

■ **The tougher question is: If I can sometimes *dish out* tough love when necessary, how do I *take* tough love when I'm on the receiving end?**

Our Weakness, God's Power

Three times I pleaded with the Lord to take it away from me. But he said to me, "My grace is sufficient for you, for my power is made perfect in weakness."

2 CORINTHIANS 12:8-9

Just what was Paul's "thorn in the flesh"? All we know is that this "thorn" was inflicted to keep Paul humble in the wake of that incredible revelation in which he was allowed a sneak preview of the celestial realm. You and I might think it a worthwhile trade-off to be shown something of heaven's glory, but Paul pleaded with God three times, to no avail, for the "thorn" to be taken from him. Seems that God intended to use that "thorn in the flesh" to demonstrate his own power to overcome Paul's weaknesses. Various other passages tend to suggest that Paul's "thorn" might have been obscured sight, which would certainly be fitting, given the forbidden celestial wonders he had seen. This raises an intriguing question about why God allows for all sorts of incapacitating disabilities. Why does God permit blindness, or deafness, or scores of other physical and mental handicaps? We don't have to look far to find at least one instance in which Jesus gives us an explanation. Remember the man Jesus healed who was born blind? When various ones offered misguided explanations for the man's blindness, Jesus cut them all short, saying, "This happened so that the work of God might be displayed in his life" (John 9:3).

Is it not possible, then, that the same is true of everyone who comes into this world as one of God's "special people"? If they are mirrors to us of our own spiritual blindness, deafness, and moral deficiencies, in what way might our own physical ailments and diseases be a reminder to us of God's power working through whatever adverse circumstances we face?

■ **The question worth asking is: If I've prayed to God that he might take away some "thorn" in my flesh, what might I miss out on if that "thorn" were actually removed?**

A More Mature Path to Righteousness

For in the gospel the righteousness of God is revealed—a righteousness that is by faith from first to last, just as it is written: "The righteous will live by faith."

ROMANS 1:17

If asked, most of us would say that we ought to be people of faith, characterized by righteous living—and, for the most part, we *are* such people. Yet if it were that simple, why do you suppose Paul explores at such length the relationship between *faith* and *righteousness?* The short answer is that the Jews were notorious for thinking that righteousness came through strict law-keeping. While we might chide the Jews for practicing a futile "works righteousness," is it possible that even we easily confuse *being* good with *doing* good? Herein lies a dangerous trap. To whatever extent we *don't* do good (would anyone claim perfection?), to that same extent we cannot possibly claim to be righteous. So where does that leave us? As believers who are hopelessly unrighteous? Oh, no, we quickly protest! Our righteousness comes through Christ alone, not anything we might do. Herein lies an equally dangerous trap. To whatever extent we don't *have* to be good to be righteous, to that extent we often *aren't*. The temptation is to think that having a professed faith in Jesus is all we need in order to be adjudged righteous. We forget that Abraham's faith was credited to him as righteousness precisely because it was a *complete* faith, joining trust and belief with faith-prompted action.

Righteousness that is "by faith from first to last," is not a righteousness devoid of conscious acts of holiness, purity, and godliness. It is a righteousness that flows *toward* such actions, not *from* them. The difference in direction is not a matter of indifference. While deep faith invariably motivates action, actions alone can never prompt deep faith.

■ **The intriguing question is: If I struggle with being righteous, could it be because I am still relying on my own effort rather than being truly transformed?**

The Good in Things Not So Good

And we know that in all things God works for the good of those who love him, who have been called according to his purpose.

ROMANS 8:28

Maxims trip ever so lightly off the tongue, no matter how inconsistent they may be when paired with each other. Consider, for example, the adage "Look before you leap." Good advice to be sure. Then again, there is that other adage "He who hesitates is lost." In the proper context, both maxims give wise counsel. It's just that every adage has its limitations, not to be unduly stretched into absurdity. Perhaps this principle can help us better understand the complex truth contained in today's featured verse. No one has to tell us that this world is full of trouble and pain. Scripture itself tells us that suffering should come as no surprise to Christians—the very same Christians for whom all things, says Paul, are supposed to work together for good! The fact that suffering is not *good* in and of itself does not rule out the possibility that there might actually be much good in suffering. Or, at the least, that good can emerge *out of* suffering, and even that God might well use suffering as a means of bringing about the very good he intends. (Did he not cause Israel to suffer in order to bring about her redemption?)

To claim today's passage as a "Get Out of Jail Free" card for all Christians is to overstate its intended meaning. We are not promised (as we are often glibly told) that because we are Christians life will be good or even that everything will turn out good in the long run. What we *are* promised is that whether we experience good or the most horrible thing imaginable, God is working behind the scenes to bring about a good that we might never fully appreciate on this side of heaven.

■ **The difficult question is: Do I fully trust that God is bringing about good even in the most dire circumstance I might face?**

The Blame Game

One of you will say to me: "Then why does God still blame us? For who is able to resist his will?"

ROMANS 9:19

If children do not always play fair, they certainly have an innate sense of fair play. "But it's not *my* fault," they protest when the finger is wrongly pointed at them. "You can't blame *me*!" None of us likes being blamed for something we didn't do or for events beyond our control. So Paul's hypothetical question resonates with us on a deep level. If God is in complete control, why should we be blamed for our sins? It is not unlike that often heard feeble excuse, "Hey, I didn't ask to be born," which is as much to say that God brought my wretched self into this world, so what else can he expect?

In today's text Paul is addressing that very issue. Making the case to the Jews that it is God's sovereign prerogative to do whatever he wills in blessing the Gentiles with salvation, Paul anticipates what could be a logical enough extension of his argument. "If no one can resist God's sovereign master plan," one might ask, "how can even the sin in my life not be an outworking of God's will? Why then should God blame me for spiritual rebellion that he himself has divinely orchestrated?" Where the logic breaks down, of course, is in the faulty assumption that everything that happens is God's will. That God providentially works among nations and individuals to bring about his eternal plan is not to say that God wills evil or sin into existence. What God wills is right living! So when you and I sin, we are wholly outside of God's will and solely to blame. To confuse God's sovereign will with our own willful insolence is to compound the very blame we are trying so desperately to evade.

■ **The soul-searching question is: Even if I intellectually acknowledge that I alone am to blame for my sin, are there yet seductively subtle ways I attempt to throw the blame back on God?**

The Powers That Be

The authorities that exist have been established by God. Consequently, whoever rebels against the authority is rebelling against what God has instituted, and those who do so will bring judgment on themselves.

ROMANS 13:1-2

Does Paul really mean to say that Hitler, Stalin, and Mussolini were all appointed to their positions of power by God himself? That world leaders from Alexander the Great to Genghis Khan to Attila the Hun all served by divine right? Or that America's presidents have been elected not just democratically but providentially? Or is Paul simply telling us that government leaders, however they rise up, are fulfilling a vital role in God's plan for man on earth? At the very least, Scripture seems to suggest that certain leaders were in fact raised up specifically to carry out some divinely ordained mission. Merely consider Pharaoh, Nebuchadnezzar, and Cyrus. It becomes more problematic, of course, when we think of Pilate, who played such a key role in Jesus' crucifixion. Did God bring Pilate to power?

Far more troubling for most of us is Paul's censure of civil rebellion against established authorities. Would that not include the American Revolution itself and even the nonviolent, yet civilly disobedient, civil rights movement? Despite the corruption inherent in first-century Rome, it is instructive that Jesus said, "Give back to Caesar what is Caesar's" (Mark 12:17). He spoke not a word about the right to rebel when government is corrupt, abusive, or even threatening to religious freedom. Was our "Christian nation" birthed through an unchristian process? Despite the many thorny questions raised by this passage, what is clear is that—short of disobeying God himself—we are under divine imperative to submit to those who govern us. The Christian life is not about anarchy, but about order, peace and, most important of all, worrying more about kingdom than country.

■ **The challenging question is: Whatever else I think of them, do I pray for my nation's leaders as if God himself had placed them in power?**

Laying Down a Life

Then Paul answered, "Why are you weeping and breaking my heart? I am ready not only to be bound, but also to die in Jerusalem for the name of the Lord Jesus."

ACTS 21:13

Who would you be willing to die for? Your husband or wife? Your children? Your neighbor? If it came down to our life lost or another's, there are any number of special relationships that would cause us to ignore self-interest and sacrifice ourselves. But suppose no other life is in the balance. We often hear talk about soldiers laying down their lives for their country. Yet even among all the brave, patriotic men and women who have died for the cause, few of them actually signed up specifically to die, as if a kamikaze pilot or suicide bomber. Shifting the focus, still others have died because of their faith, but not always intentionally so. Millions have been killed simply because they were of the *wrong* faith, but not necessarily because they chose death rather than renouncing their faith.

To be "faithful unto death" is to be faithful even in the face of dying for what you believe. It does not mean committing suicide for the sake of the kingdom or taking the lives of others in aid of some righteous cause. Terrorists who take innocent life could not be more misguided. Yet what could be nobler than to lay down one's life for a transcendent cause? As Jesus had done before him, Paul set his face toward Jerusalem knowing that it might well lead to his death. Were you and I to be given the same choice, would we have resolutely walked into Jerusalem knowing what fate awaited us? Few of us will ever face such a difficult dilemma regarding our faith, but it is well worth seriously considering "What if?"

■ **The question for the moment is: If I think I'd be willing to *die* for my faith were I actually put to the test, am I equally committed to the even greater challenge of truly *living* for my faith?**

Accommodation or Appeasement?

The next day Paul took the men and purified himself along with them. Then he went to the temple to give notice of the date when the days of purification would end and the offering would be made for each of them.

ACTS 21:26

"Circumstances alter situations," so it is said. What might be appropriate for one set of circumstances might not be appropriate for another set of circumstances. Knowing when to do what under just the right circumstances is the mark of a mature and wise person. How else are we to understand Paul's strange actions? In his various letters, Paul repeatedly chides Jewish converts for holding onto the Law, yet here we see Paul openly practicing ritual purification; and on another occasion we see Paul having Timothy circumcised pursuant to the Law. But then there was the time when Paul chastised Peter for playing to the circumcision crowd and withdrawing from Gentile converts who were not practicing circumcision or other rituals required by the Law. Either Paul is hypocritically inconsistent or he is mature and wise. Which do you think?

Perhaps the answer lies in Paul's statement that he had become all things to all people in order that he might win them to Christ. It does not mean that we are to "do" drugs in order to reach addicts for Christ. Or convert prostitutes by visiting their beds. Or even to worship alongside Hindus, Buddhists, or Muslims in hopes of showing them the path to Christ. But it does mean that we are to build whatever bridges we can so as not to offend religious sensitivities, in particular, in a bid to win hearts and souls for the Lord. If that means doing some things that might *seem* inconsistent, consistency is found in our pure motives, our uncompromised Christian commitment, and our love for a lost and dying world. If we can't take people where we find them, we can't take them anywhere.

■ **The accommodating question is: What extraordinary steps have I taken lately to win some soul to Christ?**

Taking Time for the Lost

Then Agrippa said to Paul, "Do you think that in such a short time you can persuade me to be a Christian?"

ACTS 26:28

Some wit has quipped, "Never try to teach a pig to fly. It wastes your time, and annoys the pig." More seriously, Jesus once sent out his disciples with strict instructions, "If anyone will not welcome you or listen to your words, shake the dust off your feet when you leave that home or town" (Matthew 10:14). If you have ever tried to lead some unbeliever to Christ, you may have experienced the kind of close-mindedness that makes you think you are wasting your time. Maybe (as with Jesus teaching a reluctant Nicodemus) you have planted a seed that in time will bear fruit. But with some folks it is also possible to beat your head against the wall for nothing. With so little time to reach so many lost, surely God wants us to be good stewards of our time. Yet how are we to know how much time is too much or too little?

Although Agrippa suggests that with more time he might be persuaded to become a Christian, he appears to be making excuses for not seriously responding to the gospel. Were it solely a matter of time, Agrippa easily could have arranged for further conversation with Paul. Perhaps that is a helpful clue for us today. Is the door left open for further discussion, or has it been slammed shut? Rarely is time the issue, only receptivity. For most of us, of course, the problem is not whether doors are open or closed. How can we know how firmly the door is shut when we never even knock? More often than not, the important question relevant to time spent in evangelism is quite the reverse. In the brief time you and I have consciously given to evangelism, can we possibly persuade *anyone* to be a Christian?

> ■ **The timely question is: Among all the activities that keep me busy, how much time have I spent to save even one lost soul?**

Nourishment for Life's Storms

After he said this, he took some bread and gave thanks to God in front of them all. Then he broke it and began to eat. They were all encouraged and ate some food themselves.

ACTS 27:35-36

If you've ever been seasick, you know that the last thing you want is to eat! It would be a great idea to have a full stomach, but what is likely to happen to all that food does not bear contemplating. So you can imagine what the crew of this storm-tossed ship must have first thought about Paul's crazy suggestion. However, encouraged by Paul's example, they eagerly ate what they had been afraid to eat for two whole weeks. And they all survived! Had not Paul told them, "You need it to survive"? Looking closely at Luke's account of this impromptu meal in the midst of a storm, we are struck by its similarity with another meal. When Luke tells us that "After he said this, he took some bread and gave thanks to God in front of them all," we could be excused for thinking of Jesus in the upper room. Which brings us to a wonderful analogy.

If you have ever been truly "sinsick," the last thing you might feel like doing is eating the Lord's Supper. Not that it wouldn't be a great idea to commune with God and his people, but what's likely to happen, you wonder, if you eat it but then fall back immediately into whatever sin you are struggling with? That disappointment, too, seems not worth contemplating. If that has ever been the case with you, Paul's words still stand true. Whatever storm in life you are facing—whether it is sin or suffering or something else—"You need it to survive." The Lord's Supper is not just a meaningless weekly ritual, but a life-saving reminder of Christ's saving grace.

■ **The question of endurance is: How can I survive life's storms if I do not partake regularly in both the Bread of Life and the memorial by which I remember him?**

Higher Hearts, Higher Minds

Since, then, you have been raised with Christ, set your hearts on things above, where Christ is seated at the right hand of God. Set your minds on things above, not on earthly things.

COLOSSIANS 3:1-2

Here's a quiz for you. Apart from being countries, what else do the names Luxemburg, Denmark, and Poland have in common? (Each is a small town on the east side of Green Bay, Wisconsin.) What do the words "loose," "print," and "ball" have in common? (They are all endings for foot_____.) And what about "level," "solos," and "radar"? (They are all palindromes, spelled the same both forward and backward.) More importantly, what do the words "resurrection," "baptism," and "above" have in common? (They all speak of going from something lower to something higher.) As you think about it, rising from the dead as Jesus did was a literal elevation of an entombed body to a walking, talking, *resurrected* Savior. "Up from the grave he arose!" exclaims the hymn jubilantly. In baptism, of course, the believer symbolically reenacts Jesus' resurrection as he or she surfaces joyfully from the water, a new person in Christ. But as Paul reminds us, those two visual, tangible risings mean little if there is not a third rising—from the baser instincts in which we were once mired, to the transformed behavior of people who have been saved by God's grace.

To be raised with Christ is to walk a higher road than ever before. It is to leave behind forever our lower self-expectations and "rise to the occasion." It is to lift our eyes to view with eager anticipation the pristine purity of what we are even now becoming. *Or are we?* Is our spiritual elevator going up or down? To believe in Christ's glorious rising and to participate in a "rising" mirroring his very own is never to automatically guarantee higher hearts and minds.

■ **The question beyond the quiz is: Just how high has my spiritual life soared since I first died to sin and rose to a new life in Christ?**

Deadly Spiritual Warfare

For our struggle is not against flesh and blood, but against the rulers, against the authorities, against the powers of this dark world and against the spiritual forces of evil in the heavenly realms.

EPHESIANS 6:12

There's a marvelous little book called *Flatland* by Englishman Edwin Abbott. Its premise is that there is a society of squares, triangles, circles, and other geometric figures whose world has length and breadth but not height. It knows only north, south, east, and west, not *up* or *down,* and is unable to grasp any higher perspective. One day Sphere (from Spaceland) appears to one of Flatland's inhabitants, named "A. Square." By dragging "Square" kicking and screaming into Spaceland, Sphere finally convinces him that there is such a thing as *upward,* not just *northward.* With Abbott's story in mind, it's not difficult to see the parallel analogy of Christ (the "Sphere" of spheres) coming into our own earthly "Flatland" to teach us about a spiritual dimension we comprehend only with great reluctance. When the apostle Paul speaks in today's text about a dimension in which, moment by moment, there are spiritual forces literally battling against us, we find ourselves struggling to reach beyond our familiar, carnal Flatland to appreciate the dangers of "the dark powers" and "spiritual forces of evil."

It would be easy to dismiss a parallel universe of demonic powers by acknowledging "the devil" in theory, but relegating him to some otherworldly spiritual dimension. Or, by contrast, to see the devil lurking behind every sin as a convenient scapegoat for our own guilt. But to think that we truly live in a live-action spiritual war zone, complete with "demonic bullets" constantly whizzing over our heads, somehow seems quite unthinkable. Indeed utterly absurd! And who said we don't live in Flatland?

■ **The chilling question is: If I can accept the mysterious realities of "cyberspace," why do I live in such denial that at this very moment forces of evil are penetrating my deepest thoughts?**

Excellent Thinking

Finally, brothers and sisters, whatever is true, whatever is noble, whatever is right, whatever is pure, whatever is lovely, whatever is admirable—if anything is excellent or praiseworthy— think about such things.

PHILIPPIANS 4:8

"You are what you eat," so it is said. More importantly, "You are what you think about all day long," which—when you think about it—also involves consuming. So what do you "consume" in a given day? Most of us are bombarded with countless things better left unthought and unconsumed. Language, for instance, that is not noble. Images that are not pure. Enticements that are not true. Filtering out all of the garbage is a daunting, moment-by-moment task. Indeed, whether or not we are aware of it, our minds are constantly and subconsciously storing up all the vile filth and degradation an evil world can hurl at us. Ever known any godly folks who under the influence of medication have shocked us with vulgar language? Where do you suppose that language comes from? No wonder Paul calls us to work all the harder to fill our mental reservoir with that which is true, noble, right, pure, and lovely.

Yet Paul is not warning solely against foul language and dirty pictures, otherwise why employ the word *excellent*? Excellence is not simply the opposite of foul and dirty, but speaks instead to a standard of thinking that rises above the ordinary. It is disciplined thinking. Quality thinking. Critical thinking. Careful thinking. It is thinking on the extraordinary, the exceptional, and the sublime. The idea is not simply refusing to eat whatever is found in a garbage bin, but actively seeking to eat of the finest delicacies available. What books not only inform, but inspire? What music not only delights, but uplifts? What conversations not only *fill* time, but *embellish* time? To think with excellence is to think as God himself would think.

■ **The question for the day is: Am I content with mental hamburgers when prime cuts of choice thinking are equally available?**

Working Out for an Eternity

Train yourself to be godly. For physical training is of some value, but godliness has value for all things, holding promise for both the present life and the life to come.

1 TIMOTHY 4:7-8

Are you among the millions who regularly hit the road or the gym to get a good workout? Flab is out; exercise is in—at least for those willing to commit the time and energy to lose that weight, tone those muscles, and get the heart pumping. But make no mistake, exercise is hard work! Forget all those slick television ads promising miraculous results from effortless diets and gadgets. The saying is as true as it is trite: No pain, no gain. And that would be *regular* pain. "Hit and miss" won't cut it. "On-again, off-again" only exacerbates the pain during the on-again time. So before you sign up for that pricey club membership, you had better double-check that you are committed for the long haul. One day off and the next day it's easier to skip. Two consecutive days playing hooky from the grueling routine and the third day will pass with barely a twinge of conscience. Before you know it, the flab is back and the muscle tone has gone!

For one who referred to fighting fights and finishing races, Paul certainly would have known the value of physical training. Yet Paul highlights the far greater—indeed *eternal*—value of godly exercise. Considering that even the best toned bodies will eventually die and decompose, exercising the soul must surely take top priority. Yet it would be surprising indeed if, even among believers, there was nearly as much time and effort devoted to exercising spiritual muscles as physical ones. Of course, for those who would take spiritual exercise seriously, the secret to success is no secret. For spiritual exercise, as with physical exercise, all the same rigorous rules apply.

■ **The daunting question is: How can I hope to be fit for eternity if I shrink from the painful daily routine of stretching myself spiritually?**

When Scruples Become Unscrupulous

To the pure, all things are pure, but to those who are corrupted and do not believe, nothing is pure. In fact, both their minds and consciences are corrupted.

TITUS 1:15

Would you prefer to be around a person with stringent scruples or someone who is notoriously unscrupulous? Given the connotation of *unscrupulous*, most of us would choose the person with scruples, wouldn't we? But the fact that a person has scruples doesn't guarantee he isn't unscrupulous. In today's text Paul is warning Titus about Jewish believers who continued to have scruples about eating food that was ceremonially "unclean" under the Law and were strictly enforcing those dietary scruples on Gentile converts. For Paul it was more than just a matter of doctrinal ignorance. The greater problem was the attitude behind their scruples—an attitude as "unclean" and impure as they claimed the food to be. What made it impure was a frame of mind lacking room for grace. "In the hands of those who don't understand God's grace," Paul seems to say, "even the well-intended insistence on scruples cannot help but become unscrupulous." A conscience uninformed by grace is powerless to distinguish between "clean" and "unclean" or pure and impure.

Few of us worry much about "clean" and "unclean" food. Yet we have many personal scruples that, directly or indirectly, we insist that others follow. Perhaps they are legitimate scruples dictated by doctrine or morals. However, the danger is either being so "grace-filled" that we relegate all scruples to the realm of personal opinion or—like these Jewish legalists—being so lacking in grace that we call "unclean" what God has made clean. The ability to maintain godly scruples without becoming unscrupulous in their application is itself a precious gift of grace.

■ **The question of scrupulous integrity is: Are my high standards of virtue matched by an equally high sense of God's grace?**

Making a Good Finish

I have fought the good fight, I have finished the race, I have kept the faith.

2 TIMOTHY 4:7

Think back over all the people you've read about in the Bible so far. Are you struck by the number of them who start well but don't finish well? Perhaps the prime example is Solomon. In worldly terms Solomon had it all: wisdom, wealth, fame, and glory—and even what seemed to be a deep devotion to God. But despite his celebrated wisdom, in his later years Solomon foolishly married foreign wives who led him into idolatry. How does *that* happen? If Solomon's judgment had been impaired because of senility, we could understand. But like many others who seem to lose their way in later years, wise King Solomon became just an old fool. Even today we often hear of those who disgrace themselves in a "midlife crisis." Or longtime stalwarts of the church who suddenly leave the faith. Or couples who get divorced after thirty years of marriage. In each instance, are we to believe that there were serious problems all along, bubbling just beneath the surface, or was some switch flipped due to aging?

With few exceptions, what most characterizes the young is idealism and unquenchable optimism. But life has a nasty way of dashing youthful dreams. Experience has a moderating influence on us as we grow older, perhaps because of financial limitations, health issues, or family concerns. Many become cynical, embittered, or just plain tired of fighting the good fight. If older age has an enemy, surely it is discouragement. But when the finish line is more clearly in sight than at the beginning, how can one not get a second wind and finish the course with a flourish?

■ **The challenging question is: If I ever start slipping into a mode of cynical discouragement, what new vision can I capture to keep me going?**

The Choice of All Choices

You adulterous people, don't you know that friendship with the world means enmity against God? Therefore, anyone who chooses to be a friend of the world becomes an enemy of God.

JAMES 4:4

"Choose your friends carefully" is good advice—especially for young people—for "Bad company corrupts good character." Why, then, are parents so quick to give that advice, yet so unwilling to follow it themselves when it comes to choosing either friendship with God or friendship with the world? Indeed, why do parents have such great concern for the friends their children choose, but think nothing of the worldly friendship they themselves introduce to their children? Make no mistake, none of us can be neutral about which "friend" we have chosen. There's no "casual friends" versus "close friends." No "work friends" and "social friends." With God, it's all or nothing. Not that God is unwilling to share. He simply knows that, at best, the world is only a pretend friend. With the world it's all take and no give, all promise and no fulfillment. No wonder the world is God's enemy, for only God's love is genuine, and only his promises are always fulfilled. As our Father, God wants to spare us the hurt and disappointment that comes from ill-chosen friendships.

Are you perhaps not so sure that we committed believers are "friends with the world"? If the case could be made by the use of only one word in today's culture, that word would be *materialism*. Only the most blind among us could possibly deny that we have too much, too soon, too often. That we are spoiled by the abundant life. That we are consumed by our consumables and enslaved to our possessions. If that isn't friendship with the world, what is? To claim a friendship with God that permits an ongoing friendship with God's enemy is not just to offend God, but to engage in the most dangerous self-deception.

■ **The question of choice is: Do the decisions I make reflect a greater friendship with a faithful God or with an ever-so-fickle friend?**

Warding Off Alien Invasions

Dear friends, I urge you, as foreigners and exiles, to abstain from sinful desires, which wage war against your soul.

1 PETER 2:11

The fascination with UFO's, extraterrestrials, flying saucers, and paranormal activities knows no bounds. No longer are UFO's solely the stuff of comic strips and science fiction. Devotees spend countless hours searching out evidence of extraterrestrial life. Nothing could convince them that we're not constantly being invaded by alien forces. What else explains those mysterious crop circles or Peru's intriguing Nazca Lines? Yet what a colossal waste of human enterprise! If only all the time and money expended on the search for alien life forms was redirected to a longing for God right here on this planet! Without question, there's a cosmic war going on, but in this life-and-death struggle it is *we* who are the aliens. *We* the strange, mistrusted, and despised foreigners who don't really belong. As believers in Christ, we are not of this world, or at least ought not to be. And to the extent that we are not, the world counts us its enemy, just as it did the "Chief of aliens" who invaded this world from his home in heaven.

And so the battle lines are drawn. As long as we remain physically in this world, our souls will be bombarded with every evil this world has to hurl at us, whether intellectual, sexual, or sensual. Even our natural desires conspire against us to conform to this present world. "Why be different?" comes a familiar inner voice. "Do you want everyone to think you are weird?" The gravitational pull of this world should never be underestimated. Just when we think we are hovering at a safe distance, suddenly we come crashing down into a material, carnal, and worldly dimension that couldn't be more alien.

■ **The easily identifiable question is: What success am I having in abstaining from the sinful desires hurled at me as a believing alien in a hostile world?**

_____

_____

_____

_____

So Many Virtues, So Little Time

Make every effort to add to your faith goodness; and to goodness, knowledge; and to knowledge, self-control; and to self-control, perseverance; and to perseverance, godliness; and to godliness, mutual affection; and to mutual affection, love.

2 PETER 1:5-7

Quite likely you have heard this familiar passage being taught innumerable times. It is not unusual for each virtue in the list to be defined and explained with great care (if not tedium), often with the suggestion that there is a progression from first to last. And who can argue with *faith* being foundational or *love* being the ultimate? But sustaining a logical progression throughout the list requires rather fanciful analysis. Peter's argument is not that there is an increasing scale of importance; rather, that we need to have *all* of these qualities *in increasing measure*. If we were to think of a lunch buffet, the idea would be to put more and more on our plate until there is absolutely no more room! Being filled with these virtues is how we participate in the divine nature and escape the temptations of the world. These virtues take us beyond an elementary knowledge of Christ and transform us into his likeness. If there is any progression to be considered, it is our personal progression from babes in Christ to mature citizens of the kingdom.

Since the Christian life is to be a progression, it is only natural that we should take inventory of how far we have progressed. Are we more Christlike now than when we first called upon the Lord for our salvation? Have we noticeably matured in Christ, or are we stagnant? Given what Peter repeatedly cites as a risk for all believers—being worse off at the end than at the beginning—we would do well to be brutally honest about how effectively we have incorporated this list of spiritual virtues into our lives.

■ **The question of spiritual development is: Can I see as much demonstrable growth in virtue since my spiritual rebirth as physical growth since the day I was born?**

Of Milk and Meat

In fact, though by this time you ought to be teachers, you need someone to teach you the elementary truths of God's word all over again. You need milk, not solid food!

HEBREWS 5:12

H ebrews is a book that almost anyone can understand. Who could miss its core teaching—that Christ is superior to every aspect of the old covenant? Or its urgent call to faithfulness, citing Israel's infidelity and—by sharp contrast—the steadfastness of those in "the roll call of the faithful"? Perhaps the discussion of Melchizedek's unique priesthood calls for deeper reflection, but generally Hebrews is as straightforward as the morning newspaper. Why, then, does the writer suddenly stop mid-stride to chide his readers for their inability to understand what he is saying? Why does he call them overgrown babies who still need their mother's milk? Perhaps it is because of the book's seemingly contradictory themes; first, the absolute assurance to be found in Christ, and second, the repeated warnings against falling away. Only those who still drink "milk" are disturbed by that seeming incongruity. Those mature enough to digest "meat" have no difficulty understanding both sides of the same theological coin.

Can we fall away into disbelief? Israel did! And *if Israel*, argues the Hebrew writer, then so can we. "We must pay attention so that we do not drift away," infers the writer. "See to it that you don't have an unbelieving heart that turns its back on God." "We have come to share in Christ *if* we hold our confidence in him firmly to the end." For all the doctrinal debates over "eternal security," it is clear that the Hebrew writer is warning us not to take our salvation for granted. But for meat lovers everywhere comes the reassuring promise that if we firmly and fully "fix our eyes on Jesus," nothing could be more certain than that those who are in Christ will remain in Christ for eternity!

■ **The meaty question is: Are my eyes firmly fixed on Christ, or do I find myself not just blinking, but forever looking away?**

Hope As an Anchor

Because God wanted to make the unchanging nature of his purpose very clear to the heirs of what was promised, he confirmed it with an oath…We have this hope as an anchor for the soul, firm and secure.

HEBREWS 6:17,19

Will your anchor hold in the storms of life?" is a line from the hymn by Priscilla Owens. The nineteenth century was an era of ships on the sea, storms, and anchors, so one is not surprised to read lyrics like these: "We have an anchor that keeps the soul, steadfast and sure while the billows roll; fastened to the Rock which cannot move, grounded firm and deep in the Savior's love." According to the Hebrew writer, God not only *promised* that his heirs would inherit everlasting life, but he also confirmed it with a divine *oath*. How much more assurance could anyone ask? In the midst of family crises and breathtaking health scares, you and I need something to hang onto when all seems lost. In a world of transient values, fluctuating markets, corporate buyouts, and political uncertainty, we long for strength, stability, and security. In the imagery of the Hebrew writer, our anchor for the soul is found in nothing less than God's own solemn word.

Do you find it interesting that God tells us not to swear with oaths, but rather to let our word be our bond? God's swearing in this instance is in the form of a judicial oath, not simply a crass profanity invoking the name of some deity. Unlike us, God never lies. But to give us added assurance, God swears by his own righteousness that what he has promised us is the truth, the whole truth, and nothing but the truth. So whatever the storm we face, God's own promise is our constant anchor. Just how refreshing is that in a world where truth is the first casualty of human existence!

■ **The question of truth is: If God is faithful to every word *he* utters, how faithful am I to every word *I* utter?**

_____

_____

_____

_____

Fixing Our Eyes on Jesus

Let us run with perseverance the race marked out for us, fixing our eyes on Jesus, the pioneer and perfecter of faith. For the joy set before him he endured the cross, scorning its shame, and sat down at the right hand of the throne of God.

HEBREWS 12:1-2

The enraptured shepherds who first fixed their eyes on Jesus in Bethlehem could never have guessed the scene witnessed some thirty years later by those who fixed their eyes on Jesus at Golgotha. To have beheld the babe wrapped in swaddling clothes and seen his sleepy little eyes must have been the most sublime view in all of history—apart from the horrendous scenes at the cross itself. Wouldn't you love to have been there with Joseph, Mary, and the infant Jesus? And how could one ever forget the sight of Jesus hanging in agony on that rugged Roman cross? Was there anyone, apart from Mary, who witnessed both the manger and the cross? Imagine the utter joy with which Mary must have fixed her eyes upon Jesus for the very first time. Then imagine the unspeakable maternal anguish she must have felt, seeing Jesus hanging before her in the throes of an agonizing death. What thoughts must have been running through her mind at the foot of the cross? Did she think back on the angel who announced she would soon be with child by the Holy Spirit? Did Jesus' life as a youngster in Nazareth flash before her? Or perhaps the tumultuous events of his ministry?

To fix our own eyes on Jesus is to replay the story from beginning to end. It is to see God in the person of a first-century Jewish baby who redefined history and reshaped the way of salvation. It is to see ourselves reflected in his grace-filled face and to acknowledge that only through Jesus can we find peace in whatever cross we bear.

■ **The question of joyful endurance is: Do my eyes merely glance occasionally at the person of Jesus, or are my eyes firmly fixed on every aspect of his divine person?**

Surprising Antichrists

Who is the liar? It is whoever denies that Jesus is the Christ. Such a person is the antichrist—denying the Father and the Son.

1 JOHN 2:22

Mention the word "antichrist," and many will quickly think about cataclysmic end-time scenarios and some future Satan-like figure. Yet John has a surprisingly different understanding of "the antichrist"—not the least difference being that, for John, there is no single, evil persona associated with a time of tribulation or the battle of Armageddon. As highlighted in today's text, John calls "antichrist" any person who denies the deity of Christ. Throughout his three brief Epistles, John refutes the Gnostic teaching that all flesh is evil, a position which necessarily excludes any possibility that a holy God could have appeared in human flesh. Repeatedly John insists that this Gnostic teaching is patently *anti* Jesus Christ and simply false. In fact, he says that the proposition of Christ's incarnation is a litmus test indicating which teachers are genuine and which are false. In contemporary terms, any philosopher, theologian, or person on the street who denies that Jesus of Nazareth was God in flesh is a modern-day antichrist.

Laced into John's argument about intellectual antichrists is his concern about other kinds of antichrists, including any person who does not love his brothers and sisters in Christ, anyone who claims to be a follower of Christ yet does not obey God's commands, or any person who thinks that once saved he can keep on sinning with complete impunity. All of these, says John, are living in practical denial of the Christ they profess and, thus, manifest the spirit of the antichrist—a spirit that "even now is already in the world."

■ **The question of truth is: Am I enthralled with talk of some apocalyptic Antichrist when the potential "antichrist" I need most to worry about is myself?**

Lukewarm Faith

I know your deeds, that you are neither cold nor hot. I wish you were either one or the other!
So, because you are lukewarm—neither hot nor cold—I am about to spit you out of my mouth.

REVELATION 3:15-16

Being lukewarm can be a good thing. Who wants to take a shower that is either scalding hot or freezing cold? And baby's milk needs to be *just right*. But when it comes to lukewarm faith, Christ is plenty steamed that the disciples in Laodicea aren't more on fire! Despite employing hyperbole to suggest that he'd just as soon they were "cold," clearly Christ would not want them never to have been warmed by the gospel. What particularly nauseates Christ is the Laodiceans' namby-pamby lack of commitment. Being *lukewarm* indicates that at some point they had experienced a measure of spiritual life, at least just enough to be useless! Just enough to be an embarrassment to the kingdom. Just enough to fool themselves into thinking that they were in a right relationship with God. But "just enough" is never enough!

What Christ knows is that lukewarm disciples cannot possibly survive under the intense pressures of persecution or even life's ordinary challenges. Because Christ's revelation to John is about withstanding such onslaughts, this stinging letter to Laodicea is indeed a wake-up call! Lest you and I fall into the same trap, it is worth asking what made the Laodiceans so lukewarm? From all indications it was their abundance of material wealth. Rich by the world's standards, they had been robbed of their passion for Christ. Faith and "church" had become simply a soul-satisfying balm, a comfortable habit, a guilt-chasing solace. Yet the Lord was having none of it. Such faith is not just weak and inadequate, but cause for retching!

■ **The gut-wrenching question is: Is the intensity of my faith sufficient to help me overcome whatever trials and temptations might come my way?**

The Great Anticipation

When he opened the seventh seal, there was silence in heaven for about half an hour.

REVELATION 8:1

Silence in heaven? Hard to believe, especially with all the praise being sung by the elders, the angels, and that "great multitude," not to mention all those earthquakes, cosmic gyrations, and celestial convulsions. But with the opening of the seventh seal, suddenly comes this ominous "half an hour" of silence just before the sounding of the seven trumpets and the unthinkable destruction they herald. Why the silence? Why a "half an hour"? As with all apocalyptic language, it's difficult to be dogmatic about any detail. What *is* clear is the importance of the coming judgment, breathtaking in scale. When God promises judgment against sin and evil, he means it! And so we have cause to hold our collective breath in anticipation, to make sure we don't miss the moment…or the message.

Call it the calm before the storm or that eerie hush just before the battle commences. Whatever else it is, the silence is for effect. Silence is a signal of important things to come, which might help us make sense of the lonely, quiet years of older age. It seems such a waste, those last lingering—often painful—years. Yet perhaps it is God's way of getting our attention before the moment of our mortal transition. While those who die younger might not have the benefit of that pregnant pause, what a wonder-filled time of anticipation it must be for older folks. Have you listened to what they say during those final days? They want to go home! The home they are living in is not *home.* If our glorious homecoming is preceded by silence, then who would wish to miss the anticipation just before the trumpet sounds?

■ **The momentous question is: If God announces his coming with silence as well as sound, does the silence I experience lead to awful dread or glorious anticipation?**

To Those Who Overcome

This calls for patient endurance and faithfulness on the part of God's people.

REVELATION 13:10

For all the mystery surrounding John's apocalypse, it is virtually impossible to miss its clarion call to faithful endurance. In fact today's verse is repeated virtually verbatim in the very next chapter. Strikingly, the theme of overcoming is central to the seven letters to the seven churches. Each and every one of them concludes with a specific promise for those who endure. To those who overcome, says Christ, I will give: the right to eat from the tree of life in God's paradise; the crown of life that will keep them from being destroyed by the second death; both the "hidden manna" and a white stone with a new name written on it; and authority over nations; and being dressed in white; and being made a pillar of the temple of God; and the right to sit with me on my throne. Wow! Is it any wonder that "We Shall Overcome" was adopted as the anthem of the civil rights movement? While its use as a protest song might suggest the idea of winning some victory, "overcoming" is not about *conquering*, but *enduring*. Or is it?

In order to *endure*, we must first *conquer*. Conquer our fears, conquer our desires, and conquer the temptation to give up and give in. John's apocalypse was written as a letter of encouragement for a beleaguered generation of Christians who had become objects of persecution and even martyrdom. It was important for them to be reminded of the end game—to know that in the world to come they would be rewarded for their steadfastness in the face of fear. Maybe we don't face the same prospect of martyrdom as they—so far—but overcoming what spiritual challenges we do face is just as crucial.

■ **The question of overcoming is: Do I have the depth of faith and commitment that would keep me faithful no matter what the consequences?**

It's the Pure Who Endure

No one could learn the song except the 144,000 who had been redeemed from the earth. These are those who did not defile themselves with women, for they remained virgins…No lie was found in their mouths; they are blameless.

REVELATION 14:3-5

W ant to know the meaning of the 144,000 of Revelation? Ask around and there are plenty of people ready to tell you. But they don't all agree—so let the debates begin! But maybe we have all been overlooking the obvious. Whatever other symbolism might lie in the number itself, in today's text John tells us plainly who these "144,000" are. They are the followers of Christ who keep themselves morally pure. Pure and simple! Along with Revelation's other major theme of "overcoming," the second central theme in John's apocalypse is a call for moral rectitude. In the letter to Thyatira, Christ speaks of a certain Jezebel whose teaching is leading Christians into sexual immorality. And toward the end of John's vision comes the scene where the vile, the sexually immoral, and all liars are cast into the fiery lake. Finally, there's that scene where those who have washed their robes enter the gates of the heavenly city, while the morally impure languish without. In the rush to understand the obscure, have we ignored that which is painfully clear? While speculation demands very little of us, God himself expects pristine holiness.

Although maintaining faith even to the point of martyrdom is an important way of overcoming, in some respects that is the easy part. That kind of faithfulness is a simple, straightforward, intellectual choice. Either we deny our faith and live, or we proclaim our faith and die. By contrast, it is not *dying for Christ* that is the greater challenge, but *living for Christ*. To be a martyr is to die at the hands of others. Remaining morally pure means putting our sinful self to death by our own hand.

■ **The real "144,000" question is: In the battle to remain pure, am I *overcoming* or *succumbing*?**

God's Universal Invitation

The Spirit and the bride say, "Come!" And let the one who hears say, "Come!" Let the one who is thirsty come; and let the one who wishes take the free gift of the water of life.

REVELATION 22:17

D inner invitations. Wedding invitations. Invitations of all sorts. Some come by mail; others in person. Some invitations are fancy; some are plain. Some are exclusive, while others are for everyone. Of all the many invitations we receive, none honors us more than the invitation offered in our final passage. It is an invitation from the Lord of the universe to come into his holy presence and share in his divine nature. It is an invitation to all who have ever lived. Tired of the pain and tears of this life? You're invited to move beyond them. Had enough of a world whose divine beauty is matched only by its human ugliness? You're invited into a realm where upside down is right side up. Longing for fulfillment in an otherwise empty life? You're invited to drink in all the purpose and meaning that a world specially created for you can possibly give.

If you have been reading these devotionals throughout the year, hopefully you have come to know God in a more intimate way than ever before. How could one not love such a wondrous God! But not to assume too much, have you actually given your heart to the Lord? If not, the invitation of Christ is likewise the invitation of this book. Before yet another year rolls around, is it not time to trust in Jesus alone for your salvation? To confess his name before a disbelieving world; to penitently walk in holiness and purity; to identify yourself with Christ in the waters of baptism; to become an active part of Christ's body on earth, serving your fellow man with gladness and humility? Given such a personal, divine invitation, how could anyone possibly refuse?

◼ **The ultimate question for all of us simply has to be: Have I truly and completely submitted my life to the loving lordship of Jesus?**

_____

_____

_____

_____

Age	3/13; 5/31; 7/12; 12/19		Discernment	1/15; 2/3; 2/17; 3/4; 3/11; 3/19; 3/31; 4/6; 4/16; 5/12; 5/30; 6/30; 7/4; 9/13; 12/2; 12/18
Ambition	11/28		Discipline	3/3; 4/13; 5/17; 5/18; 9/29; 12/4
Angels	3/23		Discipling	11/21
Anticipation	12/28		Doctrine	6/27; 7/6
Appearances	6/23		Doubt	10/27; 11/1
Atonement	2/20; 7/15; 8/10		Dreams	1/18; 5/14
Attitude	7/13		Education	8/8; 10/29
Baptism	2/25; 7/28		Equality	1/30; 4/17; 6/21; 11/14
Beauty	5/11		Evangelism	10/24; 12/11; 12/12
Betrayal	4/21		Evil	12/15
Blame	3/8; 12/8		Excellence	12/16
Brokenness	11/18		Faith	6/7; 7/7; 7/26; 7/28; 8/23; 9/23; 11/3; 11/13; 11/19; 12/6; 12/27
Calling	1/5; 6/22; 6/24			
Choices	3/15; 3/22; 6/1; 11/9; 12/16; 12/20		Faithfulness	2/13; 2/21; 3/21; 5/1; 7/25; 7/26; 9/3; 10/14; 12/10; 12/23; 12/24; 12/25; 12/29; 12/30
Comfort	7/20			
Commitment	1/6; 1/14; 5/27; 6/4; 7/23; 7/25; 9/4; 9/22; 10/31; 11/9			
Communion	10/5; 12/13		Favoritism	1/12
Community	2/23; 4/22; 9/18		Fear	6/29
Compassion	3/5; 5/2		Forgiveness	1/19; 2/24; 4/14; 8/13; 11/11
Confession	5/6		Freedom	10/2; 12/1
Conflict	8/9; 12/15		Gender	3/18; 5/25
Contentment	4/28; 11/28		Gloating	6/9
Conversion	11/23; 12/14		God	1/3; 1/7; 1/31; 2/5; 2/27; 2/28; 3/12; 4/19; 6/5; 6/12; 6/19; 8/15
Courage	5/24; 8/9; 9/4; 10/3; 10/6; 11/13; 12/10			
Creativity	1/1			
Death	3/10; 4/12; 4/24; 6/2; 6/15; 7/3; 9/11; 10/20; 11/8; 11/26			
Deliverance	1/26			
Denial	12/26			
Disappointment	3/9; 4/11; 7/17		Government	12/9

Guilt	4/27; 5/6; 8/18		Love	1/13; 11/15; 12/2; 12/4
Healing	6/3; 8/4; 10/30; 11/18		Marriage	1/16; 5/29; 10/23
Heaven	12/3		Materialism	10/28; 12/20; 12/27
Heritage	1/25; 8/6; 9/13; 9/23; 10/19		Meaning	5/28; 10/21
Holiness	1/28; 2/2; 2/9; 2/18; 7/5; 9/14; 9/15; 12/6; 12/30		Mercy	1/31; 10/7; 10/25; 12/18
			Morality	3/2; 3/25; 5/26
Hope	3/9; 5/9; 6/26; 7/17; 7/20; 8/22; 8/30; 9/30; 12/24		Mothers	4/15
			Motives	5/19
Humility	2/8; 4/17; 4/28; 5/8; 7/16; 9/9; 10/17; 11/4; 11/14		Names	6/17; 9/6
			Obedience	1/29; 2/11; 3/7; 4/5; 4/7; 5/8; 6/10; 6/16; 8/5
Hypocrisy	1/17; 3/7; 6/11		Parenting	2/16; 3/17; 3/25; 3/26; 5/18; 8/6; 11/28
Impulsiveness	1/11			
Influence	7/31; 9/13; 10/12; 10/19; 12/1		Passion	5/7; 5/10; 6/14; 8/1
Integrity	10/10; 12/18		Patience	4/5; 5/20; 7/18; 10/24
Introspection	2/10; 5/7		Prayer	1/10; 1/23; 1/27; 6/3; 6/6; 7/4; 7/29; 8/11; 8/31; 9/10; 9/21; 10/13; 11/16; 11/17; 11/22; 11/24
Jealousy	4/1			
Joy	10/1; 10/11			
Judging	1/20; 2/12; 3/3; 4/6; 6/9; 11/4			
			Pride	1/4; 7/18; 7/19; 8/26
Judgment	6/13; 6/20; 8/17; 9/12; 10/15; 11/26		Priorities	4/9; 7/2; 11/7
Justice	2/28; 6/21; 8/25; 9/12; 11/12		Promises	3/14; 8/10; 8/21; 12/24
Kingdom	9/20; 11/2; 11/25; 12/9		Providence	1/21; 1/24; 5/4; 7/1; 8/21; 11/29; 12/7
Language	2/19		Provision	1/9
Law	2/28; 7/6; 8/24		Purpose	1/24; 6/22; 10/21
Leadership	3/20; 4/2; 6/22; 10/10; 12/9		Renewal	9/2; 9/26; 9/29; 10/30; 12/22
Listening	3/27; 7/9; 8/5; 9/1; 9/16; 9/17		Repentance	7/21; 7/29; 8/14; 9/29; 10/11; 11/20

Resurrection	9/24	Study	2/4; 2/11; 4/3; 4/23; 5/22; 6/18; 7/11; 7/14; 8/2; 8/7; 8/16; 9/9; 10/9; 10/16; 11/2
Retrospect	2/15; 8/20		
Revenge	8/25; 10/4		
Reverence	1/22; 8/5	Substitution	2/6
Salvation	9/30; 10/20; 12/31	Suffering	2/7; 9/8; 10/1; 11/25; 12/5
Seeking	11/10; 11/19		
Self-esteem	3/28	Superstition	7/24
Selfishness	5/21	Temptation	1/2; 3/6; 3/30; 4/25; 5/26; 6/28; 10/22; 11/16; 12/21
Separation	2/14; 3/4; 8/11		
Sharing	2/1; 3/1; 4/4; 4/30; 11/12		
Significance	4/29; 6/24	Trust	1/26; 1/27; 3/10; 3/14; 3/16; 3/24; 3/29; 4/11; 4/26; 5/23; 6/5; 7/7; 7/10; 7/15; 8/28; 9/10; 9/25; 10/6; 12/7
Sin	1/2; 1/8; 2/12; 2/22; 4/10; 4/18; 4/20; 4/27; 6/28; 7/22; 7/27; 8/4; 8/12; 8/13; 8/18; 8/29; 10/11; 10/22; 11/5		
Singing	4/8; 9/19	Truth	7/30; 8/3; 8/27; 10/16; 11/27
Solitude	5/13; 6/8; 8/5; 11/28	Vision	9/5; 10/21; 11/5; 12/19; 12/25; 12/29
Soul	5/5; 10/8; 10/18	Vows	1/6; 2/26; 3/21
Spirituality	9/7; 9/20; 10/8; 10/18; 11/2; 11/6; 11/30; 12/14; 12/17; 12/22	Wisdom	5/3; 5/8; 5/12; 5/15; 5/16; 5/17; 8/19
		Worry	10/26
		Worship	6/25; 6/27; 7/8; 9/28; 10/11; 11/6

ABOUT THE AUTHOR

As a Bible scholar, attorney, and classroom teacher, F. LaGard Smith brings a unique blend of thorough biblical research, objective analysis, and personal insight to his writing.

Smith is the author of some 35 books on a wide variety of topics ranging from doctrinal discussions and current social and moral issues to books of inspiration and devotion. Smith does much of his writing in the quiet Cotswold countryside of England, which inspired his own bestselling reflective journal, *Meeting God in Quiet Places*. In the States, he has spent a lifetime teaching both law and religion at Christian universities.

The Daily Bible is the outgrowth of a suggestion by Smith's father, who early on implanted the idea that "somebody ought to put the Bible in the right order." Upon his father's death, Smith decided to launch just such a project. In the nearly three decades since its original publication, *The Daily Bible* has blessed countless readers with its unique chronological approach and informative narrative.

Now with the publication of this companion volume, *The Daily Bible Experience*, Smith has joined heart and mind together for a rich spiritual journey that you are invited to share each and every day.

Unlike Any Other **Bible**
You Have Ever Read

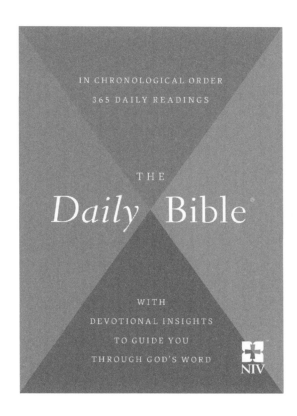

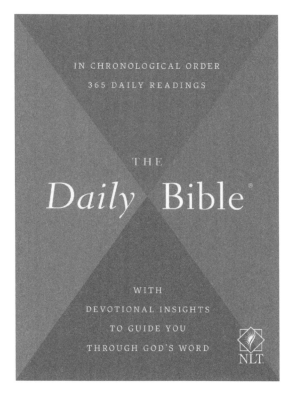

As the unique, chronological presentation of God's story daily unfolds before you,

you will begin to appreciate God's plan for your life as never before.

Reading the Bible will become a fresh, inviting, more informative experience.